Big Book of
Questions
&Answers

What does the chimpanzee eat in its natural habitat?

Which alphabet is the most widely used in the world?

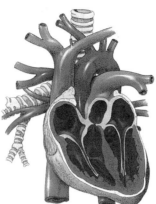

Where is this organ in the body and what does it pump?

In heraldry, where might you find a charge on a field?

Which famous cycling race, lasting 26 days, takes place in France?

Which country has 20 sheep for every human?

Clowns are sometimes called "Joey." How did they get this nickname?

For 700 years, samurai dominated Japan. Who were they?

What color would a pair of red shoes appear in blue light?

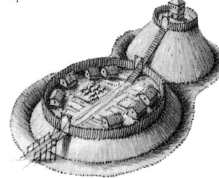

What kind of castle is this and when was it built?

What does this instrument record?

How does the deadly black widow spider get its name?

Why is the arrow-poison
frog so brightly colored?

In ancient Greece, what were the Spartans famous for?

What kind of musical
instrument is this?

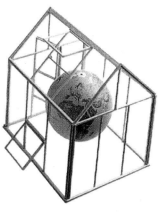

How is carbon dioxide
contributing to the
warming of our globe?

Big Book of
Questions
&Answers

Written by
Ann Kramer,
Theodore Rowland-Entwistle,
John Farndon

On which island off the east coast
of Africa does this animal live?

What is this structure
called and where would
you see it?

What is this theater called
and when was it built?

COVENT
GARDEN
BOOKS

Can you name this
modern building, and
say what it is used for?

DK PUBLISHING
www.dk.com

Produced for Dorling Kindersley by
PAGEOne, United Kingdom

Project Editors
Liza Bruml, Helena Spiteri, David Pickering

Art Editors
Sarah Scrutton, Diane Clouting, Jill Plank, Sharon Spencer

US Editor
B. Alison Weir

Managing Editors
Simon Adams, Gillian Denton, Helen Parker

Managing Art Editor
Julia Harris

Picture Researchers
Fergus Muir, Charlotte Bush, Ola Rudowska

Production
Catherine Semark, Samantha Larmour

Editorial Consultants
Neil Ardley, Ted Hart, Richard Platt, Barbara Taylor

First American Edition, 1999
10 9 8 7 6 5 4 3 2 1

Published in the United States by
Dorling Kindersley Publishing, Inc., 95 Madison Avenue
New York, New York 10016

A catalog record is available from the Library of Congress

ISBN 0-7894-4383-X

Color reproduction by Colourscan, Singapore
Printed in Hong Kong

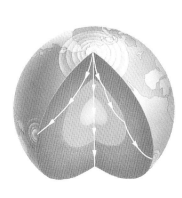

Contents of part 1

Contents of part 2

Contents of part 3

What do you know about nature?

What makes a home?

When did it happen?

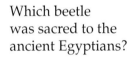

Which beetle was sacred to the ancient Egyptians?

Why did the ancient Egyptians value the wedjat eye?

Who invented it?

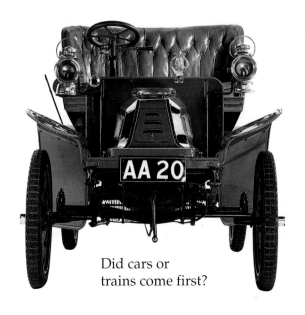

Did cars or trains come first?

Test yourself on people and places

1 What is the name of the kind of government where there is "rule by the people"?

11 What is the origin of the American celebration Thanksgiving?

Thanksgiving supper

2 Why are windmills a common sight in the Netherlands?

Windmill

12 Which Italian city was built on a small group of islands in a lagoon?

3 Which single country produces about one fifth of the world's wine?

Grape harvesting

13 What is UNICEF and what does it do?

4 What is a stupa, and with which religion is it associated?

14 Can you name the canal that links the Mediterranean and Red seas?

Painted egg faces

5 Sometimes a clown in a circus is called "Joey." Where did this nickname come from?

15 Which city was specially built to replace Rio de Janeiro as the capital of Brazil?

6 Which vast region in the Russian Federation stretches from the Ural Mountains to Alaska?

16 Shiva, Vishnu, and Brahma are gods of which religion?

Vishnu   Brahma   Shiva

7 Where might you find Tuareg, Ashanti, and Masai people?

Tuareg

Ashanti   Masai

17 In which sport might you race for the America's Cup, and how did the winner's trophy get its name?

8 What is karma, and why is it so important to Buddhists?

Sitting Buddha

18 These national symbols represent which four countries?

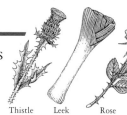

Shamrock   Thistle   Leek   Rose

9 What do the tabla, tambura, and sitar have in common?

19 In an orchestra, what does the conductor use a small stick, called a baton, for?

10 Where was Parcheesi first played?

20 How did the cuddly teddy bear get its name?

Teddy bears

Test yourself on people and places

The Silk Road

Huskies pulling sled

21 What are the people who live in the Arctic called?

22 The Silk Road runs through Central Asia. What was it first used for?

23 Why do lots of tourists flock to the town of Oberammergau every ten years?

Intensive agriculture

24 Which is the most widely used alphabet in the world?

Diviner

25 Why does a dowser, or diviner, use a Y-shaped hazel or willow twig?

26 There are many kinds of puppets. What sort is a marionette?

The Koran

27 The Bible is sacred to both Jews and Christians. Which religion believes in the Koran?

28 In which religion do the men wear a shawl called a tallith and a skullcap called a yarmulke?

Boating on the lake

29 What is so special about Lake Titicaca?

30 The Japanese are proud of their traditional culture. What is their national sport?

Japanese flag

31 Some of the people of the modern state of Israel live on kibbutzim. What is unusual about the kibbutz way of life?

32 What is the difference between intensive and subsistence farming?

33 Scandinavia, in northern Europe, is made up of which countries?

34 Indonesia consists of thousands of islands. Where is its capital?

35 Which nation has 20 times more sheep than people?

Sheep shearing

36 More than one-fifth of the world's population lives in just one country. Which one?

Processional dragon

37 Many people work on a movie set. What is the director responsible for?

38 Which is Europe's longest river, and where does it flow?

39 If guerrillas are not a kind of ape, what are they?

TURN TO PAGES 12 AND 13 FOR THE ANSWERS

Answers for people and places quiz

1 Democracy. In this kind of government the people play a part, usually by voting for representatives to make decisions on their behalf.

Voting at a ballot box

2 Much of the land in the Netherlands is below sea level. To prevent flooding, barriers called dykes have been built. The water is then pumped from the enclosed areas, which are known as polders. Windmills were once used to power the pumps that drained the land.

3 France, the largest country in western Europe. It has many very famous wine-growing regions, including Bordeaux, Burgundy, and Champagne. France is also well-known for its good food, particularly cheeses such as Brie and Camembert, and goat's cheese.

French flag

4 A stupa is a dome-shaped mound of brick or stone covering a site or object sacred to Buddha. Many stupas are found in India, the birthplace of Buddhism about 2,500 years ago.

Indian stupa

5 Clowns take their nickname, and their white faces, from the Englishman Joseph Grimaldi (1779-1837). With his painted face, he is considered to be the first real stage clown.

Joseph Grimaldi

6 Siberia. Much of northern Siberia lies inside the Arctic Circle. Most of the population live close to the Trans-Siberian Railway, which runs from Moscow to Vladivostok.

Sunset in Siberia

7 In the African continent. The Tuareg are Muslim nomads who inhabit the Sahara. Ashantis live in the dense forests of West Africa. The tall Masai people herd cattle on the open plains of Kenya.

Africa

Buddhist wheel of life

8 Buddhists believe that everyone is reborn. They think that karma, or the sum of good and bad deeds that a person did in one life, will affect the quality of their next life.

9 They are all traditional Indian musical instruments. The tabla is a drum; the sitar and tambura are stringed. The musicians improvise melodies that are based on ragas — a fixed series of notes.

Tambura
Sitar
Tabla

10 The ancient board game of pachisi was first played in India, and is still the national game. The modern version, called Parcheesi, is based on its Indian predecessor.

Parcheesi

Answers for people and places quiz

11 In November 1621, the English settlers in North America held a thanksgiving feast to celebrate their first harvest. Every year Thanksgiving Day is repeated on the fourth Thursday in November.

Venice, Italy

12 Venice, a beautiful city built on 118 islands. It is linked to the mainland by a causeway, but most people travel by gondola or motorboat on the network of canals.

13 UNICEF is the United Nations Children's Fund. It was set up in 1946 by the United Nations to help child victims of World War II. The fund now provides medical help and education to children around the world.

UNICEF symbol

14 The Suez Canal, a major waterway and trade route that was completed in 1869. Cutting through the Isthmus of Suez to link the two seas, it reduces the sailing distance around the world.

Suez Canal

15 Brasilia. In 1960, it was made the seat of government and the capital of Brazil. The city was designed in the shape of an aircraft, and its futuristic architecture contrasts with its rural surroundings.

Brasilia

16 Shiva the destroyer, Vishnu the preserver, and Brahma the creator are the three most important gods of the Hindu religion. One of the world's oldest religions, Hinduism began in India more than 5,000 years ago.

Hindu "Om" symbol

17 Ocean racing. Two yachts from different nations race a triangular course. The trophy is named after the first winner of the race, the U.S. yacht *America*.

Sailing

18 The shamrock is the national emblem of Ireland, the thistle belongs to Scotland, the leek is the national emblem of Wales, and the rose is England's national flower. Scotland, Wales, England, and Northern Ireland make up the United Kingdom. Its flag is the Union Jack.

Union Jack

19 Some orchestras may contain as many as 90 musicians. To make sure they keep time, the conductor uses a baton or hand motions to give the orchestra the correct tempo, or speed. The conductor also interprets the composer's music.

Conductor with his baton

20 The teddy bear is said to have been named after U.S. president Theodore Roosevelt, whose nickname was Teddy. In 1902, on a hunting trip, Roosevelt refused to kill a bear cub. Later, a shopkeeper began selling toy bears, calling them teddy bears.

Answers for people and places quiz

Inuit hunt seal to eat

21 Inuit, which means "real men." The name "Eskimo", means "eaters of meat," and was given to the Inuit by Native North Americans.

26 A marionette is a string puppet. It is worked from above by tilting a bar, which pulls the strings. This moves the puppet's arms, legs, and head.

String puppets

22 From the 1st century BC until the development of a sea route in the 1600s, traders and merchants traveled the perilous Silk Road to bring silks and other precious goods from China to Europe.

Camels are led along the route

27 The followers of the religion Islam, who are called Muslims (or Moslems), read the Koran, which is the holy book of Islam. Muslims believe it is the direct word of God, or Allah, as revealed to his prophet, Muhammad. The Koran consists of 114 *suras*, or chapters, that are written in verse.

23 Every ten years the inhabitants of Oberammergau in Germany reenact Jesus Christ's crucifixion. Visitors come from all over the country and abroad to see the passion play performances.

Passion play

28 The tallith, a shawl worn by men during prayers, and the yarmulke, or kipa, are both used in Judaism, the Jewish religion.

Menorah
Yarmulke
Tallith
Torah

24 All western languages, as well as the written languages of Africa, are based on the Roman alphabet, which was developed in about the 7th century BC. Then it had only 21 letters; J, U, W, Y, and Z were added later.

Roman letters in alphabetic order

29 High in the Andes mountains, 12,507 ft (3,812 m) above sea level, Lake Titicaca is the world's highest navigable lake. It lies between Bolivia and Peru, covering an area of about 3,200 sq miles (8,300 sq km). Both ships and traditional reed boats use the lake.

South America

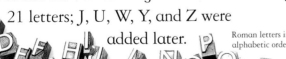

25 Dowsing is an ancient way of finding water. The dowser holds one end of the Y-shaped twig in each hand, and walks around until the stem twitches downward, showing where water is buried.

30 Sumo wrestling. In this sport the two contestants, who follow a special diet for strength and weight, try to push each other out of a small ring.
Sumo wrestlers

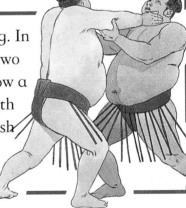

Answers for people and places quiz

Kibbutz inhabitants working together as a community on the farm

31

A kibbutz (which means "gathering") is a special kind of farm. The people who live on these farms are all equal. They work together, sharing the land, food, and decision making. The children are brought up collectively.

Intensive chicken houses

Subsistence farming

32 Intensive farming produces surpluses of crops and livestock for a farmer to sell for profit. Subsistence farming produces only just enough produce for a farmer to live on.

33 Historically the region

Scandinavia

known as Scandinavia consisted of Norway and Sweden. Today, it also includes other places where Nordic people live. Denmark, Finland, and Iceland are now considered part of Scandinavia, as is Greenland.

34 Indonesia's many islands straddle the equator from Malaysia to Australia.

Borobudur Temple, Java

Most Indonesians live on the island of Java, which is also the site of the country's capital, Jakarta.

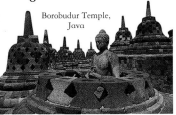

35

New Zealand flag

New Zealand. With its warm, moist climate, the country is ideal for farming, especially sheep and cattle. New Zealand is the world's leading exporter of lamb and dairy produce, and is the second largest exporter of wool.

36 China. This vast country is the third largest in the world. More than a billion people live in China, which makes it the most populated country in the world.

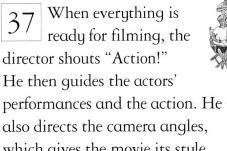

The family is very important in the Chinese way of life

37 When everything is ready for filming, the director shouts "Action!" He then guides the actors' performances and the action. He also directs the camera angles, which gives the movie its style.

Movie set

38 Europe's longest river is the Volga River, which flows 2,290 miles (3,688 km) through Russia from the Valdai Hills to the Caspian Sea. Boats use it to transport goods across the country.

Volga River

39 Named after the Spanish for "little war," guerrillas are fighters who are not regular soldiers. Working in small groups, guerrillas make sudden raids on invading forces.

Modern guerrillas

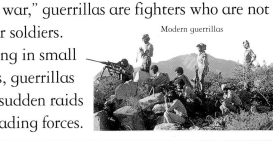

The amazing world of buildings

Q In which colossal theater did gladiators fight wild animals?

Elevator lifted animals into the arena

A Nearly 2,000 years ago in ancient Rome, spectators flocked to the Colosseum to watch public "games" featuring fights between hungry animals and human gladiators, chariot races, and mock battles.

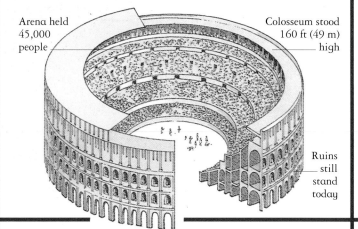

Arena held 45,000 people

Colosseum stood 160 ft (49 m) high

Ruins still stand today

Q Where in Spain might you find a fantastic, unfinished Holy Family?

A The fantastic wrought-iron spires of the cathedral of Sagrada Familia, or Holy Family, are among the most famous sights in Barcelona. Designed by the great Catalan architect Antonio Gaudi (1852-1926), work began on the cathedral in 1882 but is still unfinished today.

Spires reach high into the sky

Q This famous modern English building has its insides on the outside. What is its name, and who occupies it?

A In 1986 the famous insurance company Lloyds of London moved to new offices – the Lloyds Building. It was designed by the British architect Richard Rogers. The appearance of the building caused much argument because all its internal services, such as the plumbing, are on the outside.

Q Which spectacular Indian temple was built for the love of a woman?

A Covered with marble and inlaid with semiprecious stones, the Taj Mahal is one of the world's most beautiful buildings. It was built by the Mogul emperor, Shah Jahan, in memory of his wife, Mumtaz Mahal, who died in 1631.

Towers are called minarets

Magnificent natural wonders

Q Why are the Himalayas sometimes known as the "roof of the world"?

A With their rugged peaks and valleys, the mighty Himalayas form the highest mountain range in the world. They lie on the border between China and Nepal. The range includes Mount Everest, which, at 29,028 ft (8,848 m), is the world's tallest mountain.

The summit of Everest was first reached by E. Hillary and T. Norgay in 1953

Q Where in Arizona might you ride a mule through years and years of history?

A Northwestern Arizona is home to the spectacular Grand Canyon. Carved out by the Colorado River, the eroded rock represents millions of years of the Earth's history. The canyon is 18 miles (29 km) wide in places, and more than 6,000 ft (1,820 m) deep. Tourists can ride down, past layers of geological history, to the very bottom.

Q How did Monument Valley, in Arizona and Utah, get its name?

A This arid wilderness in the American Southwest is famous for its remarkable columns of rock. These tall sandstone structures look like monuments.

Extraordinary shapes have been formed by wind-borne sand

Q At what time of day does Ayers Rock in central Australia change color?

Aboriginals

A Ayers Rock (Uluru) is a huge mass of sandstone, rising 1,142 ft (348 m) above a flat desert floor. It is sacred to the Aboriginals. Caves at the base are decorated with traditional Aboriginal paintings. At sunset, when rays from the setting sun strike the rock, it glows a deep red.

Guess the flags

Do you know what these flags represent? Most of them are the flags of countries, but two represent organizations and two are sports flags.

1

2

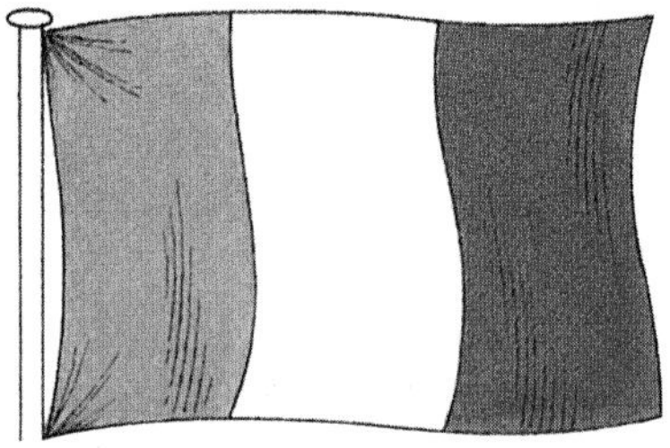

3

4

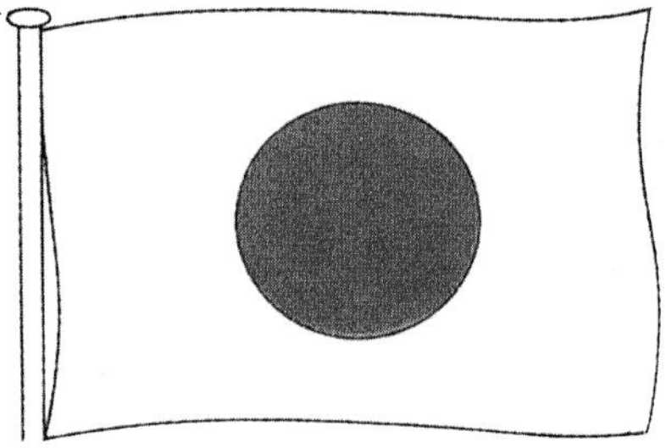

5

6

7

8

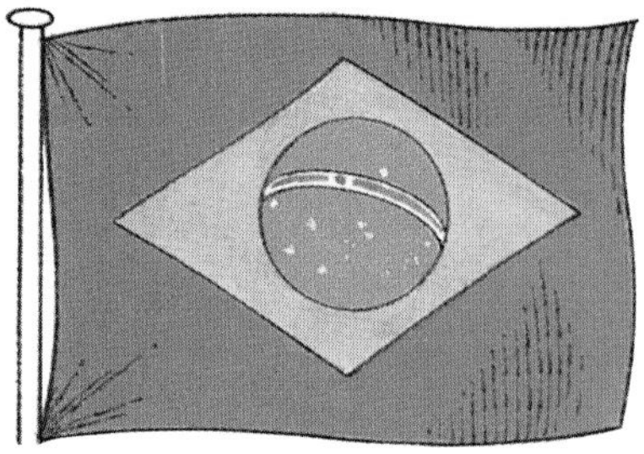

9

10

11

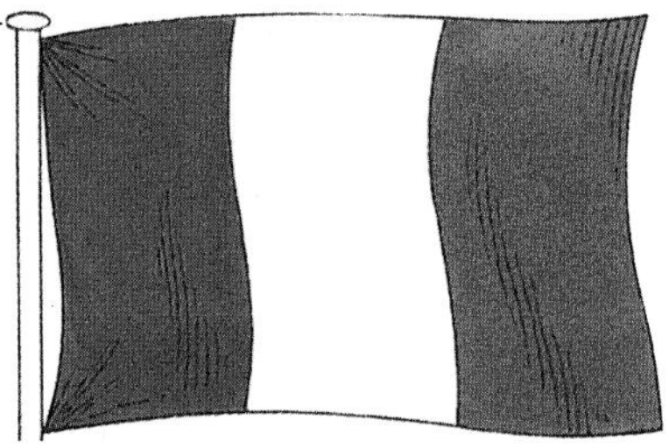

12

13

14

TURN TO PAGE 64 FOR THE ANSWERS

Name the countries and continents

Some of these shapes are countries and some are continents. Can you name them? There are extra questions for you to answer about each country or continent to help you guess the right answers.

1

a) Which tropic is this, Cancer or Capricorn?

b) What is this city called?

2

a) This is the longest river in the world. Do you know its name?

b) This imaginary line goes all the way around the world. What is it called?

3

a) These are the highest mountains in the world. What is this chain of mountains called?

b) Do you know what this island is called?

4

a) What is the name of this mighty river?

b) Do you know the name of this mountain range?

5

a) What is the name of this city?

b) This is the largest canyon in the world. Do you know its name?

6

a) What is the name of this sea?

a) Can you name this famous capital city?

7

a) What is the name of the ocean that surrounds these islands?

b) What is the capital city of this country called?

8

a) This country is made up of islands. Do you know the names of the two largest islands?

b) What is the name of the biggest city in this country?

TURN TO PAGE 64 FOR THE ANSWERS   17

Sports facts

Q What is the origin of modern tennis?

A An indoor game known as royal tennis was first played in France about 800 years ago. The court had open windows, doors, and a sloping roof. It was not until the 19th century that tennis was played on grass.

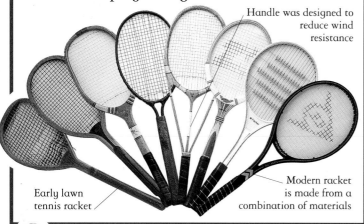

Handle was designed to reduce wind resistance

Early lawn tennis racket

Modern racket is made from a combination of materials

Q Which famous cycling race, lasting 26 days, takes place in France?

A Every summer, some of the world's finest cyclists travel to France to take part in the Tour de France. It is an extremely grueling road race covering a course of about 2,200 miles (3,500 km). A yellow jersey is awarded to the overall leader at the end of each stage of the race.

Yellow jersey is worn by the overall leader of the race

Q When and where were the first Olympic Games held?

A The world's first Olympic Games began as a men-only religious festival at Olympia in ancient Greece, more than 2,000 years ago. There was only one race. More events were added later. The first modern Olympics were held in Athens, Greece, in 1896.

The Olympic Flame is lit from a burning torch

Runners carry the torch from Olympia to the site of the games

Cowboys skillfully lasso and bring down cattle

Q The word "rodeo" is from the Spanish word meaning "roundup." How did the sport of rodeo begin?

A In the American West many years ago, cattle roamed freely instead of being fenced in. Cowboys had to round up the cattle in spring and fall. During breaks, the cowboys often competed against one another at skills such as steer wrestling and calf roping. These competitions developed into the modern rodeo.

Remarkable cities of the world

Aztec pyramid
with a temple
on top

Causeways link islands

Temple precinct

Q Mexico City stands on the site of which ancient Aztec city?

A The Aztecs, who ruled Mexico until 1519, founded a mighty empire. Their capital, Tenochtitlan, was a "floating city." It was built on islands in Lake Texcoco. Today Mexico City, the capital of Mexico, lies on the site of Tenochtitlan.

Mexico City is the most populated city in the world today

Q Which city-within-a-city is the smallest independent state in the world?

A Tucked inside Rome, the historic capital of Italy, is another city. Known as Vatican City and ruled by the Pope, it is the world's tiniest independent state. It covers an area of just 0.17 sq miles (0.44 sq km).

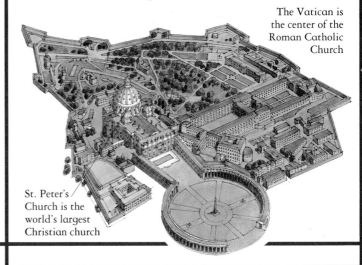

The Vatican is the center of the Roman Catholic Church

St. Peter's Church is the world's largest Christian church

Q The Brandenburg Gate stands on an east/west line that once divided which German city?

A After World War II, the German capital of Berlin was split in two. In 1989, the dividing wall was demolished and Berlin was reunited.

The Brandenburg Gate formed part of the wall that separated East and West Berlin

Berlin was reinstated as the capital of Germany in 1990

Q For the followers of which three great religions is Jerusalem holy?

A Every year millions of people flock to Jerusalem. Christians visit the Church of the Holy Sepulcher, where they believe Christ was buried. Jews pray at the Wailing Wall, the ruins of Herod's temple. Muslims worship at the Dome of the Rock Mosque, where they believe Muhammad ascended to heaven.

Jerusalem, Israel

Islamic star and moon

Christian cross

Jewish Star of David

Name these famous buildings

ANCIENT BUILDINGS
Here are two monuments and one temple. What are they called, and where in the world can you find them?

1

2

3

MODERN BUILDINGS
Can you name these 20th-century buildings and say what they are used for?

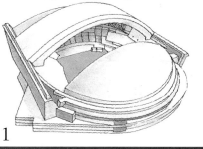

1

2

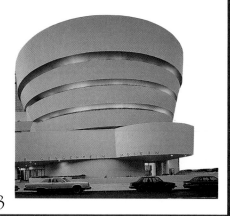

3

TALL STRUCTURES
What are the names of these six structures, where would you see them, and which one of them stands the tallest? Hint: They are not shown to scale.

1

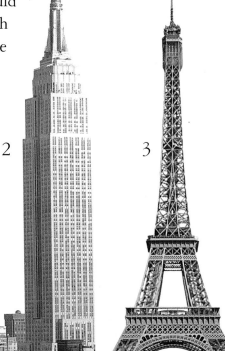

2

3

4

5

6

Find the picture that does not belong

Except for one picture, all the pictures in each of these boxes are linked in some way. Can you figure out the connection, and also find the picture in each box that does not belong?

ARTISTS

1

2

3

MUSICAL INSTRUMENTS

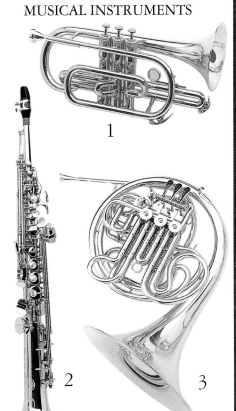

1

2

3

FLAGS

1

2

3

SPORTS

1

2

3

4

UNIFORMS

1

2

3

4

BUILDINGS

1

2

3

4

TURN TO PAGE 64 FOR THE ANSWERS

Test yourself on nature

1 Swimming in the sea, why would you avoid a Portuguese man-of-war?

Portuguese man-of-war

2 Why is the arrow-poison frog that lives in rain forests so brightly colored?

Arrow-poison frog

3 Which huge, flightless bird lays the world's largest egg?

Huge egg and hen's egg

4 Smooth and skeletal muscles are both found in the human body. How do they differ from each other?

5 Over short distances, which animal can run at about 60 mph (100 km/h) – as fast as a car?

Adult horse

6 A sett is an underground system of tunnels. Which nocturnal animal lives in this kind of home, and how is it built?

7 Cows are often seen lying down chewing the cud. What is cud, and why do they chew it?

8 How are the pearls that come from oysters and some other shellfish made?

Blister pearl

9 Inside which sea mammal would you find spermaceti oil?

10 Why do beavers spend their time cutting down trees?

Beaver gnaws at tree

11 What is a mermaid's purse, and where would you find one?

Mermaid

12 Bacon and ham come from which farm animal?

13 What are the three kinds of blood cells found in the human body, and what are their jobs?

14 A lizard sometimes sheds its tail. When might it do this, and what happens to the tail?

Tailless tree skunk

15 Can you name the three main types of horses, and say which type is the smallest?

16 Where would you find anthers, stigmas, and styles?

The whale shark can be 49 ft (15 m) long

17 The whale shark is the biggest fish, but there are other larger creatures living in the sea. What is the largest sea creature?

18 There are about 40 cacao beans in every pod, or fruit, of the cacao tree. What are the beans used for?

19 Why was the marine toad taken to Australia in the 1930s?

Marine toad

TURN TO PAGES 24 AND 25 FOR THE ANSWERS

Test yourself on nature

20 The common flea jumps onto people to bite them. How far is it able to leap?

Flea gets airborne

21 Why does a dog sometimes hang its tongue out of its mouth and pant?

Panting dog

22 Can flying squirrels and flying lemurs really fly through the air?

Flying squirrel

23 Fossils of ammonites are some of the most commonly found stony remains. What were ammonites?

24 Why do leafcutter ants march back to their nest carrying bits of leaf?

Ants bite off huge pieces of leaf

25 Why are the boa snakes of tropical America and the pythons of Africa, Asia, and Australia known as "constrictors"?

26 A dromedary camel has one hump and a Bactrian camel has two humps. What is in the hump (or humps)?

27 Why do some warm-blooded animals hibernate?

Hibernating dormouse

28 What kind of tree grows to be the tallest in the world?

29 Which dinosaur was the largest known meat-eating creature of all time?

30 Why do snakes stick out their tongues and flick them?

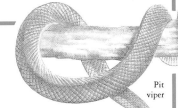

Pit viper

31 The mudskipper, unlike most other fish, can spend long periods out of water. How does it survive on land?

32 Crocodiles and alligators look very similar. How can you tell them apart?

33 When a honeybee "dances" in a figure eight, what is it telling other bees in the hive?

Figure–eight pattern

34 The coldest place on Earth is on the ice of the Antarctic. How do newborn emperor penguins survive in this cold?

35 How are the spiny anteater and the platypus different from other kinds of mammals?

Platypus

Spiny anteater

36 Bats are nighttime creatures. What special noises do they make to help them find their way in the dark?

African elephant

37 What animal is the closest living land relative to the elephant?

38 Which group of animals feed their young on milk?

39 Why do male grasshoppers and crickets make a chirping sound?

Chirping grasshopper

TURN TO PAGES 26 AND 27 FOR THE ANSWERS

Answers for nature quiz

1 The Portuguese man-of-war is a floating colony of hundreds of jellyfish-like creatures called polyps. Some of the polyps trail tentacles with stinging cells. If you touch a tentacle, you trigger one of these cells, which will then sting you with a poison.

2 The arrow-poison frog's skin contains poison. The bright colors of the skin, which include yellow, orange, blue, and red, warn predators that the frog is poisonous to eat.

3 The world's largest egg is laid by the ostrich, the world's biggest living bird. The egg is about 8 in (20 cm) tall and weighs 3 lb 8 oz (1.6 kg), 30 times as much as a hen's egg.

Ostrich with her chicks

4 Smooth muscle is found in your digestive system, bladder, and blood vessels. It works automatically, even when you are asleep. Skeletal, or striated, muscle is different because you can control it at will. It covers your bones and is used to move them.

Skeletal muscle

Smooth muscle

5 In a sprint the fastest land animal is the cheetah, a member of the cat family. Over a long distance the pronghorn antelope of North America holds the record.

Cheetah bounds after prey and then pounces

6 The badger, a member of the weasel family, lives in a sett. It uses its strong claws to build the tunnels of the sett in the side of a bank or among tree roots. Over the years more tunnels are added. A large sett may be 100 years old.

Badger

7 Cows eat grass, which has to be well chewed before it can be fully digested. The cow has four stomachs. Grass is stored in the first stomach and later brought up in a wad, the cud, which is chewed thoroughly and then passed to the other stomachs.

Cow has four stomachs

8 A pearl is created when a piece of grit lodges in the shell. The shellfish covers the grit with a layer of shell lining known as mother-of-pearl, or nacre. The pearl that is formed removes the irritating grit.

Irritating grit in shell   Nacre forms around grit   Pearl comes free from shell

9 Spermaceti oil is a waxy substance that fills the huge square forehead of the sperm whale. Scientists believe that it may help the whale keep its balance when deep diving.

Enormous sperm whale

10 A beaver uses branches to dam streams and to make its home, called a lodge. The lodge is built from sticks and mud in the pool of water formed by the dam. In the lodge the beaver hollows out a dry chamber above water level to live in. Beavers eat bark, twigs, and leaves.

Answers for nature quiz

11 A mermaid's purse is the case of eggs laid by a shark or ray. The fish lay their eggs near the seashore, anchored to seaweed or rocks by tendrils. After the eggs have hatched, the rubbery cases are often washed up onto the beach.

Egg cases

12 The pig. Pork is the name given to fresh pig meat. Bacon is pork that has been "cured" by treating it with salt, and sometimes smoking it. Ham, which also comes from the pig, is usually from the hind leg of the animal. It can be either smoked or cured.

Different types of meat come from the pig

13 A tiny drop of blood contains about five million cells. Some are red cells, which carry oxygen around the body. Others are white cells, which fight infection. Platelets are the third kind of cell. They help make the blood clot.

Red cell *White cell* *Platelet*

14 The end of a lizard's tail breaks off if it is seized by a predator, such as a bird or a cat. The broken-off piece of tail twitches for a bit. This confuses the enemy while the lizard escapes. The lizard's tail will regrow in about eight months.

Tree skunk's tail has regrown

15 The three main types are draft horses, light horses, and ponies. Draft horses, such as Shires, are used to pull plows; light horses, such as Arabians, take part in races. The pony is the smallest type, less than 5 ft (1.5 m) high at the shoulder.

Shetland pony is the smallest

16 Anthers, stigmas, and styles are parts of a flower. The anthers contain pollen and are male flower parts. The stigmas, which receive the pollen, are held on styles and are female flower parts.

Stigma
Style
Anther

17 The blue whale is not only the largest sea creature but also the largest animal that has ever lived. It grows to about 100 ft (30 m) long and weighs up to 134 tons (136 tonnes) – about as heavy as 2,000 people!

Blue whale

18 Cacao beans are roasted, shelled, and then ground into a paste called cocoa butter. Cocoa butter and sugar are the main ingredients of chocolate. Cocoa is an ancient mis-spelling of the Mayan word cacao.

Chocolate

19 The marine toad was originally found only in Central and South America. In the 1930s it was taken to Australia to eat cane beetles, which are pests of the sugarcane crop. The toad bred so successfully that it is now a serious pest itself.

Australia

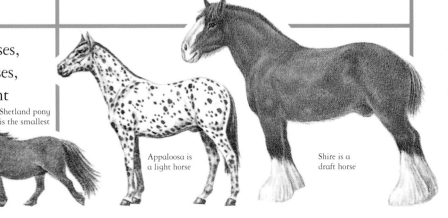

Appaloosa is a light horse

Shire is a draft horse

Answers for nature quiz

20 A common flea can jump more than 12 in (30 cm). That is the same as a person jumping 800 ft (245 m), which is higher than a 70-story building, or St. Paul's Cathedral in London, England.

Flea

St. Paul's

21 Unlike humans, dogs do not sweat through their skin to cool themselves. There are sweat glands on a dog's paw pads, but not much heat can be lost through the feet. To cool itself down quickly the dog pants, or breathes rapidly, to give off heat from its mouth and tongue.

22 Neither of these animals can really fly. They have no wings to flap so they cannot climb upward into the air under their own power. They can only swoop or glide, using their tails to steer.

Flying lemur

23 Ammonites were sea creatures with spiral shells, similar to the modern nautilus. They were common in prehistoric times but they died out, along with the dinosaurs, about 65 million years ago.

Fossil

24 Leafcutter ants feed on fungus. In their nest the ants chew the pieces of leaf they have cut. Then they mix the leaf with saliva to make a compost, on which the fungus grows.

25 These snakes are known as constrictors because they constrict, or squeeze, their prey. Instead of giving their prey a poisonous bite to kill it, they coil their bodies tightly around the victim until it is squeezed to death.

Emerald tree boa

26 A camel's hump stores reserves of fat. This fat allows it to travel for long periods across the desert without eating or drinking. It survives by living off the fatty fluid in its hump. The hump shrinks when the camel is hungry.

Dromedary camel

27 Animals hibernate – a sleeplike state – in a sheltered place to survive the cold winter months. Some desert animals, such as snails, have to "sleep" through summer to survive the intense heat. This is called estivation.

Estivating snails

28 A giant sequoia tree, which is named *General Sherman,* is the largest tree in the world. It grows in Sequoia National Park, California. It is over 270 ft (82 m) tall and its weight is estimated at 2,500 tons.

Giant sequoia

29 The ferocious *Tyrannosaurus rex* was the largest carnivorous dinosaur. It lived between 67 and 65 millions of years ago, so all the details known about this monster have come from its fossils.

Tyrannosaurus rex was about 46 ft (14 m) long

Answers for nature quiz

30 Animals have to be aware of their surroundings to survive. A snake flicks out its tongue to detect odors in the air. The smells that stick to its wet tongue are tasted and help the snake to follow prey, find a mate, and avoid danger.

31 The mudskipper is able to leave the water and skip across mudflats and swamps using its fins as "legs." Like a diver with an Aqua-Lung, the mudskipper carries its air supply in the form of water kept in its large gill chambers.

Mudskippers clinging onto a reed

Crocodile shows its tooth

32 Look at their teeth! When its mouth is closed an alligator shows no teeth. But a crocodile always shows the fourth tooth on each side of its lower jaw. Both animals are meat eaters, and they use their teeth to grab prey.

Alligator shows no teeth

33 A honeybee dances the figure–eight pattern to inform other bees in the hive of the location, in relation to the sun, of a source of pollen or nectar.

Emperor penguins

34 The male penguin keeps the eggs warm between his feet and belly. When the eggs hatch, the chicks stay warm by standing on their parents' feet to keep off the cold ice.

35 Unlike most mammals, the spiny anteater, or echidna, and the platypus lay eggs instead of giving birth to live young. When the eggs hatch, the mother feeds the babies on milk. These animals are known as monotremes, and they are both found in Australia.

36 Bats find their way – and their prey – by making very high-pitched squeaks and clicks. The sounds bounce back off nearby objects and are detected by the bat's large ears. This is called echolocation and gives the bat information about the object.

37 Believe it or not, it is the rock hyrax, which looks like a guinea pig and is about the size of a rabbit. Like the elephant, hyraxes are vegetarian, have long front teeth that grow throughout their lives, and have similar foot bones.

Small furry rock hyrax

38 The only creatures that feed their young with milk are mammals. The milk is produced in mammary glands on the chest or abdomen. The young babies suck the milk from the mother's teats.

Mother dog and suckling puppies

Grasshopper

39 The males chirp to attract a female or to warn off rival males. The noise is made by rubbing together the ridged veins on the front wings, or by rubbing the toothed ridge on the back leg against the wing vein.

Ridged veins on wing

Toothed ridges on back leg

Strange creatures of the sea

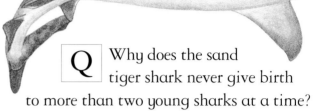

Q What is unusual about the way in which sea horses breed?

A Unlike most living creatures, it is the male sea horse that gives birth. In the breeding season the female lays as many as 200 eggs in a special pouch on the front of the male's abdomen. The eggs develop in the pouch, and after about four weeks the baby sea horses are born.

Tail is used to hold on to the coral

Male rests after giving birth to baby sea horses

Q Why does the sand tiger shark never give birth to more than two young sharks at a time?

A There can be as many as 15 embryo sharks in a mother sand tiger shark's womb at first. But as the babies develop, they eat each other until there are just two left. The lucky survivors are born fully formed and are already ferocious creatures. They immediately leave their mother and swim away in search of other fish to eat.

Q In the depths of the sea, why is the viperfish such a fearsome hunter?

A The viperfish has a long, flexible spike on its back, which it uses like a fishing rod. When it hunts, it holds the spike over its head. Curious fish are attracted to the spike's glowing tip. Once lured, the viperfish uses its long fangs to stab its victim. The prey, trapped in the hunter's mouth by its curved teeth, is then swallowed whole.

Long spike

Curved teeth prevent the victim from escaping

Long fangs

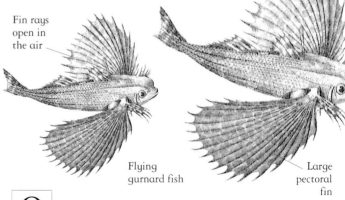

Fin rays open in the air

Flying gurnard fish

Large pectoral fin

Q Is it true that some fish can fly?

A No fish can actually fly. But some fish, called flying fish, can leap out of the water using their strong tails. Their pectoral fins act as "wings," helping them glide through the air. Out of water, flying fish look like giant dragonflies. When they swim they fold in their fins to make a streamlined shape.

Surprising feathery friends

Q Why does a cassowary have a bony helmet on its head?

A All three species of the cassowary bird live in the thick forests of Australasia. They are huge flightless birds that feed on fruits, berries, and seeds. The tall horny casque on its head is used to push aside the tangled forest undergrowth. The survival of these birds is threatened by the destruction of forests.

Horny casque

Two-wattled cassowary

Cassowary chick is reared by the male

Q Which tiny bird hums to stay still in midair?

A To stay in one place in the air, the hummingbird flaps its wings nonstop, just as a swimmer treads water to stay afloat. Its wings beat between 20 and 50 times a second to keep it hovering. This fast beating makes the humming sound you hear when the bird feeds from a flower.

Blades spin fast when the helicopter hovers

Q Which majestic bird is the national emblem of the United States?

A Probably chosen for its large size and super strength, the bald eagle is the national emblem of the United States. It is not really bald but looks that way because the white feathers on its head, which grow only when the bird is four years old, contrast with its dark body.

White head feathers

Eagle has excellent eyesight

Large, powerful wings for soaring and diving

Toes have long, sharp talons to grasp prey

Q Which bird makes a journey every year from the top of the world to the bottom, and back again?

Male Arctic tern brings his mate fish during courtship

A The Arctic tern makes the longest migration in the world. Flying from pole to pole it migrates about 22,000 miles (35,500 km) a year. The tern spends the short Arctic summer breeding and feeding on insects and fish. It then flies south toward the South Pole for another summer near the Antarctic.

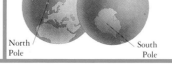

The poles are among the coldest places on Earth

North Pole

South Pole

Identify these wild animals

Can you name the animal shown in each box? There is also a question to answer about each animal, which may help you identify it.

1 What does this animal lick up with its long sticky tongue?

2 The young of these mammals are called leverets. What are the adult males and females known as?

3 In a matter of minutes what can this reptile change about the way it looks?

4 What kind of surroundings does this brightly colored tropical fish live in?

5 Why does this animal have wide, flat feet?

6 This marsupial lives in Australia. What does it do to avoid the heat of the day?

7 Where does this large South American bird build its nest?

8 All 22 kinds of this animal live on which island off the east coast of Africa?

Guess the animal from the part

TAILS

Can you guess which creatures these tails belong to? Two of the creatures live in the sea, one is a member of the same group of animals as spiders, and the others are all mammals.

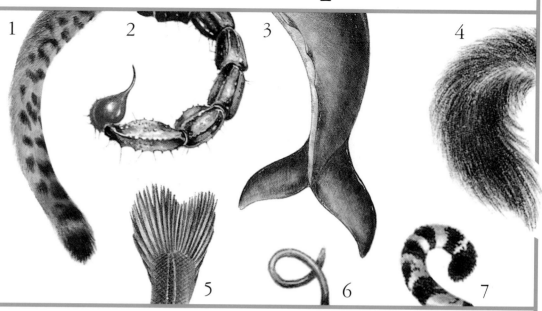

1 2 3 4

5 6 7

SKINS AND FURS

Some skins are scaly, others are bumpy. Lots of animals have fur, which often has a special pattern. Do you know which animals these skins cover?

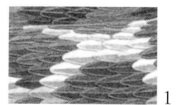
1

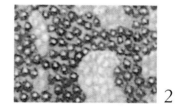
2

3

4

5

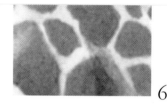
6

LEGS

Animal legs are all different. Some are made to make long leaps, to run fast, or to walk on sand. Others are adapted for life in or by water. Can you guess which creatures these legs belong to?

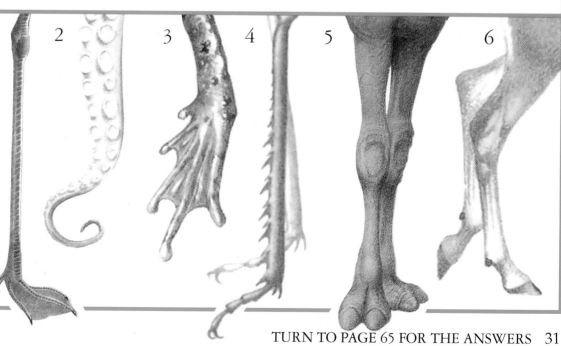

1 2 3 4 5 6

TURN TO PAGE 65 FOR THE ANSWERS

Creepy crawly facts

Q How does the deadly black widow spider get its name?

A This shiny, black-bodied spider is so called because, after mating, the female sometimes eats the smaller male spider. The female is also one of the few spiders that can kill people. Her body is no bigger than a pea, but her bite contains poison that is 15 times more deadly than the poison of a rattlesnake.

Q Which insect uses a sticklike disguise to hide from its predators?

A With a body that looks like a dried-up leaf, the spiny stick insect blends in perfectly with the prickles and curly leaves on which it perches. It moves slowly and sways as it walks, so that it looks like part of the tree moving in the wind.

The legs look like the veins of dead leaves

Sharp spines are like the thorns on the twigs

Body is brownish yellow, like the leaves

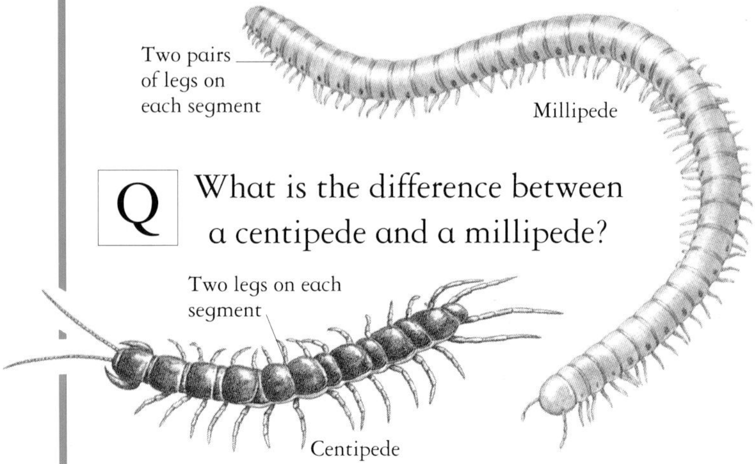

Two pairs of legs on each segment

Millipede

Q What is the difference between a centipede and a millipede?

Two legs on each segment

Centipede

A The centipede has one pair of legs on each body segment. It is an active hunter and can run swiftly after insects and other small prey. The millipede does not need to be as quick on its feet because it feeds on decaying plant matter. It has two pairs of legs on each segment. The legs move in waves, pushing it slowly through the soil.

Q When would you see a stag beetle using its huge, antlerlike jaws?

A Only the male stag beetle has such large mandibles (jaws). In fact they are so heavy that they cannot give a strong bite. Instead they are used mainly for show. Just like real stags, males use their "antlers" to threaten and wrestle with other males during the breeding season, to compete for a female.

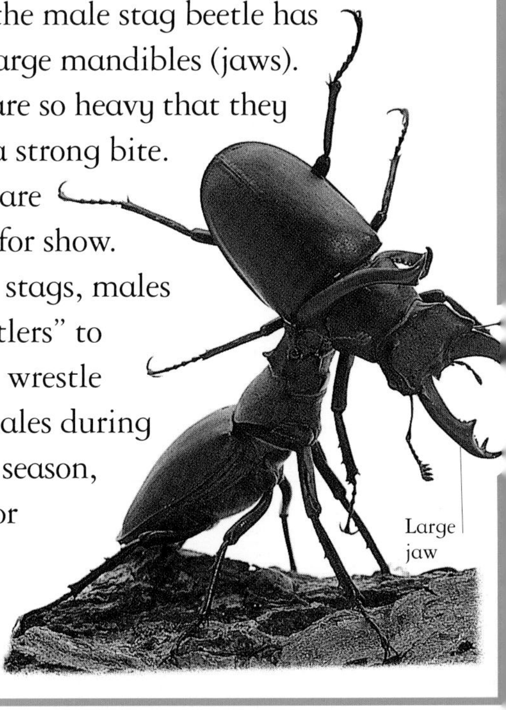

Large jaw

Attack and defense

Q Is the frilled lizard of Australia really as fierce as it looks?

A This lizard is quite harmless. The "frill" is a large flap of loose skin around its neck. When the lizard is startled by a predator, it opens its mouth wide. This makes the frill, which is usually folded flat, open to show a huge ruffle-like collar. If this display does not scare off the enemy, the lizard runs away.

Frill stands up to frighten away the enemy

Q How and why does a Venus's-flytrap plant catch insects?

A This plant has two kidney-shaped lobes at the tip of its leaves. The lobes are hinged at the midrib. When an insect lands on the leaf, it touches sensitive bristles, which trigger the lobes to snap shut. Once trapped inside, the insect is eaten — it is digested and absorbed by glands on the leaf.

Teeth along the edge form a cage around the insect

Trigger bristles

Damselfly lands on the lobe

Q How does the crested porcupine defend itself from an enemy?

Quills, or stiff spines, protect the body

Tail quills are barbed like arrows

A When the crested porcupine feels endangered it rattles the quills, or hollow spines, on its tail to warn predators to stay away. Attackers who come too close are struck with the tail. The sharp quills come out easily and stick into the enemy like arrows.

Q Which sea creatures confuse their enemies by hiding behind a cloud of ink?

A Squids, octupuses, and cuttlefish have an ink gland attached to their digestive system. If they are threatened they squirt a dark-colored ink, called sepia, out of a syphon at the end of their digestive tract. The ink forms a cloud in the water, which confuses the enemy about which shape to follow.

Cloud is like an underwater smokescreen

Common squid

33

Match the animal to its diet

All the creatures in this box live in the wild. Can you pair each one with the animal or plant (in the box beneath) that it eats in its natural habitat?

 TURN TO PAGE 65 FOR THE ANSWERS

Spot the one that does not belong

In each of these boxes two of the three objects have something in common. Can you spot the picture that does not belong with the others, and say why?

FUNGI

BIRDS

REPTILES

TREES

BUGS

ANIMALS

TURN TO PAGE 65 FOR THE ANSWERS   35

Test yourself on history

1 A ruthless dynasty ruled China between 221 B.C. and 206 B.C. What was its name?

Army officers in chariots

2 North American colonists issued which famous declaration on July 4, 1776?

William I

3 What is the Domesday Book, and why was it written?

4 Who were the Samurai, and where did they rule?

5 Which general rode into battle on a wild horse called Bucephalus? *Bucephalus was a beautiful horse*

Disaster strikes Pompeii

6 In A.D. 79, what terrible disaster overtook Pompeii?

7 Sailors used an astrolabe to help them navigate. When and where was it developed?

8 The Phoenicians produced purple color to dye cloth. How did they make it? *Phoenicians dyeing cloth*

9 Books were first made by the Egyptians 5,000 years ago. What did they use to make the paper?

10 Who led the first expeditions to the South Pole, and what happened to the party of British explorers? *Husky-drawn sled*

11 Which sea battle stopped the French invading Britain in 1805?

Battleships at sea

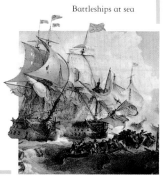

12 World War I broke out in 1914. Why was it so called?

13 Who did the Sioux fight at the Battle of Little Bighorn in 1876, and who won? *The Sioux are a native North American tribe*

14 Which religious movement was begun with Martin Luther's list of 95 complaints?

Luther pins up his list

15 Between 1788 and 1868, who was sent to Botany Bay?

16 Harappa and Mohenjo-Daro were the world's first cities. Who built them?

17 Why were the Huns, and other tribes that attacked the Roman Empire, called "barbarians"?

18 What happened to the Jews during World War II? *Rounding up the Jews*

19 The ancient Egyptians mummified their dead. Why did they do this, and how were the bodies preserved? *Richly decorated coffin contains a mummy*

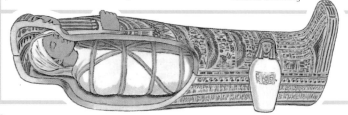

Test yourself on history

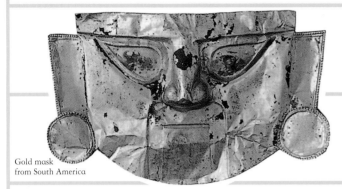

Gold mask
from South America

28 In 1963, which American made a now-famous speech that included the words: "I have a dream"?

29 Why did the Pilgrims sail across the Atlantic to North America in 1620?

The *Mayflower*, the
Pilgrims' ship

20 In the early 16th century, Spanish adventurers went to South America. What were they looking for?

21 Why did the explorer James Cook make his crew eat fresh fruit and pickled cabbage?

James Cook

Coronation of Charlemagne

30 In about A.D. 60, who led Britons in a revolt against the Romans?

31 Which empire did Charlemagne rule from Christmas Day 800?

22 The treasure that pirates stole from ships included "pieces of eight." What were they?

Pirate's flag

23 The word "spartan" means strict or brave. Who were the Spartans, why are they famous, and where did they live?

24 What happened on Wall Street in 1929, causing worldwide economic depression?

Stock market
ticker tape

25 The Vikings sailed to many countries in long-ships. Where did they come from?

El Cid

26 A knight in full armor had his face covered. What did he wear so that people could identify him?

27 Amerigo Vespucci was an Italian explorer. Which continent is named after him?

Amerigo Vespucci

32 The breastplate and gauntlet are pieces of armor. What parts of the body do they protect?

33 This eagle crest belonged to a great family. What was their name?

Black double-headed
eagle crest

34 The Assyrians ruled in the Middle East 3,000 years ago. Name their capital city.

35 El Cid is a Spanish national hero. How did he become famous, and what was his real name?

36 In about 1550 B.C, what devasted the Minoan civilization?

37 The tomb of which Egyptian boy-king was uncovered in 1922?

Scarab beetle
brooch from the tomb

TURN TO PAGES 40 AND 41 FOR THE ANSWERS

Answers for history quiz

1 The Ch'in dynasty from which China gets its name. The dynasty's emperor was Shih Huang Ti. His vast army united the country, which had previously consisted of many warring states.

Paul Revere warns colonists that the British army is coming

2 The Declaration of Independence. Each year on July 4, Americans celebrate the day when the colonists, who were fighting the British over lack of representation in the British government, declared independence.

3 The Domesday Book is a remarkable document. Commissioned by King William I in 1085, it was a detailed survey of the lands, people, animals, and other goods of all the villages in England.

The original Domesday Book can still be seen in London, England

Samurai

4 The Samurai were aristocratic warriors. They followed a strict code of honor. From 1185 to 1868 their shoguns, or lords, ruled Japan.

5 Alexander the Great (356-323 B.C.). The brilliant general and the horse were devoted to each other. When the animal died, Alexander built a city in India in its honor.

6 One summer afternoon in A.D. 79, Mount Vesuvius in Italy erupted. Burning ash from the volcano completely buried the Roman city of Pompeii, and its inhabitants.

A plaster cast of the hollow left in the ash by a body

7 The astrolabe was developed during the 8th century by astronomers in Egypt. In 971, the world's first university was founded in Cairo, Egypt, and the Arabs made great advances in astronomy, mathematics, and medical science.

Moorish astrolabe

8 The Phoenicians were Mediterranean sailors and traders. They made the expensive, vivid purple dye from crushed murex seashells. Only high government officials could afford to wear purple cloth.

9 The Egyptians pressed together strands of papyrus reed to form scrolls to write on. Later, the Romans wrote on treated animal skin called parchment. The Chinese invented the paper we use about 2,000 years ago.

Papyrus reeds

10 Captain Robert Scott led the British expedition that reached the South Pole on January 17, 1912. But they were beaten to the pole by Norwegian Roald Amundsen and his team. Only five of Scott's team of ten men reached the pole; unfortunately Scott and the rest of his team died on the return journey.

Answers for history quiz

11 In 1805 the French emperor Napoleon Bonaparte was poised to invade England. But the British fleet under Horatio Nelson destroyed the combined French and Spanish fleet at the Battle of Trafalgar.

Planes were first used in World War I

12 In 1914 a terrible war engulfed Europe. It was called the Great War, or World War I, because fighting took place in every continent of the world. The war lasted until 1918, and millions were killed.

13 The Sioux fought the U.S. cavalry at Little Bighorn, Montana. The warriors wiped out the cavalry, but the Native Americans were eventually forced onto reservations.

Sioux hunting buffalo

14 Martin Luther thought the Catholic Church was corrupt. His list of complaints inspired a mass movement for the reform of the Catholic Church, called the Reformation. Expelled from the Church in 1521, Luther founded Protestantism.

15 Lying south of Sydney, Botany Bay was where James Cook first landed in Australia. From 1788 to 1868 the British sent convicts to Botany Bay to relieve over-crowding in British prisons.

British convicts

Beautiful stone carving

16 In about 2500 B.C. a great civilization flourished around the Indus River in southern Asia. The people of the region were highly skilled. They built the world's first cities: Mohenjo-Daro in what is now Pakistan, and Harappa, in modern India.

Gold buckle set with garnet

Gold and enameled cloak fastener

17 As the Roman Empire began to decline, it was threatened by tribal people who lived outside the empire, such as the Huns, Visigoths, and Vandals. The Romans called them "barbarians," which means "uncivilized"; in fact they were skilled warriors and craftspeople.

18 In Nazi Germany, Jews were persecuted and imprisoned. By 1945, about six million Jews had been rounded up and murdered in specially built concentration camps. The slaughter of Jews during World War II is called the Holocaust.

Jews were forced to wear a yellow star

19 The Egyptians believed in life after death. They therefore preserved the bodies of the dead as mummies. The internal organs were removed, and the body was then treated to prevent decay.

Answers for history quiz

20 The Spanish soldiers, known as conquistadors, were looking for gold, silver, and land. Two of the most famous conquistadors were Hernando Cortes and Francisco Pizarro.

Cortes, Spanish conqueror

21 Many sailors used to suffer from the disease scurvy, which is caused by a lack of vitamin C. James Cook was an enlightened captain. When he sailed to Australia, Cook kept his crew healthy by insisting that they eat fresh fruit and pickled cabbage.

22 The currency stolen by pirates was doubloons, or "pieces of eight." A doubloon was a Spanish gold dollar that was worth eight Spanish gold escudos.

Gold doubloon

23 The Spartans were the inhabitants of Sparta, the second major city-state of ancient Greece. They were renowned throughout Greece for their courage and discipline. Male Spartans began military training at the age of seven, and remained soldiers until they were 60.

Spartan hoplites (foot soldiers) were very fierce

24 On October 24, 1929, the New York Stock Exchange, on Wall Street, crashed. Stock prices fell, the economy of the country collapsed, and millions lost their jobs. The effects were felt across the world throughout the 1930s.

25 The Vikings were seafarers from Norway, Sweden, and Denmark. They sailed magnificent longships, and settled in many lands, reaching North America in around AD 1000.

Viking longship

26 A knight in armor could be recognized by his coat of arms. The "arms" consisted of two elements – the field (background color or pattern), and charge (symbol or picture).

The coats of arms were diplayed on shields

27 In 1499, Amerigo Vespucci became the first European to explore the coast of Brazil. His maps of the New World were so good that sailors referred to the newly found continent as "Amerigo's Land" and it is now known as South America.

United States' flag

28 The influential civil rights leader, Martin Luther King, Jr., made a speech including these words when he led 250,000 people to Washington to demand equal rights for black Americans. In 1964-65, equal rights laws were passed. King was assassinated in 1968.

Martin Luther King, Jr.

Answers for history quiz

29 The Puritans, or Pilgrims, sailed from England to North America in a small ship, the *Mayflower*. The 102 settlers on board were seeking freedom of worship in the New World.

Puritan families lived simple lives, following the teachings of the Bible

30 After Britain had been invaded and conquered by the Romans, the warrior-queen Boudicca led the Iceni tribe in a fierce revolt. But they were no match for the Romans and were brutally crushed.

Boudicca leads her warriors

31 Charlemagne, king of the Franks (the ancestors of today's French) was crowned emperor of the Romans at St. Peter's Basilica in Rome. He created the first important empire in western Europe after the fall of Rome. (It later became the Holy Roman Empire.)

32 The breastplate of a suit of armor protected the chest. It was flared so that sword strokes bounced off. The gauntlet protected the hand, and was made of many small pieces, which allowed the hand to move freely.

Knight in armor

33 Hapsburg (or Habsburg). By the 1500s, this family dominated central and southern Europe, including Italy and Spain. They ruled the Holy Roman Empire, then the Austrian Empire, until their overthrow in 1918.

18th-century Hapsburgs

34 Nineveh was the capital of the Assyrian Empire. The Assyrians were famed for their strength in battle, but their empire collapsed when Nineveh was destroyed by the Babylonians and Medes in 612 BC.

Statues guarded buildings

35 El Cid, from the Arabic word "sidi" meaning lord, was a Spanish nobleman, Rodrigo Diaz de Vivar. In 1094, he recaptured Valencia from the ruling Muslim Moors of North Africa, who had invaded Spain in AD 711.

Frieze of bull leaping, a dangerous Minoan sport

36 The Minoans were seafarers who settled on Crete about 4,000 years ago. They built huge palaces and had a rich culture. In about 1550 BC, a volcanic eruption destroyed their civilization. Early this century archaeologists uncovered a Minoan palace at Knossos.

37 Tutankhamen's. He was a boy-king who ruled Egypt some 3,500 years ago. The British archaeologist, Howard Carter, found the boy's tomb, which contained his body and many treasures, in the Valley of the Kings.

Tutankhamen's coffin

Historical events

The dead were carried away on carts and buried in large graves

Q What killed approximately one third of the people in Europe at the end of the Middle Ages?

A In 1347, a terrible disease from Asia swept across Europe. The people who caught it developed black patches on their bodies and usually died within a few days. The plague became known as the Black Death because of the dark patches. Today we know that it was bubonic plague, which was spread by fleas that lived on infected black rats.

Q Why did people rush to California in 1849?

Gold nugget

A The first gold fields were discovered in northern California in January 1848. The following year, many thousands flocked to the region hoping to make their fortunes from prospecting (looking) for gold. It was the greatest gold rush in American history. In 1849 alone, the state's population soared from 20,000 to over 100,000 people.

Prospector sifts for gold

Q Who believed that they had to offer human hearts to their sun god Huitzilopochtli?

Jade mask

A From the 13th to the 16th centuries, the Mexican valley was dominated by the Aztecs. They founded a great empire and captured many prisoners. Believing that the world would come to an end unless they sacrificed people to their sun god, the Aztecs built temples where priests offered the hearts of as many as 1,000 prisoners every week to Huitzilopochtli.

Sacrificial knife

Stone blade

Q Which Chinese army has stood guard for more than 2,000 years?

A Standing in rows, a magnificent army of over 8,000 terra-cotta clay figures watches over the tomb of the first emperor of all China, Shih Huang Ti. Made in 210 BC, the life-size models are exact copies of the army that had helped the emperor unite the rival kingdoms of China.

Some 700,000 slaves and craftspeople made the hollow figures

People in history

Q Which French heroine heard the "voices of angels"?

A In 1429 the French army, led by Joan of Arc, finally defeated the English, who had ruled much of France for the past 100 years. Joan of Arc was very religious, and claimed that she had heard the voices of angels and saints telling her to restore the rightful king of France to his throne.

Joan of Arc led French troops to victory at Orleans

Q In 1492 the Italian sailor Christopher Columbus set sail in search of a new sea route to India. What did he find?

A After sailing westward from Spain for two months Columbus sighted land, which he believed was India. In fact, it was an island in the Caribbean. He was welcomed ashore by native peoples. Since then, these people have been called "Indians" because the explorers thought that they were in India.

Mao Zedong

Q Who led the Long March through China in 1934-5?

A Mao Zedong, head of the Communist Party in China, led about 100,000 people from Kiangshi province, the communist stronghold. They marched to Shensi province in northwest China to avoid attack from the opposition National Party. Only 30,000 people survived the Long March.

The march covered 6,000 miles (9,700 km)

Q How did Charles Darwin shock the world in 1859?

A Charles Darwin was an English naturalist. His book, called *On the Origin of Species*, was published in 1859. In it he put forward his theory of evolution based on natural selection, or "survival of the fittest," and made the then shocking suggestion that humans were descended from apes.

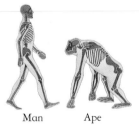

Man   Ape

Darwin shown as a monkey

Name these well-known people

Look carefully at these pictures. Each panel contains portraits of people that are famous for a similar reason. Can you figure out which country they are from, and who they are? The small pictures by the side give you a clue to help you identify them.

CHIEFS

1

2

RULERS

1

2

3

ARTISTS

1

2

3

MODERN LEADERS

PRESIDENT IS KILLED
Texas Sniper Escapes; Johnson Sworn In

1

2

3

Make the link and name the event

All the pictures in each of these seven panels are linked either to a war or a revolution. Can you recognize the elements, make the connection, and name the event?

1
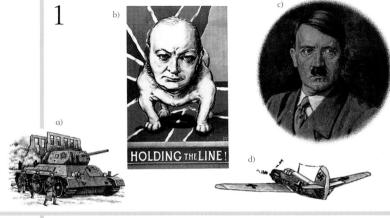

2

3

4

5

6

7
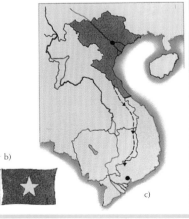

TURN TO PAGE 66 FOR THE ANSWERS

What people believe

Q What do the gods Ra, Surya, and Apollo have in common?

A People all around the world have told stories abouts gods and goddesses. Although they may have lived far apart and had different cultures, the myths told were often about the same subjects, such as the rain, the sea, the moon, and the sun. Ra from Egypt, Surya in India, and the Greek Apollo were all ancient sun gods.

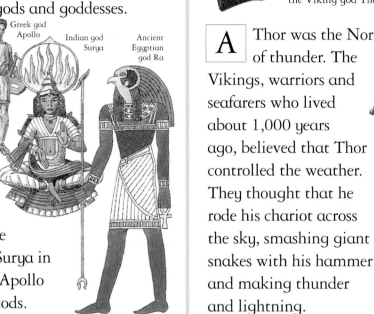

Greek god Apollo

Indian god Surya

Ancient Egyptian god Ra

Q Who was Thor, and why did he carry a hammer?

Hammer, symbol of the Viking god Thor

A Thor was the Norse god of thunder. The Vikings, warriors and seafarers who lived about 1,000 years ago, believed that Thor controlled the weather. They thought that he rode his chariot across the sky, smashing giant snakes with his hammer and making thunder and lightning.

Thor's hammer was thought to be a thunderbolt

Q Why were 200 people tried in Salem, Massachusetts, in 1692?

A Four hundred years ago, many people believed in witches. They accused old or peculiar women of being in league with the devil, and blamed them for misfortune. During the last big witch hunt, in Salem, 200 women were accused of witchcraft; 19 were hanged.

Q Why was Mother Teresa awarded a Nobel Peace Prize in 1979 ?

A Mother Teresa, who died in 1997, was a Christian and believed that she had a duty to ease human suffering. Born in Albania in 1910, she spent most of her life in India . She founded the Missionaries of Charity and won the Nobel Peace Prize for her work with the homeless and the dying.

Mother Teresa wearing a flowing dress called a sari

Art through the ages

Clay tablet

Detail of the *Standard of Ur*

Q With what two inventions did the Sumerians of Mesopotamia transform daily life nearly 5,000 years ago?

A During the Bronze Age, the Sumerians developed the system of picture writing known as cuneiform. The pictures were drawn on tablets of damp clay with wedge-shaped pens. They also invented the wheel, which they used on wagons and war chariots, and to make pottery.

Q What was the "Renaissance" and where did it begin?

A The Renaissance, a French word that means "rebirth," was a period in history that began in Italy in the 15th century. It lasted about 200 years, during which time educated people developed new ideas about the world around them, and rediscovered the arts and learning of ancient Greece and Rome. It produced great artists such as Michelangelo, whose painting on the Sistine Chapel ceiling survives to this day.

Chapel ceiling

Q Which two great composers were born in 1685?

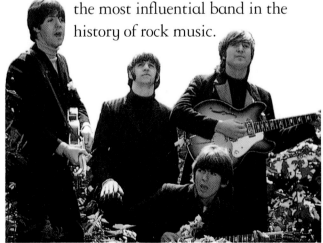
Royal Fireworks

A Johann Sebastian Bach and George Frideric Handel. Both born in Germany, they were great composers of Baroque music – a musical form that dominated the 17th and early 18th centuries. The *Brandenburg Concertos* are among Bach's best-known works; Handel's include *Music for the Royal Fireworks*.

Bach 1685-1750

Q Which musical insects gave 1960's rock music its distinctive sound?

A The Beatles. The band consisted of John Lennon, Paul McCartney, Ringo Starr, and George Harrison, all from Liverpool, England. The Beatles were probably the most influential band in the history of rock music.

Put the pictures in date order

Look at the pictures in each of these six boxes. Can you say who or what they are, and put them in the correct date order? Begin with the one that lived or was built the longest time ago.

FLIGHT

1

2

3

THEATER

1

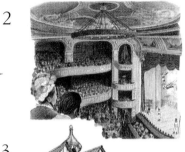
2

3

CASTLES

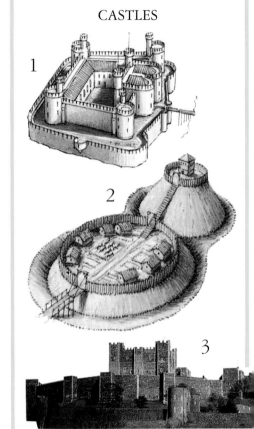
1

2

3

SHIPS

1

2

3

WRITERS

1

2

3

CITIES

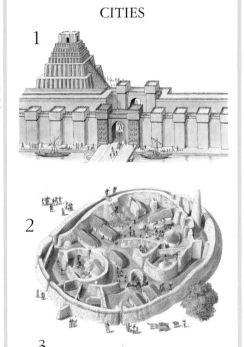

1

2

3

Match the art to the people

All the objects of art in this panel belong to a definite period of history or a certain group of people. Can you match the art to its origins, shown in the panel beneath?

TURN TO PAGE 66 FOR THE ANSWERS 49

Test yourself on science

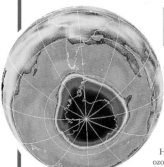

Hole in ozone layer

1 What is the scale that is used to measure the loudness of sound called?

2 Why is the ozone layer surrounding the Earth so important?

3 A jet of boiling water that suddenly shoots up from the ground is called a geyser. When does a geyser blow?

4 What did the scientist Galileo suggest could be controlled by the swing of a suspended weight?

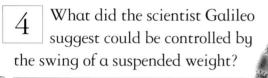

Shivering

5 When you are very cold, you shiver and get goose bumps on your skin. Why?

6 The moon has no light of its own. Why is it then that it can be seen shining brightly in the night sky?

7 There is only one kind of rock that can float on water. What is it called, and why is it so light?

8 What is created when electricity flows through a coil of wire?

Eastman

9 Why are store items marked with panels of black and white stripes?

10 In 1888, what did George Eastman invent?

Shoes in white light

11 What color would a pair of red shoes appear in blue light?

12 Why do the names of many plastics begin with the word "poly"?

13 What sort of picture will a camera that registers infrared rays take, and what information will be given by the picture?

14 A communication satellite is held in orbit by gravity. How long does it take to orbit the Earth?

Fractal pattern

15 This pattern is called a fractal. What produces it, and why is it never-ending?

16 Why do astronauts have to wear a special space suit when they venture outside their spacecraft?

17 What is the longest road system in the world called, how long is it, and where is the longest stretch?

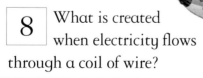

Harrier

18 What is so special about a *Harrier* jump jet?

19 A nuclear power station produces energy from the nuclear fission of uranium atoms. What is fission?

20 Many bicycles have gears. When does a cyclist choose the lowest gear?

Racing cyclist

Test yourself on science

21 The word "radar" stands for RAdio Detecting And Ranging. How can a radar scanner be used to check car speeds?

22 What is a sextant and who used such a device?

Sextant

23 A cyclist relies on the friction created by the brakes to stop. What is friction?

24 Which woman revolutionized nursing and the care of the sick in hospitals during the 19th century?

25 In the world of computers, what do the technical terms "hardware" and "software" mean?

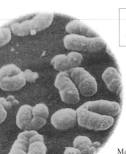

26 What world-shaking events are measured on the Richter Scale?

27 Where would you find chromosomes, and what do they do?

Magnified chromosomes

28 What is the name of the wave that might be produced if there is an earthquake on the ocean floor?

29 Which do you think will hit the ground first when dropped – an egg or a stone of the same size and shape?

H₂O

30 What familiar substance does the chemical symbol H₂O stand for?

Chemical symbol

31 How much of the air is made up of the gas oxygen?

32 What type of lens is used in a magnifying glass?

Straw appears bigger under magnifying glass

33 Which was the first aircraft to fly faster than the speed of sound, and when did it first do so?

34 Optics, acoustics, and statics are all branches of the same science. What is this science called?

35 Why is the kind of wildlife different at the top and bottom of a mountain?

Baby

36 Medicine has many different branches. What is the name of the branch that specializes in the care of children?

37 Where would you expect to find a crust, a mantle, and an inner and outer core?

38 Contour lines appear on some maps. What do they show?

39 What did Guglielmo Marconi invent?

Marconi

TURN TO PAGES 54 AND 55 FOR THE ANSWERS

Answers for science quiz

1 The loudness of a sound depends on the amount of energy sound waves carry. It is measured on a logarithmic scale, the Decibel Scale. This means each time ten decibels is added to the level, the loudness is multiplied by ten.

Megaphone amplifies sound

2 Ozone forms a layer in the Earth's atmosphere that shields the Earth from the sun's dangerous ultraviolet rays. Too much ultraviolet can harm the nucleus in the cells of plants and animals.

Hole in the ozone layer over the Antarctic lets in harmful rays

3 Deep underground, hot rock can heat water in chambers. When the water boils, the steam increases the pressure and the water is blasted up and forced out in a boiling fountain.

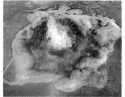
Geyser with a boiling fountain

4 At the end of the 16th century Galileo noticed that a suspended weight, or pendulum, moved back and forth regularly. He suggested that this swing could be used to control a clock.

Pendulum clock

5 Shivering is the body's automatic way of making the muscles move to produce heat. The bumps appear on your skin because tiny muscles lift your body hairs upright. The erect hairs help trap air close to the skin and so conserve heat.

Erect hair

Goose bump

6 The moon shines because it reflects light, like a mirror, from the sun. As the moon orbits the Earth, different shapes, or phases, appear depending on how much of the sunlit side of the moon you can see.

The moon appears to grow (wax) and shrink (wane)

7 Pumice, a unique rock that is peppered with tiny holes. It is formed when volcanic lava froth, containing bubbles of gas, hardens. Pumice stone is rough and some people use it to scrub their skin.

Gray pumice stone

8 The current in the coil makes a magnet, called an electromagnet, with a field that can be switched on and off. The electromagnet can be made stronger by winding the wire around a piece of iron.

Electro-magnetic crane

Coil with iron core

9 These striped labels on many items are known as bar codes. The bar code identifies the item and contains other computerized information about it, such as its price. A scanner with semiconductor laser is used to read the code.

Bar code scanner

10 George Eastman invented the handy Kodak camera and the roll film to go in it. His inventions replaced glass plates and bulky cameras, and made photography easy for millions of people.

Brownie box camera

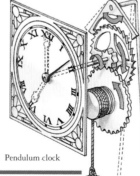

Answers for science quiz

11 In ordinary light, the shoes appear red as they reflect red, absorbing all other colors in the light. In blue light, the same shoes look black, because they absorb all the blue light and reflect no red light.

Red shoes look black

12 Plastics have names like polyethylene, polystyrene, and polyvinyl chloride (PVC) because they are made from molecules called polymers. The word "poly" means many and all polymer molecules are composed of long chains of atoms.

Molecule of polyethylene

13 A camera that uses infrared rays produces a picture known as a thermogram. All objects give out invisible infrared rays. The hotter an object the stronger the infrared rays produced. A thermogram shows the heat of different parts of the object.

Heat picure

14 A communication satellite takes 24 hours to orbit the Earth. It appears to stay stationary over the same part of the globe all the time, so it can receive and send signals. This kind of orbit is called geostationary.

Geostationary orbit

15 The fractal is made by a supercomputer. It is infinite because an equally intricate pattern is made no matter how often a part of the pattern is enlarged.

Powerful super-computer

16 In space there is no air and it is extremely cold. The pressurized space suit provides the astronaut with air to breathe. Without the suit the astronaut would explode. The suit also protects the body from harmful radiation and the cold.

Astronaut in a space suit

17 Covering a distance of at least 29,000 miles (47,000 km), the Pan-American Highway holds the world record. The longest stretch of the road runs from Alaska to Chile, with a small gap in Panama and Colombia.

Route of Pan-American Highway

18 The *Harrier* jump jet is one of few aircraft able to take off and land vertically. The powerful jet nozzles can be rotated downward so that the plane can fly vertically. This means it does not need a long runway, so it can take off and land in confined spaces, such as on a ship.

19 Normally, nothing can enter the nucleus of an atom because it is surrounded by circling electrons. However, if high-speed particles, called neutrons, are fired at atoms of uranium, the nuclei are split. This splitting, which produces heat, is known as fission.

Uranium atoms are split

20 The lowest gear is the one with the largest cog. It is selected to climb hills because it turns the wheel of the bicycle more slowly but with more force. The cyclist has to pedal faster but the extra force makes climbing easier.

A large cog turns the wheel slowly

Answers for science quiz

21 The scanner bounces radio waves off the car. The movement of the car makes the return waves shorter, and from the change in wavelength, the car's speed can be calculated.

Radar speed trap

22 The sextant was used by early surveyors and navigators. It can measure the angle between two distant objects, such as two stars. From the angle, they could calculate their position or find their way.

23 Friction is a force that opposes motion. It is created when two surfaces, such as a brake pad and wheel, rub against each other. Friction, which produces heat and wastes energy, slows down the bicycle wheel.

Brakes rely on friction

24 The woman known as "the lady with the lamp" is Florence Nightingale. After nursing soldiers in the Crimean War, she opened a school in London, England, to improve the standards of nursing.

Nurse Florence Nightingale

25 Hardware is the computer equipment and includes the central processing unit, keyboard, monitor, and printer. The software describes the instructions or programs the computer uses.

Computer harware

26 The Richter Scale measures the force of earthquakes. The scale runs from 0-9, each number marking a force ten times greater than that of the previous number.

Shock waves radiate from epicenter, or focus, of earthquake

27 Chromosomes are miscroscopic thread-like structures made up of genes. They are found in the nuclei of cells and they carry genetic information. Sex is determined by the chromosomes X and Y. A female has two Xs; a male has an X and a Y.

Genes control your looks

28 A tsunami. This huge wave, often wrongly described as a tidal wave, can be 250 ft (76 m) high when it reaches land. When it crashes onto the shore it may cause great destruction. A tsunami can also be caused by a volcanic eruption.

29 The two objects will fall at the same rate and hit the ground at the same time. Falling is controlled by the force of gravity. Gravity is affected by the object's mass (the amount of material in it) rather than the heaviness of the object.

Egg and rock fall together

30 H_2O stands for water. It is chemists' shorthand meaning that each molecule of water contains two atoms of the gas hydrogen (H) combined with one atom of the gas oxygen (O). All chemical elements have a shorthand symbol.

Answers for science quiz

31 Oxygen accounts for 21 percent of air. Nothing can burn without oxygen and it is needed by our bodies to make energy from food. Most of the air – 76 percent – is nitrogen gas. Argon forms 1 percent. The rest is tiny amounts of carbon dioxide, helium, methane, hydrogen, krypton, neon, ozone, and xenon.

Water is sucked up from the saucer into the jar, taking the place of the oxygen in the air that has been burned by the candle

32 A magnifying glass has a convex lens, which is thicker in the middle than at the edges. It magnifies the image by bending the light rays that pass through it so that they come together at a point (focus) after they have passed through the lens.

Convex lens

33 Bell X-1

Flown by American pilot Chuck Yeager on October 14, 1947, the rocket-powered *Bell X-1* was the first aircraft to break the sound barrier. A sonic boom is produced when an aircraft flies faster than the speed of sound.

34 Physics, which is the science of energy and matter. Optics is concerned with the physics of light; the study of sound and how it travels is known as acoustics; statics is the study of the forces that support structures.

A loud sound can make a glass vibrate so strongly that it shatters

35 As you climb a high mountain the temperature drops. It is much colder nearer the top, so only animals and plants adapted to a cold climate can survive.

No trees grow on the peak

36 The branch of medicine dealing with the care of children is called pediatrics. It comes from a Greek word meaning boy or child. It takes years of study to become an expert in a single area of medicine such as pediatrics.

37 The crust, mantle, and core are the layers that make up the Earth. The core at the middle of the Earth is made up of an outer core of liquid iron and an inner ball of solid iron and nickel.

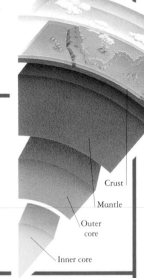
Crust
Mantle
Outer core
Inner core

38 Contour lines on a map connect points that are of equal height above or below sea level. They indicate how the land slopes and show the position of hills and valleys. They are the brown lines on the map shown here.

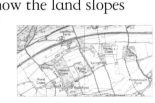
Map showing contour lines

39 Italian electronic engineer Guglielmo Marconi (1874-1937) invented the first radio system in 1895. Six years later he sent a radio signal across the Atlantic. Today radio waves carry many kinds of information.

Radio receiver

Universal facts

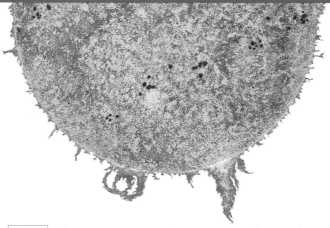

Q The sun's surrounding atmosphere, the corona, emits solar wind. What is this wind and how does it affect the Earth?

A Solar wind is made up of electrically charged particles. The Earth is protected from the wind by its magnetic field, which is pushed into a teardrop shape as the charged particles flow past.

Q What is a star made of, and how does it come into being?

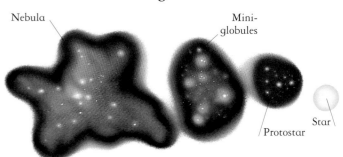

Nebula

Mini-globules

Protostar

Star

A A star is a ball of burning gas. It is born out of a huge cloud of hydrogen gas and dust particles, called a nebula. Gravity pulls some of the dust and gas into a spinning globule, which gradually splits into many smaller mini-globules. Each of these eventually becomes a protostar, and then a star, as its center compresses, heats up, and starts to shine.

Q How is carbon dioxide contributing to the warming of our globe?

A The glass in a greenhouse allows heat from the sun to come in. The glass traps some of the heat when the air outside cools down. The Earth's atmosphere works like the glass. Pollution in the air, such as the gas carbon dioxide, makes the atmosphere trap even more heat, causing the planet to get warmer. Too much carbon dioxide may change our climate.

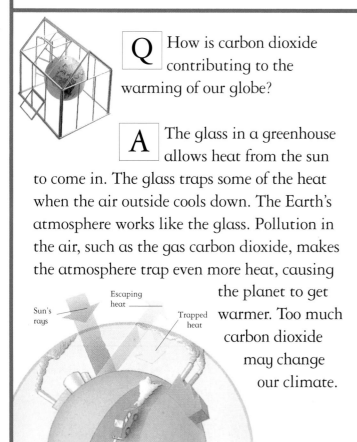

Sun's rays

Escaping heat

Trapped heat

Q Who first understood the force of gravity, and what is it?

A The famous English scientist Isaac Newton started thinking about gravity in 1666 when he saw an apple falling from a tree. Gravity is a force in every object that pulls things toward it. The heavier the object, the stronger its gravity. Newton went on to prove that the moon is kept in orbit by the Earth's gravity.

The world of weather

Q Tornadoes leave a trail of terrible destruction. What are they and what causes them?

A A tornado is a violent storm, sometimes called a whirlwind. It starts in a thundercloud. High winds streaming over the cloud set a column of rising warm air spinning. More air rushes into the swirling column to replace the rising air. Like a spiraling funnel coming down from the cloud, the tornado sucks up dirt and other objects off the ground.

Q A weather forecaster can predict the day's weather using a chart. What does the chart show?

Low pressure storm

A The word "high" shows an area of high atmospheric pressure, indicating settled weather. The word "low" shows an area of low pressure, meaning windy, wet weather. The lines around the words are isobars that connect regions of equal pressure. The blue triangles show a cold front; the red semicircles, a warm front.

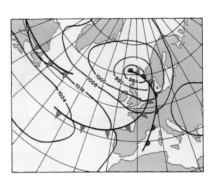

Weather chart

Q How does a glacier change the shape of the landscape it flows through?

A The snow that falls on the tops of high mountains never melts. It builds up in hollows and the lower layers turn to ice. This ice then flows very slowly down the mountain like a river. As it flows, this river, or glacier, grinds away at the landscape to form valleys. Moraine, or rocks, carried in the flow, build up to make walls, behind which lakes form.

Deep U-shaped valley carved out by glacier

Lake forms behind moraines

Q What might you see when it is both sunny and raining at the same time?

A You may see a rainbow if you look toward rain, with the sun shining from behind you. This is because the raindrops reflect the sun's light back to you. Each drop acts like a miniature prism, splitting ordinary white light into a band of colors.

Match the items to their raw material

The same main raw material is used to produce all the items in each numbered box. The raw materials are shown in the center box. Can you figure out which items come from which raw material?

1
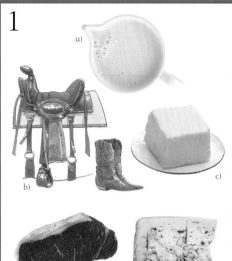
a)
b)
c)
d)
e)

2

a)
b)
c)
d)
e)
f)
g)

3
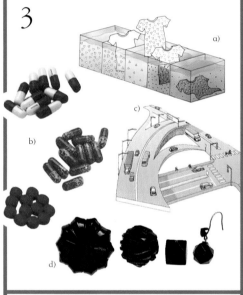
a)
b)
c)
d)

RAW MATERIALS

	Bauxite
Iron ore	Sand
Tree	Coal
Oil	Cow

4

a)
b)
c)
d)

5

a)
b)
c)
d)

6
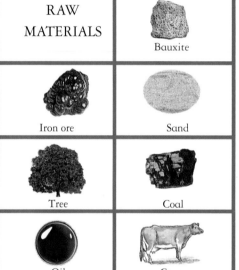
a)
b)
c)
d)

7
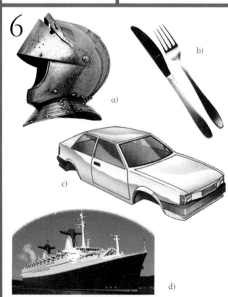
a)
b)
c)
d)
e)

Find the misfit

All but one of the pictures in each of these six boxes are connected in some way. Can you find the link, and name the object that does not fit with the others?

POWER

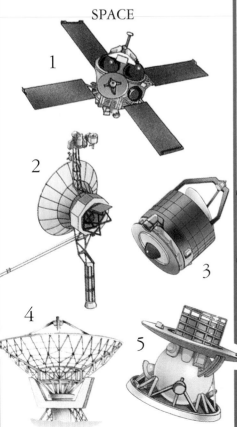

1
2
3

MEASURING

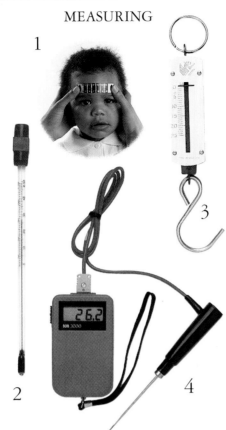

1
2
3
4

EXPLORATION

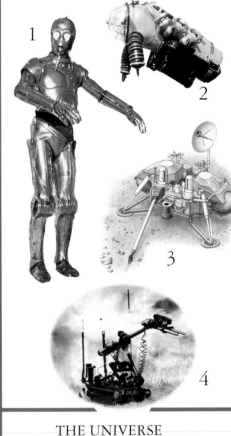

1
2
3
4

SPACE

1
2
3
4
5

RECORDING

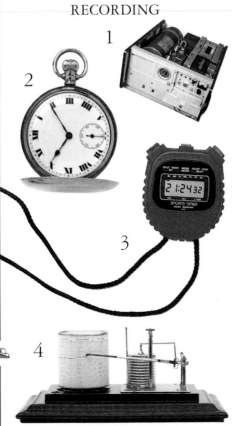

1
2
3
4

THE UNIVERSE

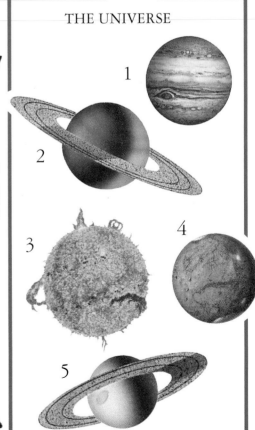

1
2
3
4
5

TURN TO PAGE 67 FOR THE ANSWERS

Famous inventions

Bell's box telephone

Q What invention enabled speech to be sent along wires?

A Alexander Graham Bell sent the first message, "Mr. Watson, come here. I want you," by telephone in 1876. Bell, a Scottish-born American teacher of the deaf, became interested in the way in which sounds are produced by vibrations in the air. He discovered how to transmit the human voice while trying to improve the telegraph.

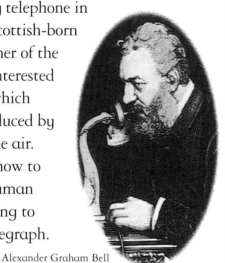
Alexander Graham Bell (1847-1922)

Thomas Edison (1847-1931)

Q Which two men invented the electric light bulb?

A Thomas Alva Edison in the US and Joseph Swan in England. Working independently, they each demonstrated their first lamps in the same year. Edison began producing lamps for sale in 1880. After Edison unsuccessfully sued Swan, the two men formed a joint company to make bulbs in Britain.

Early electric light bulb

Frank Whittle

Q Which English engineer and pilot suggested the idea of the jet engine?

A Frank Whittle had the original idea for the jet engine in 1928. The first jet-powered flight was made during the 1930s in Germany, but it was not until 1941 that Whittle's engine powered an experimental aircraft in Britain.

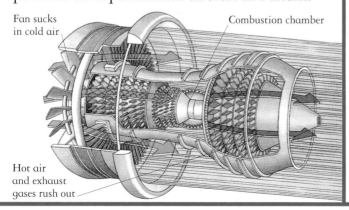
Fan sucks in cold air

Combustion chamber

Hot air and exhaust gases rush out

Metal type

Movable type arranged on composing stick

Grip

Q Who produced the first printed book in Europe?

A In the 1400s Johannes Gutenberg, from Mainz, Germany, invented a printing press. He developed movable type by casting metal in molds to form individual letters, and adapted a wine press to make a printing press. One of the first books he printed was the Bible. The Chinese began printing with wooden blocks in AD 868.

Great discoveries

Q Who discovered X rays in 1895, and why were they given this strange name?

X-ray photograph

Microsurgery

A X rays, like light and radio waves, are a type of radiation. They were first identified by the German scientist Wilhelm Roentgen. The letter X is a symbol for the unknown. Roentgen called the rays X rays because he did not understand what they were. Today X rays have many uses. In medicine they can be used to look inside the body without using surgery.

Q Francis Crick and James Watson worked out the structure of deoxyribonucleic acid (DNA) in 1953. What is DNA?

Model of DNA showing double helix structure

Chemical link

A DNA is found in the nucleus, or control center, of almost every cell. It is a long molecule that has a double helix (spiral) structure. Chemical "bridges" link the two strands of the helix. The genetic code of the cell, which is like a recipe for what the cell does and how it works, is determined by the sequence of the chemical bridges.

Q What is so special about the Hubble Space Telescope?

Hubble Space Telescope

A Launched in 1990, the Hubble Space Telescope is an optical telescope that flies 310 miles (500 km) up in the sky, in an orbit beyond the Earth's atmosphere. In this position, it avoids the blurring effect of the Earth's atmosphere and can collect much clearer images than telescopes on the ground.

Aperture door opens to let in light

Solar panels turn sunlight into electricity to power telescope

Q Who discovered how blood circulates around the body?

A In 1628, an English doctor named William Harvey (1578-1657) put forward his theory of circulation. He found that blood constantly circulates around the body in arteries and veins. He showed that the heart pumped the blood and that valves in the veins stopped the blood from flowing backward. He drew detailed diagrams to explain his theory.

William Harvey

Diagram showing circulation in the arm

Pair the device to the image it makes

All these components, instruments, or machines are used to produce a different kind of image. Can you match them to the pictures in the panel below?

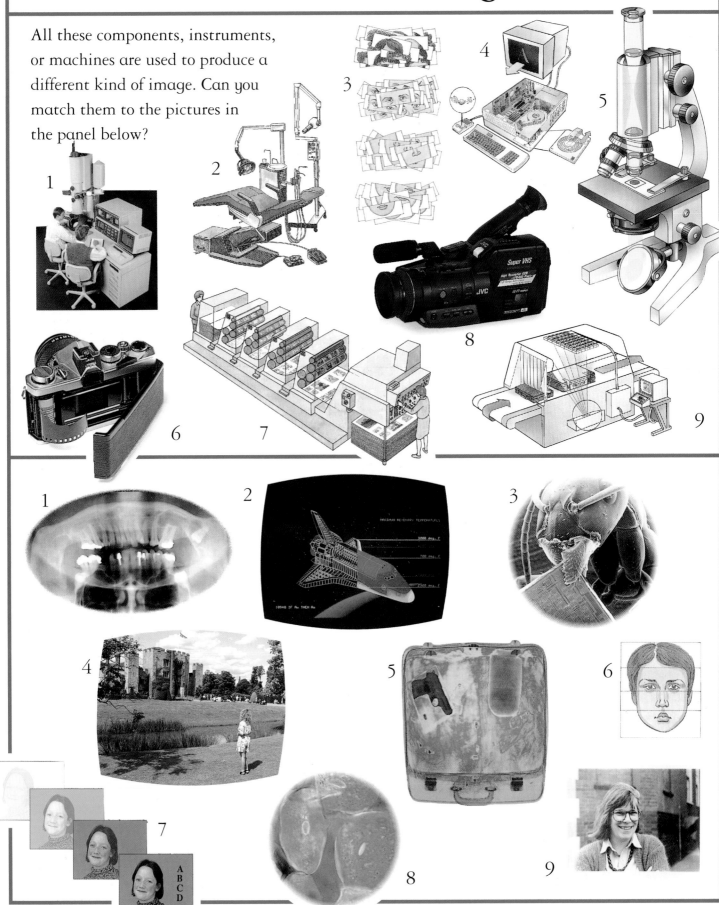

TURN TO PAGE 67 FOR THE ANSWERS

Put the body part in the correct place

The boxes around the girl show a body part and ask a question. Can you identify the part, put it in the correct place on the girl's body (marked with a letter), and answer the question?

1 How many bones make up this part of the skeleton?

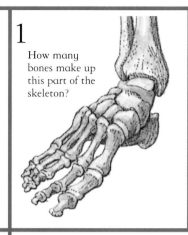

2

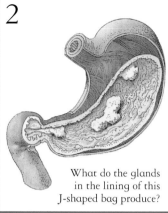

What do the glands in the lining of this J-shaped bag produce?

3

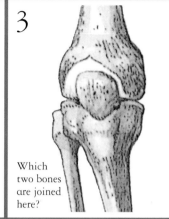

Which two bones are joined here?

4

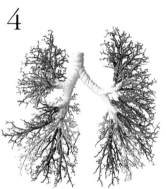

Which gas do we need to live?

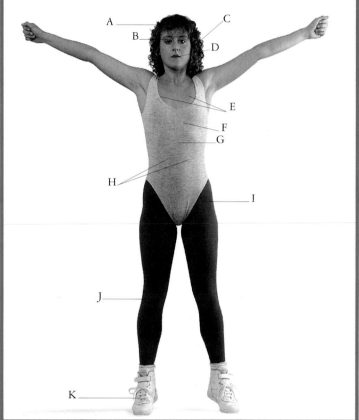

5

Can you name the hole that lets light into this structure?

6 What is the name given to an automatic reaction that we make without thinking?

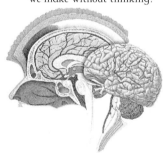

7 The middle part of this organ contains three tiny bones. Can you name them?

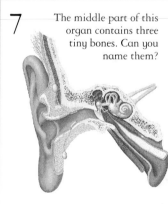

8

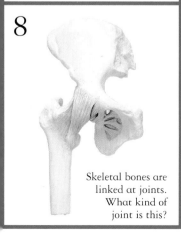

Skeletal bones are linked at joints. What kind of joint is this?

9

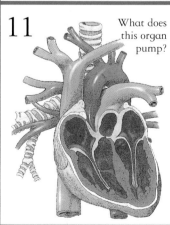

What is the name of the fluid produced by this filtering organ?

10

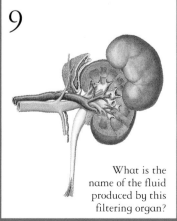

Which four types of taste can this muscular organ detect?

11

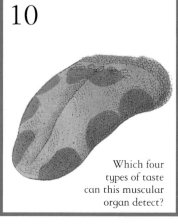

What does this organ pump?

TURN TO PAGE 67 FOR THE ANSWERS 63

People and places puzzle answers

Page 16   Guess the flags

 1. Olympic flag

 2. Italy

 3. United States of America

 4. Japan

 5. Israel

 6. India

 7. United Kingdom

 8. Brazil

 9. Canada

10. United Nations

 11. France

 12. European Union

 13. Australia

 14. Race car finish flag (checkered flag)

Page 17   Name the countries and continents

1. Australia
a) Tropic of Capricorn
b) Sydney

2. Africa
a) Nile River
b) Equator

3. India and subcontinent
a) Himalayas
b) Sri Lanka

4. South America
a) Amazon River
b) Andes Mountains

5. United States of America
a) New York
b) Grand Canyon

6. United Kingdom
a) North Sea
b) London

7. Japan
a) Pacific Ocean
b) Tokyo

8. New Zealand
a) Auckland
b) North Island and South Island

Page 20   Name these famous buildings

ANCIENT BUILDINGS
1. Golden Temple, Amritsar, India.

2. The Pyramids, Giza, Egypt.

3. The Parthenon, Athens, Greece.

MODERN BUILDINGS
1. Toronto Sky Dome Stadium in Canada is used for sports and entertainment.

2. Sydney Opera House in Australia is an arts center for theater, opera, concerts, and exhibitions.

3. The Guggenheim Museum in New York City houses modern and contemporary art.

TALL STRUCTURES
1. Statue of Liberty, New York City, NY, US 305 ft (93 m) including the pedestal and base.

2. Empire State Building, New York City, NY, US 1,250 ft (381 m).

3. Eiffel Tower, Paris, France, 1,051 ft (320 m).

4. Big Ben, Houses of Parliament clock tower, London, United Kingdom, 316 ft (96 m).

5. Canadian National Tower, Toronto, Canada, 1,815 ft (553 m): the tallest of these six buildings.

6. Leaning Tower of Pisa, Italy, 179 ft (55 m).

Page 21   Find the picture that does not belong

ARTISTS
2. *Madam Gachet in the Garden*, painting by post-impressionist Vincent van Gogh; *The Dance at the Moulin Galette* by Pierre Auguste Renoir (1) and *The Butterfly Chase* by Berthe Morisot (3) are both impressionist paintings.

MUSICAL INSTRUMENTS
2. The soprano saxophone is a wind instrument; the cornet (1) and the French horn (3) are both brass instruments.

FLAGS
1. The flag of the United Nations is the flag of an organization; the semaphore flag for the letter X (2), and the signal flag for the word "do" (3) are both flags used to send messages.

SPORTS
2. The runner competes in the summer Olympic Games; skiing (1), ski jumping (3), and ice hockey (4) are all sports included in the separate Winter Games.

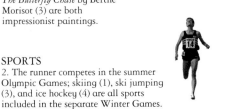

UNIFORMS
3. The ceremonial soldiers' uniform of the US; the others are naval uniforms of China (1), Russia (2), and United Kingdom (4).

BUILDINGS
3. Alcázar castle, Spain; The Blue Mosque, Turkey – Islam (1), Hindu Temple, India (2), and St. Peter's Church, Vatican City, Rome – Christian (4), are all places of worship.

Nature puzzle answers

Page 30   Identify these wild animals

1. Giant anteater.
It eats ants and termites.

2. Hare.
The males are called
jacks, the females are jills.

3. Jackson's chameleon.
It changes the color and pattern of
its skin to match its surroundings.

4. Angelfish.
It lives around coral reefs.

5. Bactrian or Asian camel.
Its wide feet splay out to keep the
camel from sinking into soft sand.

6. Wombat.
They shelter from the hot sun
in their underground burrows.

7. Toucan.
This bird nests in a hole in a tree.

8. Ring-tailed lemur.
All lemurs come from Madagascar,
the large island off Africa.

Page 31   Guess the animal from the part

TAILS

1. Snow leopard

2. Scorpion

3. Sperm whale

4. Skunk

5. Fang tooth fish

6. Pig

7. Tiger

SKINS AND FURS

1. Rattlesnake

2. Gila monster (lizard)

3. Zebra

4. Tiger

5. Nile crocodile

6. Giraffe

LEGS

1. Flamingo

2. Octopus

3. Frog

4. Grasshopper

5. Dromedary or Arabian camel

6. Fallow deer

Page 34   Match the animal to its diet

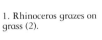

1. Rhinoceros grazes on
grass (2).

2. Giant panda eats bamboo (8).

3. Bumblebee feeds on nectar
from flowers (3).

4. Archer fish spits drops of water on bugs,
such as spiders (4), and then eats them
when they fall into the water.

5. Songthrush eats
snails (5).

6. Grizzly bear scoops
salmon from rivers (9).

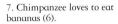

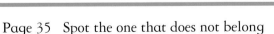

7. Chimpanzee loves to eat
bananas (6).

8. Lions are carnivores and eat
large prey, such as zebra (7).

9. Pangolin licks up ants (1)
with its long sticky tongue.

Page 35   Spot the one that does not belong

FUNGI
2. Fly agaric toadstool is poisonous;
the chanterelle mushroom (1) and
the field mushroom (3) are both edible.

BIRDS
3. The kiwi cannot fly;
the Canadian goose (1) and
the tawny owl (2) can both fly.

REPTILES
2. The marine turtle lives
in the sea; the Chilean
tortoise (1) and the
hinge-back tortoise (3)
both live on land.

TREES
2. Scotch pine is a coniferous (evergreen) tree; the
plane tree (1) and the rowan or mountain ash (3) are
both deciduous trees: they lose their leaves in winter.

BUGS
3. The spider is an arachnid and has eight legs;
the long-horned beetle (1) and the damselfly (2)
are both insects, which have 6 legs.

ANIMALS
3. The dog is alive today; the
woolly mammoth (1) and the
dodo (2) are both extinct species.

History puzzle answers

Page 44   Name these well-known people

CHIEFS

1. Geronimo, Chiricahua Apache Indian chief of North America, 1829-1909.

2. Genghis Khan, creator and leader of the Mongol Empire of northeastern Asia, 1162-1227.

RULERS

1. Louis XIV, King of France, ruled 1643-1715.

2. Tutankhamen, Egyptian pharaoh who ruled Egypt 3,500 years ago.

3. Elizabeth I, queen of England for 45 years, ruled 1558-1603.

ARTISTS

1. Elvis Presley, American "king" of rock and roll, 1935-1977.

2. Ludwig van Beethoven, German composer, 1770-1827.

3. Anna Pavlova, Russian ballerina, 1881-1931. Her most famous solo was *Dying Swan*.

MODERN LEADERS

1. John F. Kennedy, youngest American president, born 1917, assassinated 1963.

2. Mohandas Gandhi, who instigated India's independence from British rule, 1869-1948.

3. Nelson Mandela, born 1918, leader of the African National Congress against apartheid in South Africa, is still alive today.

Page 45   Make the link and name the event

1. WORLD WAR II
a) Russian T-34 tank used in 1943 tank battle b) Winston Churchill, British war-time Prime Minister, depicted as a British bulldog on a poster c) Adolf Hitler, leader of the Nazi party d) Messerschmitt fighter plane flown by the Luftwaffe – the German air force.

2. INDUSTRIAL REVOLUTION
a) Factory town b) Early steam locomotive, built by Richard Trevithick, ran on rails for the first time in 1801 c) Clifton suspension bridge, designed by Isambard Kingdom Brunel (1806-1859).

3. RUSSIAN REVOLUTION
a) Vladimir Lenin, Russian leader and founder of the Bolshevik party b) Communist red star with hammer and sickle c) Russia's last Czar, Nicholas II and his family.

4. FRENCH REVOLUTION
a) Napoleon Bonaparte (1769-1821) led military takeover in 1799 to end French Revolution b) Marianne, imaginary revolutionist shown on Republican stamp c) Execution of Louis XVI in 1793 d) Sans-culottes (without trousers), name given to revolutionaries who wore simple clothes.

5. AMERICAN CIVIL WAR
a) Abraham Lincoln, president of the US, who stopped slavery b) Union soldier, Union army defeated Confederacy in 1865 c) Auction of slaves at a slave market d) Soldier of the Confederate army of the southern states, led by General Robert E. Lee.

6. VIETNAM WAR
a) Vietnamese jungle was bombed with chemicals to strip the leaves off the trees by US Air Force b) Vietnam flag c) Map of war zone, showing North and South Vietnam.

7. CHRISTIAN CRUSADES
a) Knights hospitallers looked after hospitals on route of warring pilgrimage to Palestine b) Siege weapons c) Sultan Saladin (1137-93), leader of the Muslim forces d) Richard the Lionheart, king of England from 1189 to 1199, took part in the Third Crusade.

Page 48   Put the pictures in date order

FLIGHT
1. Montgolfier balloon, made first flight with passengers in 1783.
2. Otto Lilenthal hang glider 1890. 3. Concorde, supersonic jet, broke the sound barrier in 1970.

ENTERTAINMENT
1. Delphi amphitheater, 5th century.
2. Globe theater, 16th century.
3. Victorian playhouse, 19th century.

CASTLES
1. Wooden motte (hill) and bailey (court), 6th century. 2. Norman stone castle, 11th-13th century. 3. Spanish round tower castle, 16th century.

EXPLORERS
1. Viking ship, 9th century.
2. Capt. James Cook's ship *Endeavour*, 1768.
3. Deep sea bathyscape *Trieste*, 1960.

WRITERS
1. Shakespeare, playwright (1564-1616).
2. Karl Marx, German philosopher and writer (1818-83). 3. Anne Frank, young war diarist (1929-45).

CITIES
1. Babylon, 2000-600 BC
2. Great Zimbabwe, 14th century.
3. Contemporary New York.

Page 49   Match the art to the people

1. Louis XIV chair and French gentleman of same period (1).

2. Aboriginal dreamtime painting and Aboriginal people (3).

3. Carved wooden totem pole and American Indian (5).

4. Norman Bayeux tapestry and Norman soldiers (7).

5. Celtic engraved bowl and Celtic people (9).

6. Carved ivory snow knife and Inuit (8).

7. Greek vase and ancient Greek person (4).

8. Medieval illuminated manuscript and monks of the Middle Ages (6).

9. Egyptian hieroglyphs and ancient Egyptian scribes (2).

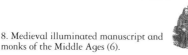

Science puzzle answers

Page 58 Match the items to their raw material

1. a) milk, b) leather goods, c) butter, d) beef, and e) cheese are all products from the COW

2. a) soap, b) paint, c) polystyrene and plastics, d) polycarbonates, e) shampoo, f) powdered soap, and g) dishwashing liquid are produced from OIL

3. a) dyes, b) drugs, c) coal tar-pitch for road surfacing, and d) jet jewel are all made from COAL

4. a) aluminum can, b) foil, c) bicycle frame, and d) aircraft body are all made from aluminum, extracted by the Bayer process from BAUXITE

5. a) window glass, b) porcelain, c) glassware, and d) silicon chips all have the same raw material — SAND

6. a) iron armor, b) stainless steel cutlery, c) low-carbon-steel car body, and d) medium-carbon-steel ship body are all smelted from IRON ORE

7. a) ship, b) paper products, c) furniture, d) wood for fuel, and e) wooden musical instruments are all products from the TREE

Page 59 Find the misfit

POWER
2. The coal-fired power station uses non-renewable fossil fuel; solar panels (1), and wind turbines (3) are both forms of renewable energy.

MEASURING
3. Spring balance measures weight; mercury thermometer (1), fever strip thermometer (2), and digital celsius thermometer (4) are all used for measuring temperature.

EXPLORATION
2. Atmospheric diving suit for a diver to explore at very deep depths; anthropoid robot C3PO (1), space probe robot (3), and bomb disposal robot (4) are all types of robots.

SPACE
4. Dish-shaped radio wave antenna; *Mariner 9* (USA) (1), *Voyager 1* (USA) (2), *Giotto* (European Space Agency) (3), and *Venera 9* (USSR) (5) are all space probes.

RECORDING
4. Barograph used to measure and record air pressure; pocket watch (1), exceptionally accurate atomic clock (2), and stopwatch (3) all record or measure time.

THE UNIVERSE
3. Sun is a star; Jupiter (1), Saturn (2), Earth (4), and Neptune (5) are all planets.

Page 62 Pair the device to the image it makes

1. A scanning electron microscope magnifies the whole object, such as an ant shown at 15 times its size (3).

2. The dental X-ray machine takes X-ray pictures such as a dental X ray (1).

3. Photofit cards are put together to make photofit picture (6).

4. A computer can be used to generate a graphic of a space shuttle (2).

5. The light microscope magnifies objects normally invisible to the naked eye, such as human cheek cells magnified 200 times (8).

6. A 35mm single lens reflex camera uses film, which can be processed to produce a photographic print (9).

7. A four-color printing press will combine magenta, cyan, yellow, and black to produce a full-color printed image (7).

8. The video camera records video film, which can be viewed on your television screen (4).

9. The baggage scanner, a type of X-ray machine, where the monitor screen shows an image of the contents of a suitcase for security purposes (5).

Page 63 Put the body part in the correct place

1. The foot is located at K
26 bones, including those of the ankle.

2. The stomach is located at G
The glands in the lining of this J-shaped bag produce acid and digestive juices.

3. The knee joint is located at J
Thighbone (femur) and shinbones (tibia and fibia).

4. The lungs are located at E
Oxygen.

5. The eye is located at B
The pupil.

6. The brain is located at A
A reflex.

7. The ear is located at C
Anvil (incus), hammer (malleus), and stirrup (stapes).

8. The hip joint is located at I
Ball-and-socket joint, which allows bones to swing in two directions and also to twist.

9. The kidneys are located at H
Urine, which is then stored in the bladder.

10. The tongue is located at D
Sweet, salty, sour, and bitter flavors.

11. The heart is located at F
Blood.

Prehistoric Life

Animal life first started about 1 billion years ago (bya), when soft-bodied creatures lived in water. These forms of early life gave rise to fish with internal bony skeletons. The first amphibians that could walk and breathe on land evolved from the fish. In turn, reptiles evolved. Dinosaurs were reptiles. Just like today's lizards, they had scaly skin and laid eggs. Fossils (animals or plants preserved over millions of years) of prehistoric life give us the clues with which we can piece together the history of our planet.

Styracosaurus skull

Q1. Were all of today's different continents once one land mass?

Q2. How long did dinosaurs inhabit the Earth: about 65, 165, or 265 million years?

Ginkgo leaves

Q3. What was the biggest development in plants in the age of the dinosaurs?

Q4. Is it true that the name dinosaur means "scaly hunter"?

Iguanodon hand

Q5. How many horns did a *Triceratops* have on its head?

Q6. Was the name "dinosaur" coined in 1792, 1842, or 1892?

Q7. Was the earliest known bird a *Pterosaur*, a *Pterodactyl*, or an *Archaeopteryx*?

Q8. Which present-day man-eating creatures are near relatives of the dinosaurs?

Q9. When did dinosaurs become extinct: 35, 65, or 95 mya (million years ago)?

Q10. Which group of reptiles is the oldest: turtles, lizards, or snakes?

Q11. Which modern creature was *Iguanodon* named after?

Q12. What do you call resin that has hardened over millions of years?

Q13. Was *Stegosaurus's* brain the size of a walnut, an apple, or a melon?

Q14. Does *Styracosaurus* mean vampire lizard, spiked lizard, or horned hunter?

Q15. Did the blades jutting from this backbone support spikes, plates, or a skin sail?

Turtle shell fossil

Ouranosaurus skeleton

Q16. *Hypselosaurus* was 39 ft (12 m) long. Was one of its eggs as long as 5, 25, or 55 hen's eggs?

TURN TO PAGE 120 FOR ANSWERS

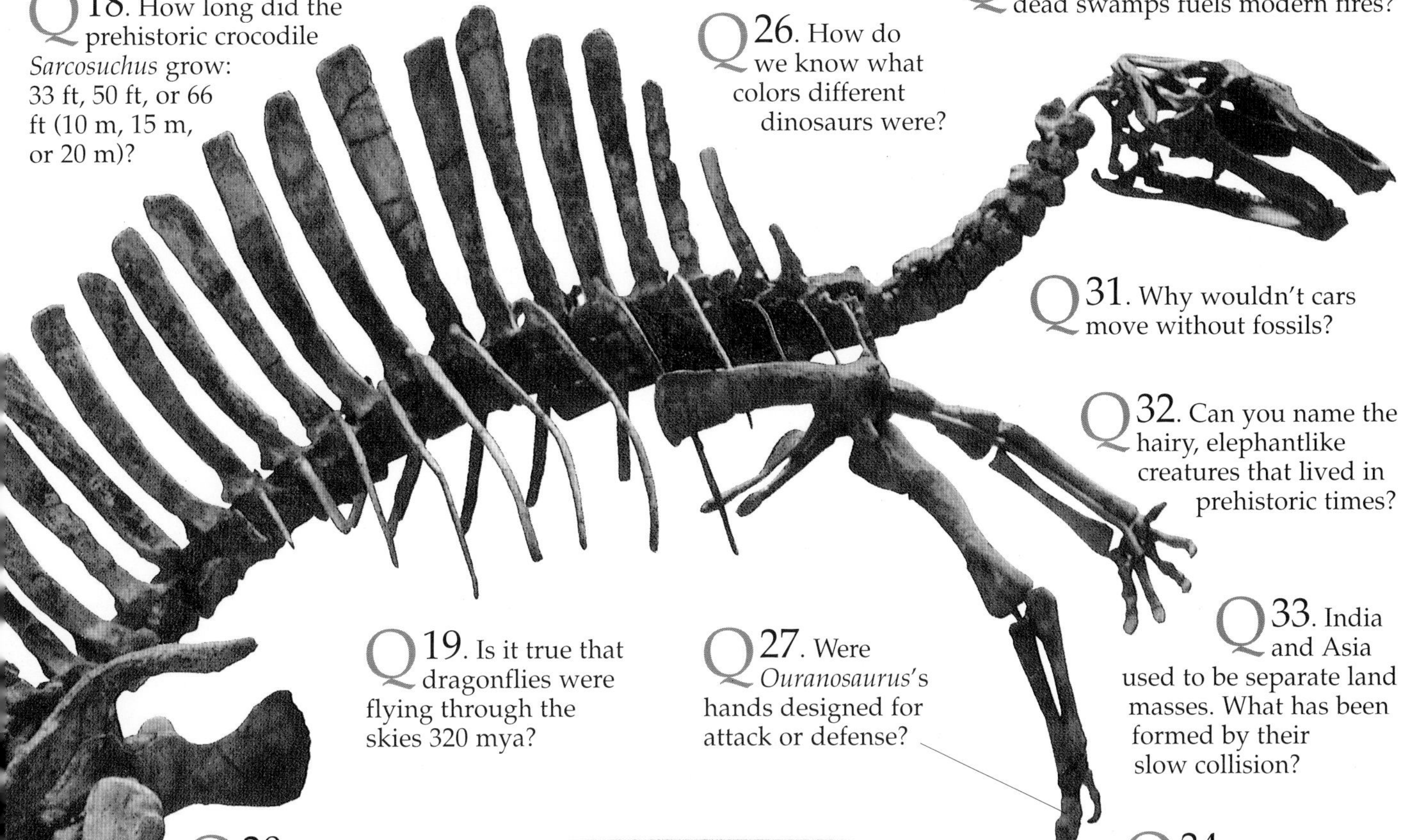

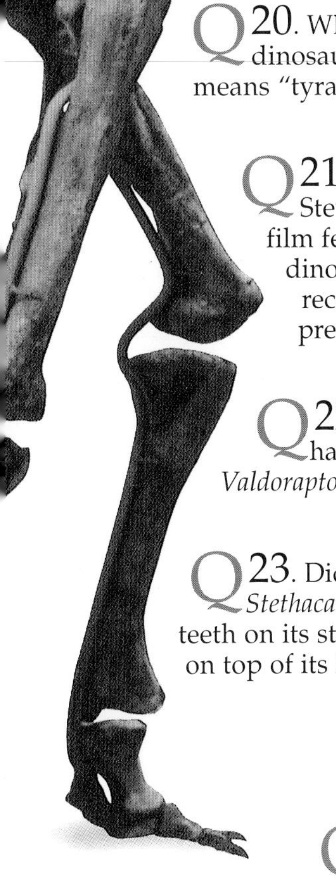

Q17. How big was *Hyracotherium*, the first horse: the size of a cat, a dog, or a deer?

Q18. How long did the prehistoric crocodile *Sarcosuchus* grow: 33 ft, 50 ft, or 66 ft (10 m, 15 m, or 20 m)?

Q19. Is it true that dragonflies were flying through the skies 320 mya?

Q20. Which dinosaur's name means "tyrant lizard"?

Q21. Which Steven Spielberg film featured dinosaurs recreated in the present day?

Q22. Which flying "dinosaurs" had a 23-ft (7-m) wingspan: *Valdoraptors*, *Kronosaurs*, or *Pteranodons*?

Q23. Did the prehistoric shark *Stethacanthus* have tiny teeth on its stomach, or on top of its head?

Q24. Was *Scelidosaurus* a meat eater or a plant eater?

Q25. The *Coelacanth* fish was discovered in the Indian Ocean in 1938. Why did it shock scientists?

Q26. How do we know what colors different dinosaurs were?

Q27. Were *Ouranosaurus*'s hands designed for attack or defense?

Fossil dragonfly

Q28. Lucy is a 3-million-year-old woman whose remains were found in Ethiopia. Which pop song was she named after?

Q29. Which TV cartoon show (now also a film) features a prehistoric family?

Q30. What material from long-dead swamps fuels modern fires?

Q31. Why wouldn't cars move without fossils?

Q32. Can you name the hairy, elephantlike creatures that lived in prehistoric times?

Q33. India and Asia used to be separate land masses. What has been formed by their slow collision?

Q34. How many limbs does a tetrapod have?

Q35. Was a dinosaur the biggest animal that has ever lived?

Q36. In which country have the most dinosaur remains been found?

Q37. Is it true that prehistoric hippopotamuses were dug up under London's Trafalgar Square?

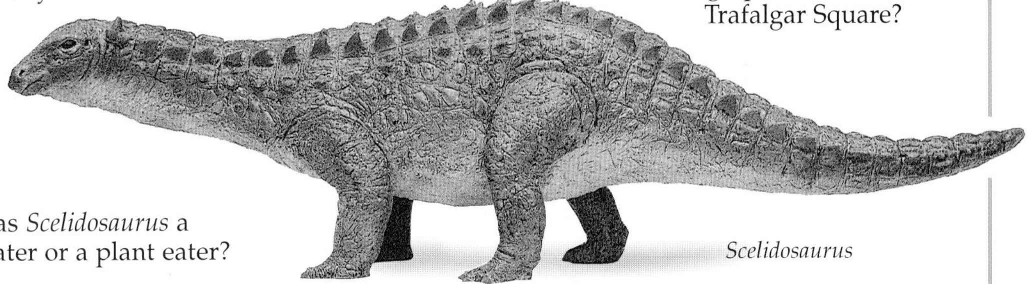

Scelidosaurus

TURN TO PAGE 120 FOR ANSWERS

69

Reptiles

Q38. Which is the largest reptile in the world?

Q39. The longest-lived reptile on record was a tortoise: did it live to be 102, 152, or 202?

Q40. Is the snake to the left poisonous?

Sinaloan milksnake

Q41. Where does the most venomous snake in the world live: Africa, South America, or Australia?

Q42. Is the smallest reptile in the world 0.3 in (8 mm) long or 0.7 in (18 mm) long?

Q43. Human beings have 24 vertebrae. How many can a snake have: up to 200, 300, or 400?

Q44. Does the length of time snake eggs take to hatch vary with moisture or with temperature?

North American rat snake hatching

Q45. Which reptile features in Aesop's fable (story) about a race between the swift and the slow?

Q46. Is a stinkpot a kind of skunk, turtle, or lizard?

Madagascar day gecko

Q47. What is a Komodo dragon: a lizard, a turtle, or a snake?

Q48. Is a crocodile's stomach the size of a lunch box, a basketball, or an oil drum?

Q49. The tuatara of New Zealand is a unique lizard with a unique number of eyes. How many?

Crocodile

Q50. What do chameleons do?

Q51. Are reptiles warm-blooded?

Q52. The biggest turtle ever found weighed 2,120 lb (961 kg). Was it an African mud turtle, a snake-necked turtle, or a leatherback turtle?

Q53. Why does the sand lizard of the Namib desert "dance"?

Q54. Crocodiles, caimans, gharials – which members of the crocodile family are missing from this list?

Q55. Why are geckos often popular house guests?

Q56. Is the snake with the longest fangs a cobra, a viper, or a rattlesnake?

Starred tortoise

Q57. How long would a starred tortoise take to plod from one end of a soccer field to the other: 30 minutes, 45 minutes, or an hour?

Q58. Is the world reptile land-speed record holder a lizard or a snake?

TURN TO PAGE 120 FOR ANSWERS

Amphibians

Tadpoles

Q59. In one fairy tale a princess kisses a frog. What happens next?

Q60. How does the green toad keep enemies away?

Green toad

Q61. Do frogs lay their eggs in water or on land?

Q62. Is a caecilian an amphibian?

Frogspawn

Q63. Do frogs or toads usually have smooth, wet skin?

Q64. Why does a frog blink as it swallows?

Q65. Where does the male hip-pocket frog carry its tadpoles?

Q66. The most active known poison comes from the skin of South American golden poison-dart frogs. The poison from just one frog could kill: 500, 1,000, or 1,500 people?

Q67. Which children's story stars a toad who is friends with a mole, a rat, and a badger?

Q68. In legend, where did salamanders choose to make their homes?

Tiger salamander

Q69. What is a hellbender: a frog, a toad, or a salamander?

Q70. What do salamanders, newts, and sirens have that other amphibians do not?

Q71. How many mosquitoes can the dwarf puddle frog (which is the size of a large peanut) eat in one night: 60, 80, or 100?

Q72. How old are these tadpoles: 4 weeks, 6 weeks, or 8 weeks?

Q73. How do poison-dart frogs warn enemies that they are poisonous to eat?

Poison-dart frog

Q74. Which human divers are named after an amphibian?

Q75. Which television show starred a frog who was loved by a pig?

Q76. Is the largest frog in the world named after Goliath, Hercules, Atlas, or Godzilla?

Q77. The word "amphibian" comes from the Greek for "double-life." Why were amphibians given this name?

Q78. Is the world frog-jumping record 10 ft, 17 ft, or 23 ft (3 m, 5 m, or 7 m) for a single jump?

European common frog going after prey

Q79. Can all frogs leap?

TURN TO PAGE 120 FOR ANSWERS

Life in the Ocean

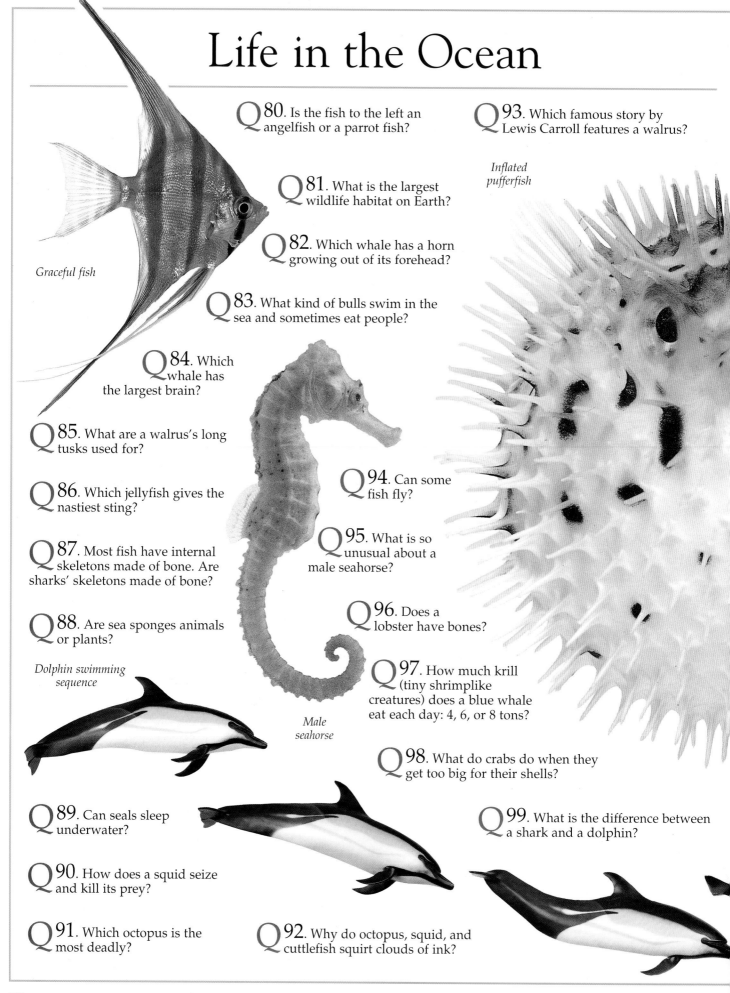

Q80. Is the fish to the left an angelfish or a parrot fish?

Q81. What is the largest wildlife habitat on Earth?

Q82. Which whale has a horn growing out of its forehead?

Q83. What kind of bulls swim in the sea and sometimes eat people?

Q84. Which whale has the largest brain?

Q85. What are a walrus's long tusks used for?

Q86. Which jellyfish gives the nastiest sting?

Q87. Most fish have internal skeletons made of bone. Are sharks' skeletons made of bone?

Q88. Are sea sponges animals or plants?

Q89. Can seals sleep underwater?

Q90. How does a squid seize and kill its prey?

Q91. Which octopus is the most deadly?

Q92. Why do octopus, squid, and cuttlefish squirt clouds of ink?

Q93. Which famous story by Lewis Carroll features a walrus?

Q94. Can some fish fly?

Q95. What is so unusual about a male seahorse?

Q96. Does a lobster have bones?

Q97. How much krill (tiny shrimplike creatures) does a blue whale eat each day: 4, 6, or 8 tons?

Q98. What do crabs do when they get too big for their shells?

Q99. What is the difference between a shark and a dolphin?

Graceful fish

Inflated pufferfish

Dolphin swimming sequence

Male seahorse

TURN TO PAGE 120 FOR ANSWERS

Q100. Is the shortest fish the Philippino dwarf pygmy goby or the minnow?

Q101. Which is the most ferocious freshwater fish?

Q102. How does a starfish feed itself?

Q103. Which fish can lay the most eggs: a sunfish, a clownfish, or a butterfly fish?

Q104. Which whale can hunt right onto the shore?

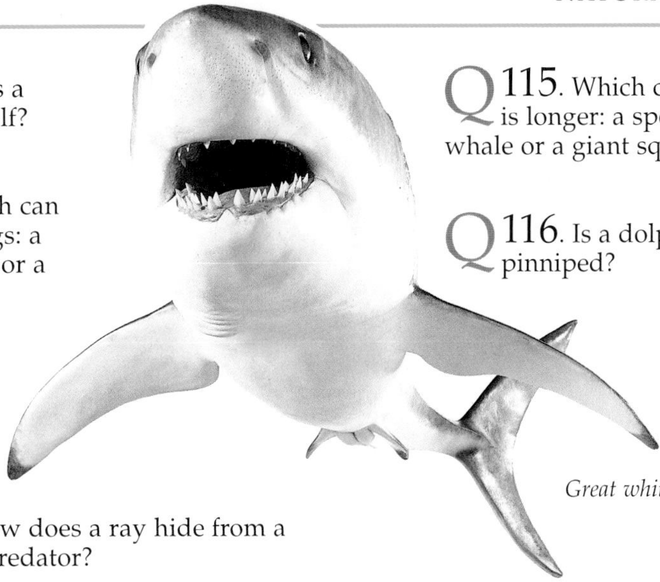

Q105. How does a ray hide from a hungry predator?

Q106. What do you call a group of fish swimming together?

Q107. Why is the beluga sturgeon such a valuable fish?

Q108. What keeps whales, walruses, seals, and sea lions so warm?

Q109. Why are sharks often called "primitive" creatures?

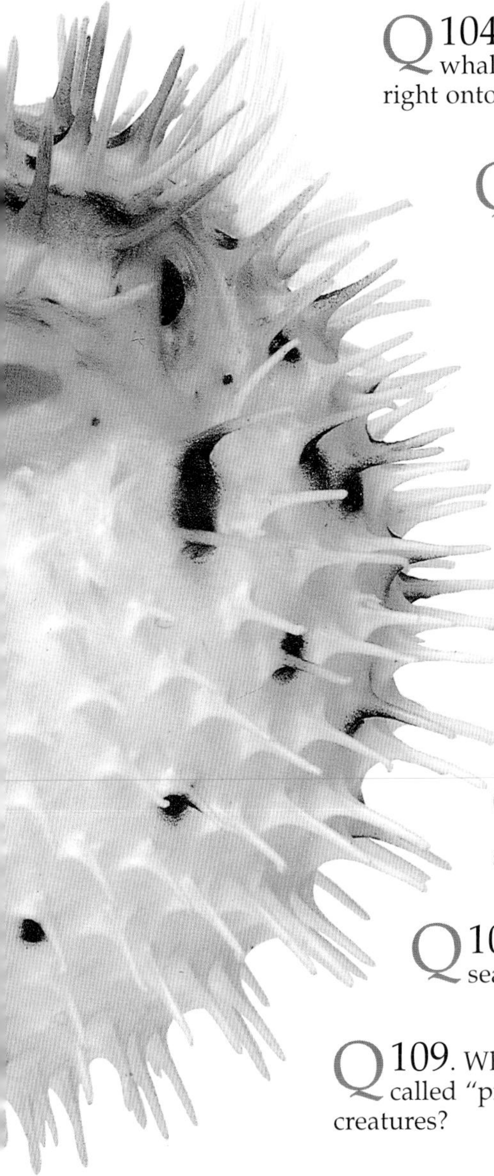

Q110. Why does the pufferfish inflate itself like a balloon?

Q111. Which sign of the zodiac is a fish?

Q112. Which fish can leap out of the water to catch prey: the archerfish or the anglerfish?

Q113. How long can the blue clam live: 10 years, 50 years, or 100 years?

Q114. Which fish can come onto land and breathe fresh air?

Q115. Which creature is longer: a sperm whale or a giant squid?

Q116. Is a dolphin a pinniped?

Great white shark

Q117. How many rows of teeth does a great white shark have?

Q118. Why does a catfish have whiskers?

Snakelocks anemone

Q119. Which fish has the longest snout: a swordfish or a saw shark?

Q120. How does the snakelocks anemone hunt and defend itself?

Q121. Which crab likes to move from one house to another?

Q122. What happens if you step on a stonefish?

Blue clam

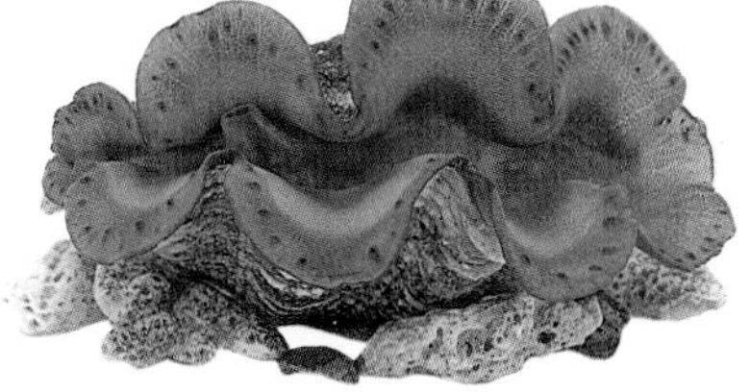

Dogs

Q123. Which wolf is not a wolf?

Q134. How do dogs make the most of their height?

Side view of skull of bat-eared fox

An obedient Doberman

Sniffing beagle

Q130. Do foxes hunt in packs or on their own?

Q135. What is a dog's most highly developed sense?

Q124. There are more than 600 breeds of domestic dogs. True or false?

Q131. Which is the smallest member of the fox family: the fennec or the Arctic?

Q136. Which star do dogs look up to: Vega, Alpha Centauri, or Sirius?

Q125. If a dog's ears are laid back, what emotions might it be communicating?

Q132. Which dog is not a dog?

Q137. What is the most unusual feature of the maned wolf's body?

Q126. What is Mickey Mouse's dog's name?

Q127. Which is the most primitive breed of dog in the world: the dingo, the dachshund, or the deerhound?

Q138. What is a female fox called?

Q139. Why do bloodhounds wish they knew a good optometrist?

Dog leash and collar

Q140. According to legend, which two brothers were suckled by a she-wolf and founded a great city?

Q141. How old is this fox cub: 6 weeks, 10 weeks, or 14 weeks?

Fox cub

Q128. Who goes to work in a dog collar?

Q133. Which was the first dog in space: Lassie, Laika, or Lulu?

Q129. Which famous Sherlock Holmes story is named after a dog?

Maned wolf

Q142. What is the maximum area over which a pack of wolves will range: 40 sq miles (100 sq km), 200 sq miles (500 sq km), or 400 sq miles (1,000 sq km)?

TURN TO PAGES 120-121 FOR ANSWERS

Cats

A roaring leopard

A snoozing cat

Q 143. How many hours a day do cats spend sleeping: 8, 12, or 16?

Q 144. Which cat did the Greek hero Hercules kill?

Q 145. Which is the fastest cat in the world?

Q 146. Which cat has no tail?

Q 147. Which cat did the author Rudyard Kipling write about?

Q 148. What is the most obvious feature that distinguishes the lion from other cats?

Q 149. Why do lions live in prides?

Q 150. Which ones do most of the hunting in a pride: lions or lionesses?

Q 151. Which is the only cat that can't retract its claws?

African male lion

Q 152. Which poet wrote a book of poems about cats that has now been turned into the successful musical *Cats*?

Q 153. Which sign of the zodiac is named after a cat?

Q 154. Which cat can live without water for the longest time: a bobcat, a sand cat, or a tomcat?

Q 155. Where was the first modern cat show held: London, Paris, or New York ?

Q 156. Which are the biggest cats: tigers or lions?

Bengal tiger

Q 157. What are black leopards better known as?

Q 158. What would the Mochica people of Peru have done with this golden puma?

Golden puma

Q 159. Which famous fictional, crafty, magical cat was created by Charles Perrault?

Q 160. Can you name the fictional lion in C. S. Lewis's Narnia stories?

Q 161. Which ancient civilization believed cats were sacred?

Q 162. Do leopards roar?

Abyssinian cat

Q 163. What is a cat's favorite plant?

TURN TO PAGE 121 FOR ANSWERS

Mammals

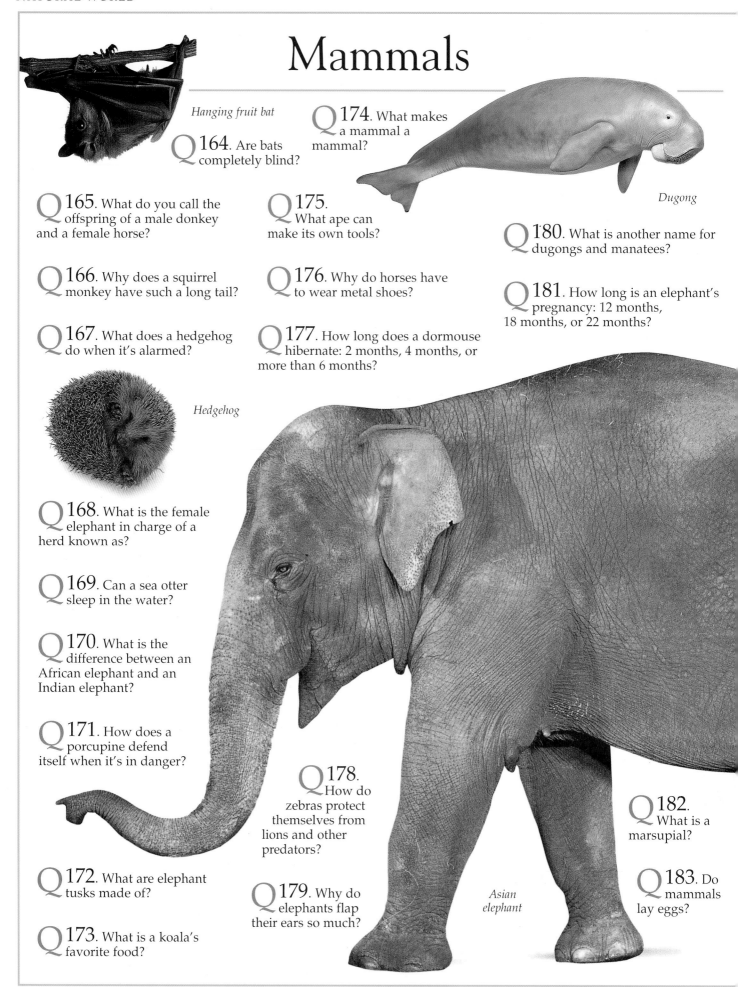

Hanging fruit bat

Q164. Are bats completely blind?

Q174. What makes a mammal a mammal?

Dugong

Q165. What do you call the offspring of a male donkey and a female horse?

Q175. What ape can make its own tools?

Q180. What is another name for dugongs and manatees?

Q166. Why does a squirrel monkey have such a long tail?

Q176. Why do horses have to wear metal shoes?

Q181. How long is an elephant's pregnancy: 12 months, 18 months, or 22 months?

Q167. What does a hedgehog do when it's alarmed?

Q177. How long does a dormouse hibernate: 2 months, 4 months, or more than 6 months?

Hedgehog

Q168. What is the female elephant in charge of a herd known as?

Q169. Can a sea otter sleep in the water?

Q170. What is the difference between an African elephant and an Indian elephant?

Q171. How does a porcupine defend itself when it's in danger?

Q178. How do zebras protect themselves from lions and other predators?

Q182. What is a marsupial?

Q172. What are elephant tusks made of?

Q179. Why do elephants flap their ears so much?

Asian elephant

Q183. Do mammals lay eggs?

Q173. What is a koala's favorite food?

TURN TO PAGE 121 FOR ANSWERS

Q184. In which continent would you find the small chinchilla rodent?

Q185. Which mammal lives, breeds, sleeps, and eats underground?

Palomino with Western-style bridle and saddle

Q186. How often can a female rat reproduce: every 4 weeks, every 6 weeks, or every 8 weeks?

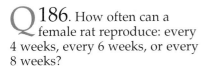

Rat cleaning itself

Q197. Bats are the only mammals that can fly. True or false?

Sperm whale

Q198. In what do you measure a horse's height?

Q187. What does a herbivore eat?

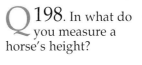

Q188. What color was Moby Dick, the sperm whale in Herman Melville's novel?

Q199. What is a baby hare called?

Q200. What does a skunk do when it's attacked?

Q189. Which are more closely related to humans: apes or monkeys?

Q190. Why are giant pandas in danger of becoming extinct?

Q201. Which large, furry mammal spends all day hanging upside down in trees in the rain forests of South America?

Q191. Is a monkey a primate?

Q202. Which country has the most elephants: Zaire or Congo?

Q192. Who lives in a warren: a rat or a rabbit?

Q203. How do rams defend their territory?

Q193. Which is the smallest mammal?

Q204. Which is the largest deer: a moose or a caribou?

Q194. Why do some mammals like to groom each other?

Q205. Can bears swim?

Q195. How does a hamster store food?

Q206. What does a beaver build?

Q196. What are the 4 ways a horse moves?

Black bear

Q207. What color does a weasel's fur turn in snowy, cold climates?

TURN TO PAGE 121 FOR ANSWERS

Birds

Guillemot egg

American robin egg

Q208. Which bird lays the biggest eggs?

Q209. Is the bird with the most feathers an eagle, a swan, a duck, or an emu?

Q210. Which bird has "eyes" in its tail?

Lanner falcon

Q211. Why do some owls have one ear higher than the other?

Q212. The male sandgrouse can carry water 18 miles (30 km) across the desert for his chicks. Where does he store it?

Q213. Which lethal creatures does the long-legged secretary bird eat?

Q214. Does air flow faster above a bird's wing or below it?

Wing of shoveler duck

Q215. How fast can a hummingbird's wings beat: 60, 90, or 120 times a second?

Q216. How high can a bird fly: up to 7, 9, or 11 miles high (11, 14, or 17 km)?

Q217. Cave swiftlets make their nests with a material from their own bodies. Is it dung, silk, or saliva?

Redstart's nest

Q218. The fastest living creature is a falcon. Which falcon is it?

Q219. One kind of bird can remain in the air continuously for up to 10 years. Is it an albatross, a tern, or a skimmer?

Q220. One species of bird probably sees more daylight than any other creature. Is it the gyrfalcon, the storm petrel, or the Arctic tern?

Q221. Which bird of which colour is a symbol of peace?

Q222. Does a robin's heart beat 400, 500, or 600 times a minute?

Q223. Is the bird with the longest bill a stork, a pelican, a penguin, or a woodpecker?

Q224. Which is the world's smallest bird: the amethyst woodstar, or the bee hummingbird?

Q225. In Greek myth, was it Icarus or Achilles who flew too close to the sun?

Q226. Is it the emperor, king, or gentoo male penguin that incubates its eggs on its feet through the world's worst winter, in Antarctica?

Q227. In 1814 the passenger pigeon population was in the billions. In 1914, how many were left?

Q228. Are most birds' bones hollow or solid?

Q229. Is the bird with the greatest wingspan an eagle, a condor, or an albatross?

Bird skeleton

Q230. What makes the wrybill unique?

78   TURN TO PAGE 121 FOR ANSWERS

Mini-beasts

Q231. The Kayapo Indians of Brazil model their society on an insect that they think lives in perfect harmony. Which insect is it?

Q232. How many pairs of shoes would an arachnid need?

Tortoise beetle

Q233. Which beetles "fire a gun": dung, camphor, or bombardier beetles?

Q234. One particular kind of weevil has a very long neck. What is it called?

Q235. In which country would you find the world's most venomous spider: Australia, China, or Brazil?

Bumblebee

Q236. Are worker bees male or female?

Q237. The sun spiders of Africa and the Middle East are arachnid world record holders. Is their world record for size, speed, or reproduction?

Madagascan moon moth

Goliath beetle

Q245. What do caterpillars turn into when they grow up?

Earthworm

Peacock butterfly

Q238. In the first World Worm Charming Championship, in 1980, competitors had 30 minutes to charm worms by vibrating a garden tool in the soil. Did the winner charm 311, 511, or 711 worms?

Q239. Which luxury clothing material is made by moths?

Q240. For its size, the rhinoceros beetle is perhaps the world's strongest creature. Can it support 250, 550, or 850 times its own weight on its back?

Gold beetle

Q241. Why are moths attracted to bright lights?

Q242. Is the smallest spider 0.1, 0.06, or 0.02 in long (2.4, 1.4, or 0.4 mm)?

Q243. Are Goliath beetles or elephant beetles the largest of all beetles?

Brimstone butterfly

Q244. This butterfly has a hidden pattern on its wings. What kind of light would make that pattern show up?

Q246. Nephila spiders' webs are very strong. Are they used to make ropes, rugs, or fishing nets?

Q247. Why do glow worms glow?

Crab spider

Q248. What was the distance around the largest spider's web ever measured: 13, 20, or 27 ft (4, 6, or 8 m)?

TURN TO PAGE 121 FOR ANSWERS

Flowers and Plants

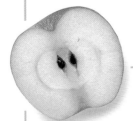

Q249. What do you call the flowers of fruit trees?

Ripe apples

Q250. Which chestnut can you eat: the horse chestnut or the sweet chestnut?

Q251. What happens to a broad-leaved tree in the fall?

Q252. Is a cedar tree a broad-leaved tree or a coniferous tree?

Q253. What is a young tree called?

Q254. How often does an annual plant flower?

Q255. Can you name a plant used in cosmetics?

Q256. Which part of the sugar maple tree produces maple syrup?

Sugar maple

Q257. Which bell-shaped flower grows in abundance in Holland?

Cross-section of oak tree

Q258. Is an oak tree a broad-leaved tree or a coniferous tree?

Iris

Q259. Do all plants flower?

Q260. What is the male reproductive part of a flower called?

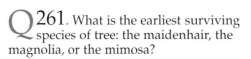

Colored lines guide bees to nectar

Q261. What is the earliest surviving species of tree: the maidenhair, the magnolia, or the mimosa?

Q262. Who first made chocolate from the cocao pod: the Aztecs or the Egyptians?

Q263. How do cacti survive living in the world's driest places?

Cross-section of cactus stem

Q264. Is a monkey puzzle a tree, a fruit, or a flower?

Q265. What is the process by which a plant uses the energy in sunlight to make food?

Pinecone

Q266. Do pinecones open in dry weather or in rainy weather?

Q267. Which is the biggest tree in the world?

Q268. Which part of a sunflower can you eat?

Q269. Why do people get hayfever in the spring?

Q270. What is the female reproductive part of a flower called?

Ox-eye daisy

Q271. This daisy is a composite flower: true or false?

Q272. What is the function of the xylem: to transport water and minerals or to store seeds?

TURN TO PAGE 121 FOR ANSWERS

Parts of a flower

Pink aster

Q**273.** What is pollination?

Q**274.** Where does the aster above most commonly grow: in deserts, by the seashore, or in fields?

Q**275.** What is the largest flower in the plant kingdom?

Daffodil

Q**276.** What is nectar?

Q**278.** What do you call the sticky sap that oozes out of coniferous trees?

Q**279.** What is the green pigment in leaves called?

Japanese maple leaf

Q Can you identify the parts of this sunflower?

292.

Sunflower

293.

294.

295.

296.

Longitudinal section through a sunflower

Q**277.** What happens to a flower once it has been pollinated?

Lily flower

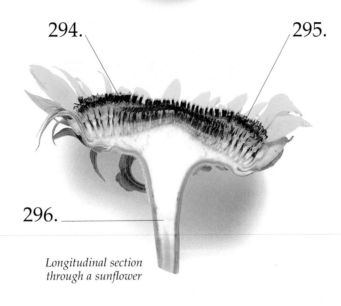

Q**280.** How is pollen carried from the male part to the female part of a flower?

Q**287.** Which plant bulb is supposed to keep vampires away?

Q**290.** How do you estimate the age of a tree?

Q**291.** Why are flowers so brightly colored?

Q**281.** What is the difference between a simple leaf and a compound leaf?

Q**282.** Do flowers smell strongest by day or by night?

Fly agaric mushroom

Q**283.** Does this mushroom help the trees it grows beside?

Q**284.** How can a plant protect itself from being eaten by a hungry animal?

Q**285.** What is a virgin forest?

Q**286.** Which tree produces acorns?

Acorns

Q**288.** Who was the Greek god of forests and flocks?

Q**289.** Can some plants eat insects?

Gerbera flower

Ancient Egypt

Understanding the past enriches our lives, and no part of history is more fascinating than the story of the land of the pyramids. The treasures of Egypt were ancient when Rome was a village, and they still inspire the world's wonder. As one proverb says, "Time laughs at all things, but the pyramids laugh at time."

Mummy case of the lady Takhenmes

Q297. What was a mummy in ancient Egypt?

Q298. Who were the pharaohs?

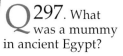

Bracelet showing the god Horus

Q303. Were the pharaohs buried on the west side of the Nile, or the east side?

Q305. Was Taweret, the goddess of childbirth, shown as a pregnant hippopotamus, stork, or cat?

Q304. Why did Egyptian priests shave their heads?

Statue of priest

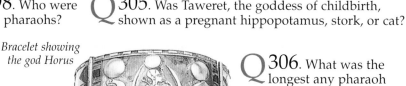

Q299. One part of the god Horus's body became a symbol of protection. Was it his hand, his heart, or his eye?

Q300. Was the Egyptian Book of the Dead a collection of spells or a list of past pharaohs?

Q301. The Egyptians did not have paper. Did they use parchment or papyrus instead?

Q302. Can you name the lion with the head of a man that guards the way to King Khafra's pyramid at Giza?

Q306. What was the longest any pharaoh reigned: 74, 84, or 94 years?

Q307. Why were the pyramids built?

Q308. Was the scarab, or dung, beetle a symbol of the Sun god or the god of the underworld?

Q309. Was the sky goddess called Fruit or Nut?

TURN TO PAGE 122 FOR ANSWERS

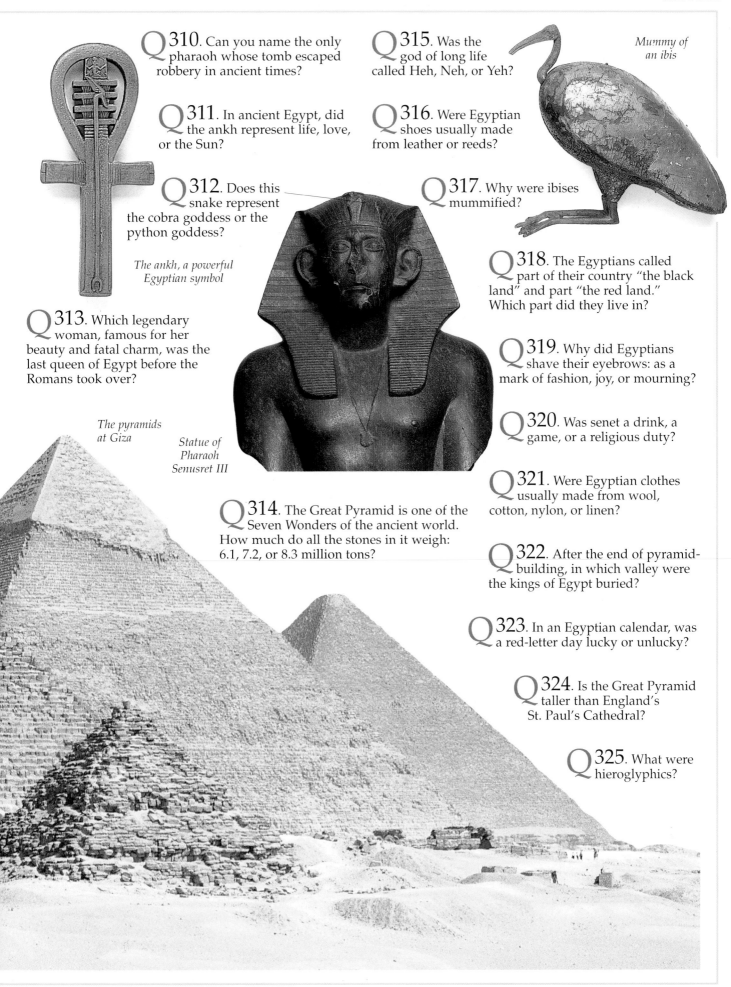

Q310. Can you name the only pharaoh whose tomb escaped robbery in ancient times?

Q311. In ancient Egypt, did the ankh represent life, love, or the Sun?

Q312. Does this snake represent the cobra goddess or the python goddess?

The ankh, a powerful Egyptian symbol

Q313. Which legendary woman, famous for her beauty and fatal charm, was the last queen of Egypt before the Romans took over?

The pyramids at Giza

Statue of Pharaoh Senusret III

Q314. The Great Pyramid is one of the Seven Wonders of the ancient world. How much do all the stones in it weigh: 6.1, 7.2, or 8.3 million tons?

Q315. Was the god of long life called Heh, Neh, or Yeh?

Q316. Were Egyptian shoes usually made from leather or reeds?

Mummy of an ibis

Q317. Why were ibises mummified?

Q318. The Egyptians called part of their country "the black land" and part "the red land." Which part did they live in?

Q319. Why did Egyptians shave their eyebrows: as a mark of fashion, joy, or mourning?

Q320. Was senet a drink, a game, or a religious duty?

Q321. Were Egyptian clothes usually made from wool, cotton, nylon, or linen?

Q322. After the end of pyramid-building, in which valley were the kings of Egypt buried?

Q323. In an Egyptian calendar, was a red-letter day lucky or unlucky?

Q324. Is the Great Pyramid taller than England's St. Paul's Cathedral?

Q325. What were hieroglyphics?

TURN TO PAGE 122 FOR ANSWERS

Ancient Greece

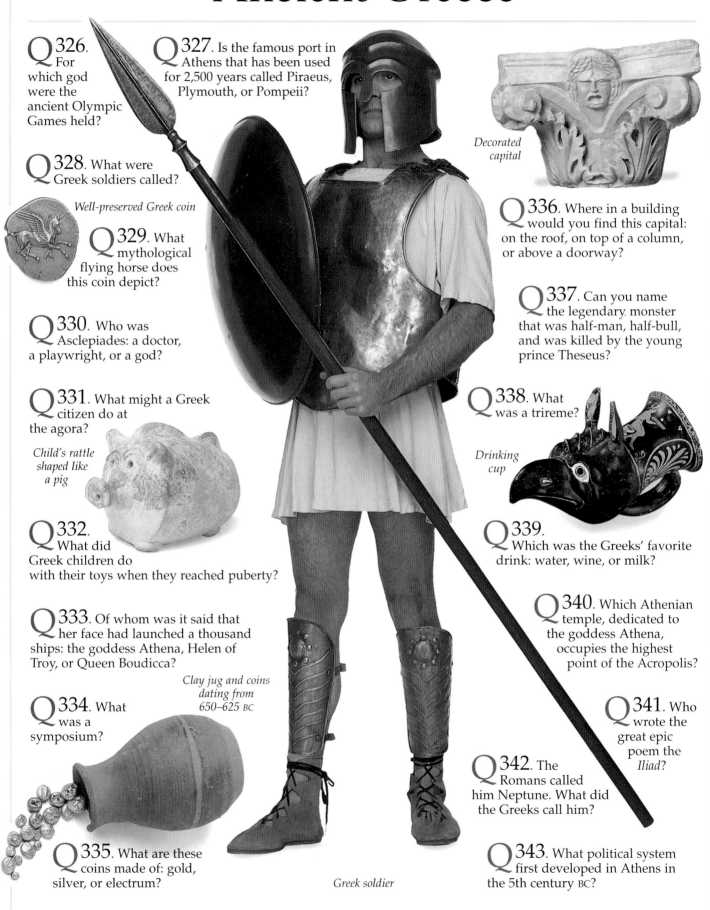

Q326. For which god were the ancient Olympic Games held?

Q327. Is the famous port in Athens that has been used for 2,500 years called Piraeus, Plymouth, or Pompeii?

Q328. What were Greek soldiers called?

Well-preserved Greek coin

Q329. What mythological flying horse does this coin depict?

Q330. Who was Asclepiades: a doctor, a playwright, or a god?

Q331. What might a Greek citizen do at the agora?

Child's rattle shaped like a pig

Q332. What did Greek children do with their toys when they reached puberty?

Q333. Of whom was it said that her face had launched a thousand ships: the goddess Athena, Helen of Troy, or Queen Boudicca?

Clay jug and coins dating from 650–625 BC

Q334. What was a symposium?

Q335. What are these coins made of: gold, silver, or electrum?

Greek soldier

Decorated capital

Q336. Where in a building would you find this capital: on the roof, on top of a column, or above a doorway?

Q337. Can you name the legendary monster that was half-man, half-bull, and was killed by the young prince Theseus?

Q338. What was a trireme?

Drinking cup

Q339. Which was the Greeks' favorite drink: water, wine, or milk?

Q340. Which Athenian temple, dedicated to the goddess Athena, occupies the highest point of the Acropolis?

Q341. Who wrote the great epic poem the *Iliad*?

Q342. The Romans called him Neptune. What did the Greeks call him?

Q343. What political system first developed in Athens in the 5th century BC?

TURN TO PAGE 122 FOR ANSWERS

Ancient Rome

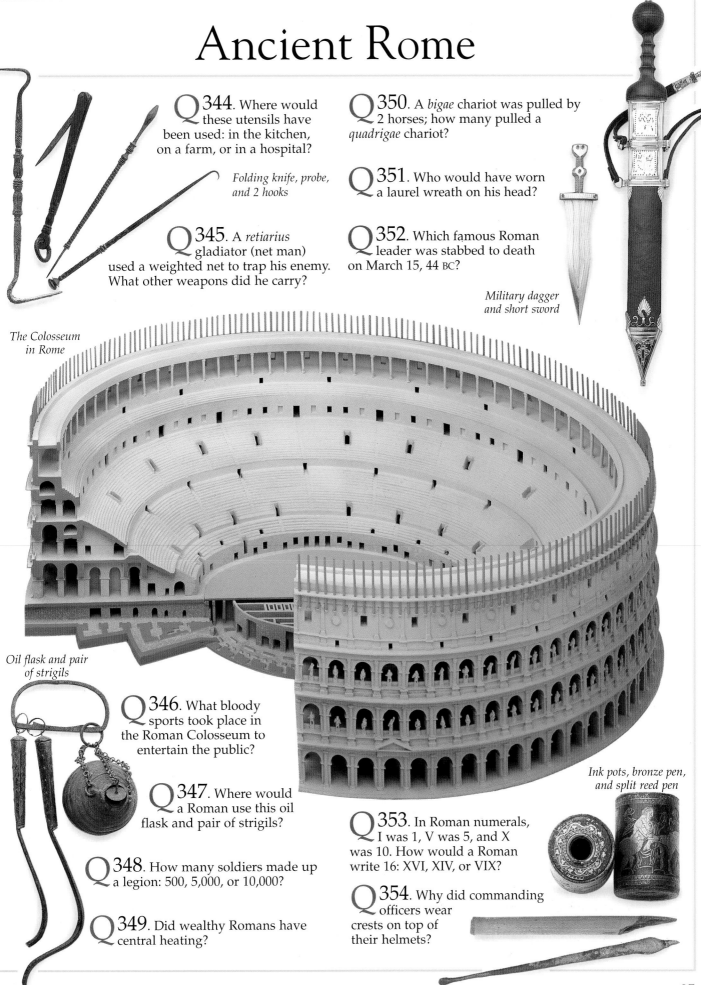

Q344. Where would these utensils have been used: in the kitchen, on a farm, or in a hospital?

Folding knife, probe, and 2 hooks

Q345. A *retiarius* gladiator (net man) used a weighted net to trap his enemy. What other weapons did he carry?

Q350. A *bigae* chariot was pulled by 2 horses; how many pulled a *quadrigae* chariot?

Q351. Who would have worn a laurel wreath on his head?

Q352. Which famous Roman leader was stabbed to death on March 15, 44 BC?

Military dagger and short sword

The Colosseum in Rome

Oil flask and pair of strigils

Q346. What bloody sports took place in the Roman Colosseum to entertain the public?

Q347. Where would a Roman use this oil flask and pair of strigils?

Q348. How many soldiers made up a legion: 500, 5,000, or 10,000?

Q349. Did wealthy Romans have central heating?

Ink pots, bronze pen, and split reed pen

Q353. In Roman numerals, I was 1, V was 5, and X was 10. How would a Roman write 16: XVI, XIV, or VIX?

Q354. Why did commanding officers wear crests on top of their helmets?

TURN TO PAGE 122 FOR ANSWERS

Medieval Life

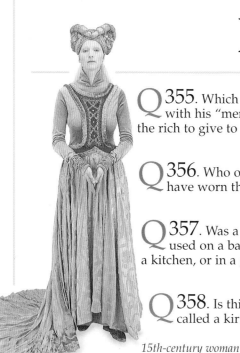

15th-century woman

Q**355**. Which legendary character, with his "merrie men," stole from the rich to give to the poor?

Q**356**. Who or what would have worn this pendant?

Q**357**. Was a flesh-hook used on a battlefield, in a kitchen, or in a graveyard?

Q**358**. Is this woman's dress called a kirtle or a skirtle?

Pendant showing coat of arms

Q**363**. The name of this instrument is the name of its parts. What is it called?

Minstrel (musician)

Q**364**. Was a villein a villain?

Q**365**. In which country did Joan of Arc live?

Q**366**. Was pannage a tax on pans, a duty on beer, or the right to pasture pigs in a forest?

Q**367**. What is the keep of a castle?

Q**368**. What was the Black Death?

Q**359**. In which century did hand knitting begin in Europe: the 9th, 12th, or 15th?

Bodiam Castle in England

Q**360**. What is the ditch around a castle called?

Q**361**. Which were easier to defend: round towers or square towers?

Q**362**. Was a morning star a weapon or a decoration?

TURN TO PAGE 122 FOR ANSWERS

Crossbow

Q369. Were pigs sometimes trained as war hounds or as retrievers for use in hunting?

Q370. What was an apprentice knight before he "won his spurs"?

Q371. What is this armor designed to protect?

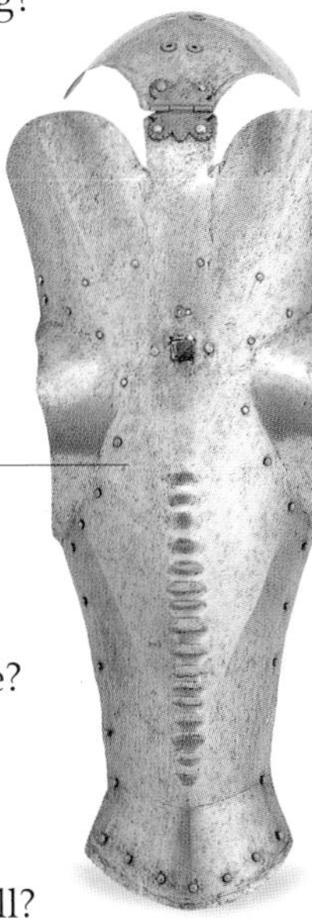

Q372. What did a knight throw on the ground to issue a challenge?

Q373. Was a castle's outer wall called the ring wall or the curtain wall?

Shaffron armor

Q374. From which flower did the English civil wars of the 1400s take their name?

Q375. In the 10th century King Wenceslaus ruled Bohemia in the Czech Republic. When is he remembered in song?

Q376. In the 1300s, which sport got in the way of archery practice and was banned by the king of England?

Q377. What were the Crusades?

Q378. What are samite, damask, and taffeta?

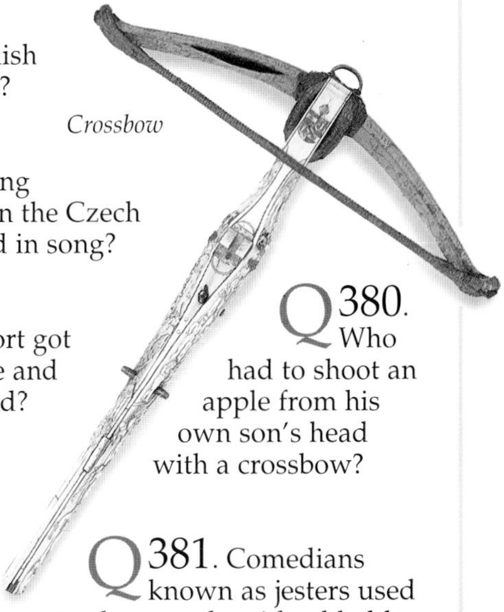

Q379. Why do these machicolations (overhanging battlements) have holes in their floors?

Q380. Who had to shoot an apple from his own son's head with a crossbow?

Q381. Comedians known as jesters used to slap people with a bladder on a stick. What was this called?

Q382. Which part of a castle was the oubliette (which means "forgotten")?

TURN TO PAGE 122 FOR ANSWERS

Renaissance

Q383. What is this young man's jacket called: a cravat, a doublet, or a stomacher?

Q384. In which Italian city-state did the Renaissance begin: Florence, Milan, or Venice?

Q385. What does the word Renaissance mean?

Fashionable Renaissance style

Q386. Is this woman's dress made of silk, velvet, or serge?

Q387. Which scholar challenged the view that the Earth was at the center of the Universe: Nicholaus Copernicus, Hans Lippershey, or Roger Bacon?

Q388. Which ancient civilization was a vital inspiration for the Renaissance?

Shield probably belonging to Charles V

Q389. Which noble family did Charles V belong to: the Hapsburgs, Tudors, or Romanovs?

Q390. Why was the 16th-century religious movement led by Martin Luther known as the Reformation?

Q391. Which great Renaissance artist and scientist designed an early tank and a flying machine?

Q392. Which 16th-century English queen owned these gloves?

Woman in 15th-century dress

Gloves belonging to a queen

Q393. Which Italian banking family used their money and influence to sponsor artists?

Q394. Can you name the romantic tragedy by William Shakespeare that was set in Verona: *Macbeth* or *Romeo and Juliet*?

An early printing press

Q395. The invention of the printing press by Johannes Gutenberg in 1450 enabled books to be mass-produced. In which country was it invented?

Q396. The Bible was the first book printed on Gutenberg's printing press. In which language was it written?

Gutenberg's Bible

Exploration

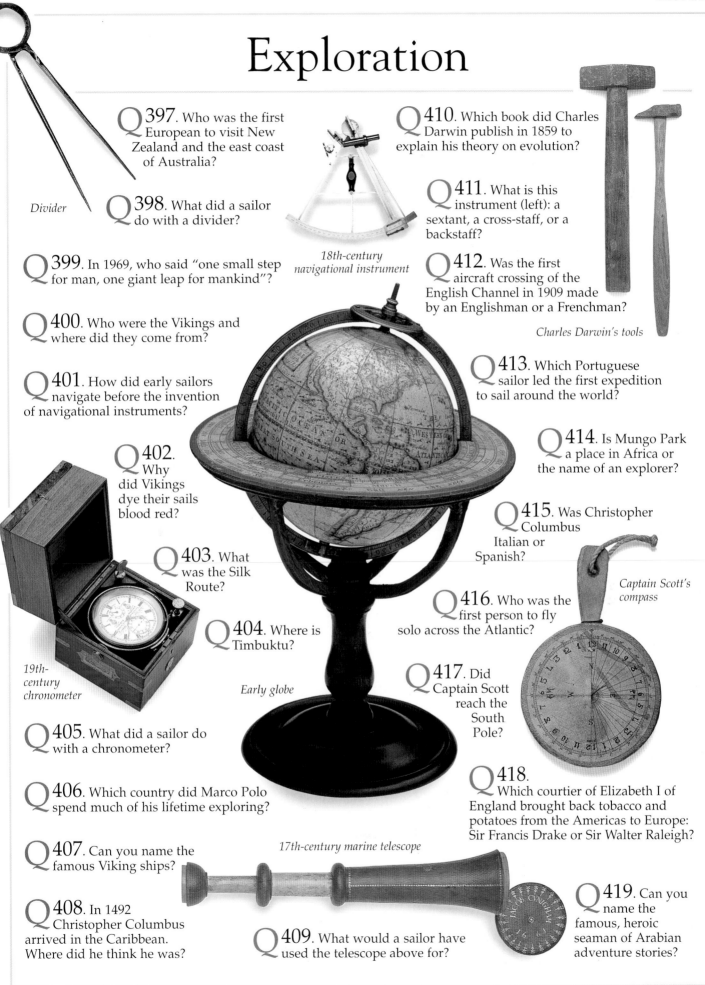

Q397. Who was the first European to visit New Zealand and the east coast of Australia?

Divider

Q398. What did a sailor do with a divider?

Q399. In 1969, who said "one small step for man, one giant leap for mankind"?

Q400. Who were the Vikings and where did they come from?

Q401. How did early sailors navigate before the invention of navigational instruments?

Q402. Why did Vikings dye their sails blood red?

Q403. What was the Silk Route?

Q404. Where is Timbuktu?

19th-century chronometer

Q405. What did a sailor do with a chronometer?

Q406. Which country did Marco Polo spend much of his lifetime exploring?

Q407. Can you name the famous Viking ships?

Q408. In 1492 Christopher Columbus arrived in the Caribbean. Where did he think he was?

18th-century navigational instrument

Early globe

17th-century marine telescope

Q409. What would a sailor have used the telescope above for?

Q410. Which book did Charles Darwin publish in 1859 to explain his theory on evolution?

Q411. What is this instrument (left): a sextant, a cross-staff, or a backstaff?

Q412. Was the first aircraft crossing of the English Channel in 1909 made by an Englishman or a Frenchman?

Charles Darwin's tools

Q413. Which Portuguese sailor led the first expedition to sail around the world?

Q414. Is Mungo Park a place in Africa or the name of an explorer?

Q415. Was Christopher Columbus Italian or Spanish?

Captain Scott's compass

Q416. Who was the first person to fly solo across the Atlantic?

Q417. Did Captain Scott reach the South Pole?

Q418. Which courtier of Elizabeth I of England brought back tobacco and potatoes from the Americas to Europe: Sir Francis Drake or Sir Walter Raleigh?

Q419. Can you name the famous, heroic seaman of Arabian adventure stories?

TURN TO PAGES 122-123 FOR ANSWERS

Aztecs and Incas

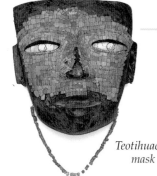

Teotihuacan mask

Q420. Which method of sacrifice did the Maya think was right for their rain god?

Maya rain god, Chac

Q421. Turquoise, coral, shell, obsidian, silver: which of these materials does not appear in the mask above?

Q422. Who lived in "the World of the Fifth Sun"?

Q423. Was Tlaloc the Aztec god of rain or the Aztec god of war?

Water vessel of Aztec god Tlaloc

Q424. Whose elite warriors were named after the jaguar and the eagle?

Q425. Which animal did the Incas use for transportation?

Q426. Which invention, *very* useful for transportation, did the Incas fail to use?

Q427. Were the Aztecs' "Wars of Flowers" fought for flowers or prisoners?

Nazca textile

Q428. In ancient Peru, did men or women carry bags like this, used to carry coca leaves and amulets (good luck charms)?

Q429. Who is Mexico named after?

Q430. Did the Nazca people live in Mexico or Peru?

Q431. From which animal does the skin on this shield come?

Aztec shield

Q432. Did the Aztecs pay taxes to chinampas, grow crops on them, or fill them with chilies and eat them?

Q433. In 1519 Spanish conquistadors arrived in Mexico on animals that the Aztecs had never seen before. What were they?

Q434. Are tomatoes, peanuts, pineapples, and sweet potatoes native to Europe or the Americas?

Peruvian bag

Q435. How was the Aztec capital, Tenochtitlan, like Venice?

Q436. In 1500, which was bigger: Tenochtitlan or London, England?

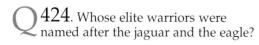

TURN TO PAGE 123 FOR ANSWERS

The Wild West

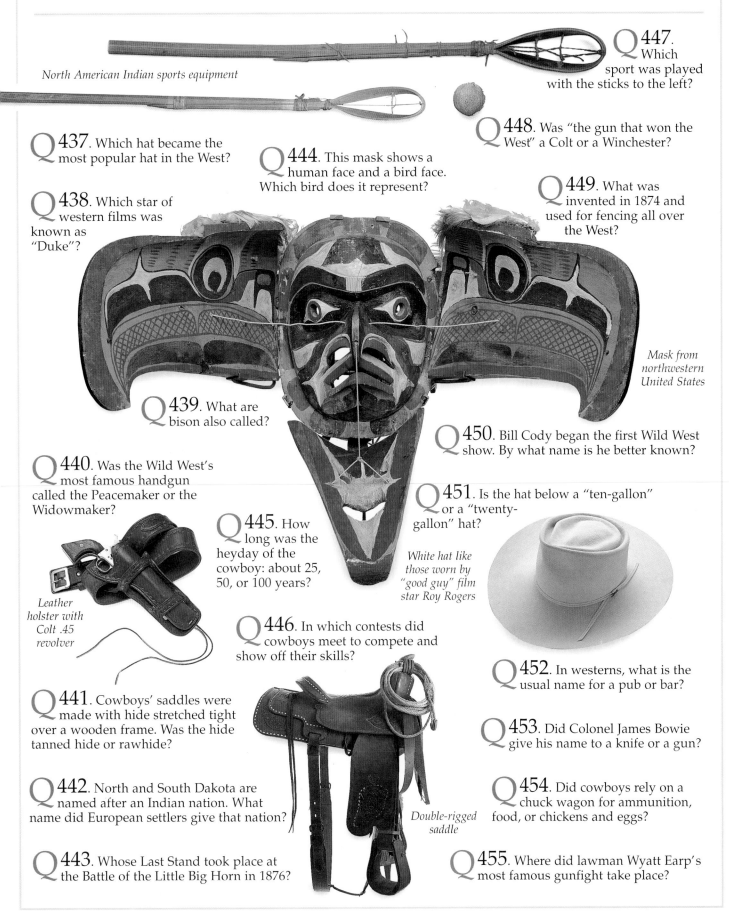

North American Indian sports equipment

Q447. Which sport was played with the sticks to the left?

Q437. Which hat became the most popular hat in the West?

Q444. This mask shows a human face and a bird face. Which bird does it represent?

Q448. Was "the gun that won the West" a Colt or a Winchester?

Q438. Which star of western films was known as "Duke"?

Q449. What was invented in 1874 and used for fencing all over the West?

Mask from northwestern United States

Q439. What are bison also called?

Q450. Bill Cody began the first Wild West show. By what name is he better known?

Q440. Was the Wild West's most famous handgun called the Peacemaker or the Widowmaker?

Q445. How long was the heyday of the cowboy: about 25, 50, or 100 years?

Q451. Is the hat below a "ten-gallon" or a "twenty-gallon" hat?

White hat like those worn by "good guy" film star Roy Rogers

Leather holster with Colt .45 revolver

Q446. In which contests did cowboys meet to compete and show off their skills?

Q452. In westerns, what is the usual name for a pub or bar?

Q441. Cowboys' saddles were made with hide stretched tight over a wooden frame. Was the hide tanned hide or rawhide?

Q453. Did Colonel James Bowie give his name to a knife or a gun?

Q442. North and South Dakota are named after an Indian nation. What name did European settlers give that nation?

Double-rigged saddle

Q454. Did cowboys rely on a chuck wagon for ammunition, food, or chickens and eggs?

Q443. Whose Last Stand took place at the Battle of the Little Big Horn in 1876?

Q455. Where did lawman Wyatt Earp's most famous gunfight take place?

TURN TO PAGE 123 FOR ANSWERS

Weaponry and War

Q456. What kind of hairy and non-military feature did General Ambrose Burnside give his name to?

Q457. Where did the largest invasion of all time take place on D-day (6 June, 1944)?

Q458. Is a scimitar a straight or a curved sword?

17th-century sword

Q459. Which can fire an arrow farther: a crossbow or a longbow?

Q460. Is the sword above a smallsword, a backsword, or a hunting sword?

Muzzle-loading cannon

Q461. From what kind of metal are bullets traditionally made?

Gun bullets

Q462. How many soldiers made up the gun crew of this cannon: about 2, 5, or 10?

Q463. How many shots could you fire from this revolver without reloading: 5, 8, or 10?

Colt police revolver

Q464. Was a musket a gun or a shield?

Q465. Dugouts are a feature of modern warfare. What are they?

Q466. In World War II, what was a U-boat?

Q467. Who led elephants across the Alps and won many battles against Rome, although in the end he lost the war?

Q468. What was the last big sea battle waged between German and British fleets: Jutland, Trafalgar, or Pearl Harbor?

Q469. He seemed invincible in battle, he crowned himself emperor of France, but in the end he was defeated at Waterloo and exiled. Who was he?

Q470. What is this hand-ax made of?

Hand-ax

Zulu Spear

Q471. Which fighting machine first rumbled into action on the battlefields of World War I?

Q472. In an army, which of these is the most senior in rank: a colonel, a captain, or a corporal?

Q473. What was the most important weapon carried by a samurai warrior?

Q474. Is an AK47 a gun, a tank, or a missile?

Q475. Is this spear designed for throwing or for thrusting?

Q476. When grenades were first used in Europe, what were the troops who were trained to use them called?

Q477. What was this nasty looking object used for?

A caltrop

TURN TO PAGE 123 FOR ANSWERS

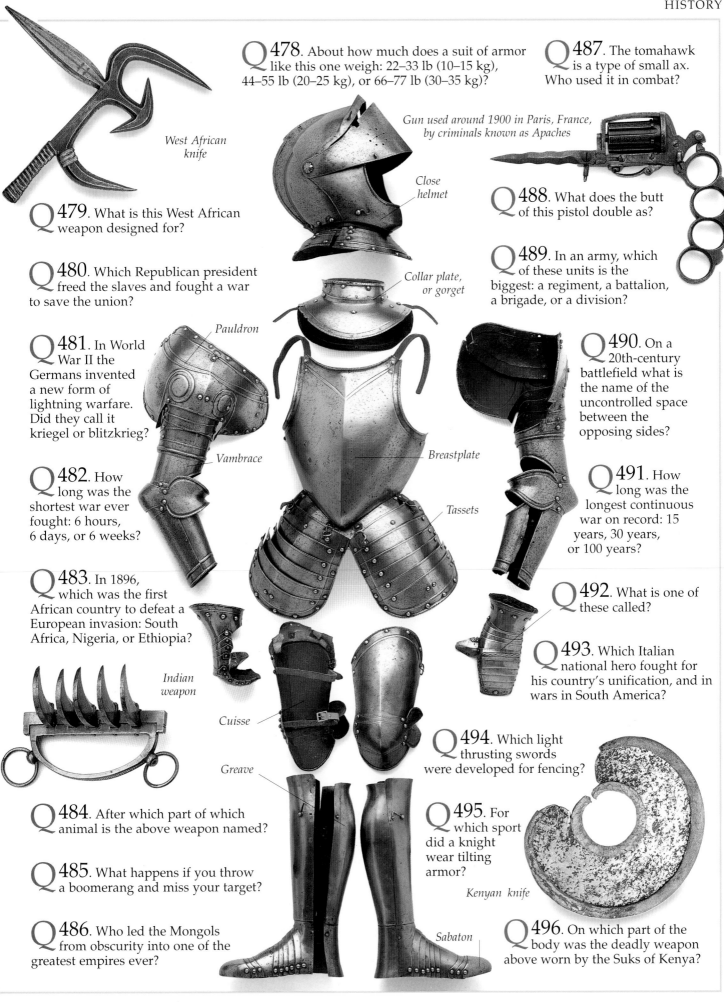

West African knife

Q478. About how much does a suit of armor like this one weigh: 22–33 lb (10–15 kg), 44–55 lb (20–25 kg), or 66–77 lb (30–35 kg)?

Gun used around 1900 in Paris, France, by criminals known as Apaches

Q487. The tomahawk is a type of small ax. Who used it in combat?

Close helmet

Q488. What does the butt of this pistol double as?

Q479. What is this West African weapon designed for?

Q480. Which Republican president freed the slaves and fought a war to save the union?

Collar plate, or gorget

Q489. In an army, which of these units is the biggest: a regiment, a battalion, a brigade, or a division?

Q481. In World War II the Germans invented a new form of lightning warfare. Did they call it kriegel or blitzkrieg?

Pauldron

Q490. On a 20th-century battlefield what is the name of the uncontrolled space between the opposing sides?

Vambrace

Breastplate

Q482. How long was the shortest war ever fought: 6 hours, 6 days, or 6 weeks?

Q491. How long was the longest continuous war on record: 15 years, 30 years, or 100 years?

Tassets

Q483. In 1896, which was the first African country to defeat a European invasion: South Africa, Nigeria, or Ethiopia?

Indian weapon

Q492. What is one of these called?

Q493. Which Italian national hero fought for his country's unification, and in wars in South America?

Cuisse

Q484. After which part of which animal is the above weapon named?

Greave

Q494. Which light thrusting swords were developed for fencing?

Q485. What happens if you throw a boomerang and miss your target?

Q495. For which sport did a knight wear tilting armor?

Kenyan knife

Q486. Who led the Mongols from obscurity into one of the greatest empires ever?

Sabaton

Q496. On which part of the body was the deadly weapon above worn by the Suks of Kenya?

TURN TO PAGE 123 FOR ANSWERS

Clothing

18th-century fan

Q **497**. What did a Viking make with a hand spindle?

Q **498**. Which French king in the 17th century began a trend for wearing wigs?

Hand spindle and bone threadpickers

Q **499**. What are made from denim, most often blue, and worn around the world?

Buckle plate

Q **500**. What did this buckle plate fasten: a belt, a cloak, or a dress?

Q **501**. Folding fans arrived in Europe in the 16th century. Where did they originate: China, Turkey, or Russia?

Detachable cuffs

Q **502**. In which century was it fashionable to wear the detachable cuffs above: the 10th, 18th, or 20th century?

Q **503**. When the first versions of the handbag appeared in the 18th century, did they belong to men or to women?

Gentleman's pouch bag

Q **504**. When did the miniskirt make its first appearance?

Woman in silk bustle dress

Q **505**. What is the main use for a fan?

Q **506**. In ancient Rome, which garment indicated Roman citizenship?

Q **507**. In the Middle Ages, were rolls, coils, steeples, butterflies, and horns headdresses, petticoats, or jewels?

Q **508**. What did wealthy men and women do with these beauty patches?

18th-century beauty patches

Q **509**. When was this straw hat fashionable: in the early 20th century or the late 18th century?

Straw hat

Roman hairpin

Q **510**. Why did Roman imperial women need hairpins?

Q **511**. In the 1500s, it was very fashionable for men to look overweight. Where did this craze originate: Norway, Italy, or Spain?

Q **512**. The lady to the left is wearing a silk bustle dress from the 1880s. What is a bustle?

TURN TO PAGE 123 FOR ANSWERS

Q513. What were chopines: shoes, buckles, or cuffs?

Gentleman's embroidered waistcoat

Q514. When was this waistcoat fashionable: in the 14th, 18th, or 20th century?

Q515. Which material, originally Chinese, was prized in the Byzantine Empire?

Accessories

Q On what part of the body would you wear these items?

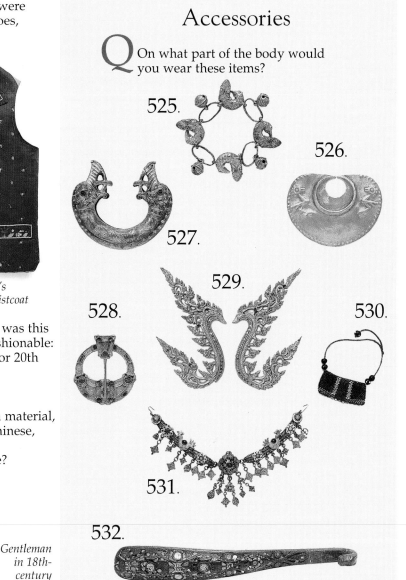

525.

526.

527.

529.

528.

530.

531.

532.

Gentleman in 18th-century suit

Hand-embroidered gloves

Q521. In the 1800s, why did upper-class European women keep their hands covered?

Wide ties

Q522. Were wide ties fashionable in the 1770s, 1870s, or 1970s?

Q516. Who were the first people to cut and fit garments, rather than just draping themselves in fabric: the Persians, the Elizabethans, or the Romans?

Q517. Can you name the stiff whalebone petticoat first worn by women in the 1850s to support their skirts?

Q518. Which country influenced fashions throughout Europe for most of the 18th century: Spain, France, or England?

Q519. Since the 1940s, nylon has been used for clothing. What is nylon?

Seamed nylon stockings

Q520. Was a pompadour a hairstyle or a parasol?

1970s platform shoes

Q523. What happened to skirts in Europe and the United States in the 1920s that some people found very shocking?

Q524. In the 1970s, did men wear platform shoes?

Inventions: to 1850

If human beings didn't have a gift for invention and scientific discovery, we would all still live in caves. Homes, clothes, jobs, schools, transportation: every part of modern life depends on the creations of science and invention. We are so surrounded by them that it's hard to imagine life without them.

Model of 17th-century clock made by Dutch mathematician and astronomer Christiaan Huygens

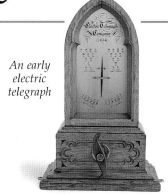

An early electric telegraph

Q533. In what did people first take to the air in 1783?

Q534. In 1656 this feature revolutionized clocks. What is it?

Q535. Which were constructed earlier, arches or tunnels?

Q536. Which was standardized first, the imperial or the metric system of measurement?

Q537. In 1530 a French invention changed the way that wine was stored and made champagne possible. What was it?

Q538. In 1802 Zachaus Winzler cooked with a substance never before used for cooking. What was it?

Bifocal eyeglasses

Q539. Was the earliest electric telegraph made in Europe or the United States?

Q540. Which were built first, baths or showers?

Q541. Was printing invented in Germany, China, or Japan?

Q542. Were eyeglasses first peered through in 300, 1300, or 1800?

Q543. Which was invented first, the violin or the piano?

Q544. Was wallpaper first produced in England, France, or India?

LIVERPOOL HUSKISSON MANCHESTER
RAILWAY — COMPANY

TURN TO PAGE 124 FOR ANSWERS

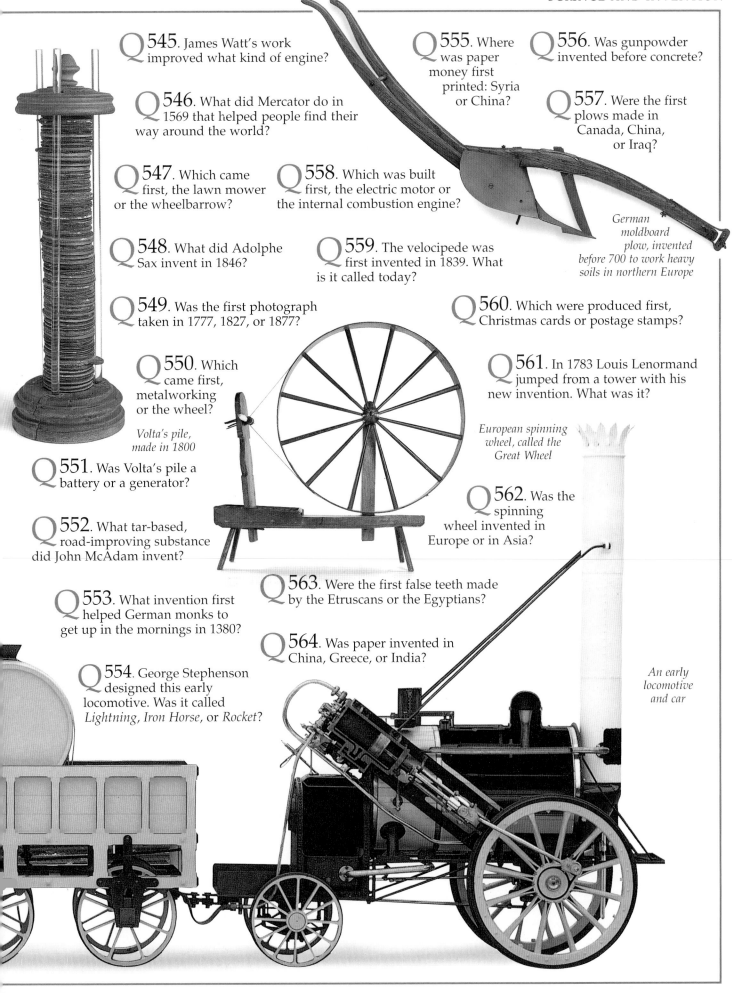

Q**545**. James Watt's work improved what kind of engine?

Q**546**. What did Mercator do in 1569 that helped people find their way around the world?

Q**547**. Which came first, the lawn mower or the wheelbarrow?

Q**548**. What did Adolphe Sax invent in 1846?

Q**549**. Was the first photograph taken in 1777, 1827, or 1877?

Q**550**. Which came first, metalworking or the wheel?

Volta's pile, made in 1800

Q**551**. Was Volta's pile a battery or a generator?

Q**552**. What tar-based, road-improving substance did John McAdam invent?

Q**553**. What invention first helped German monks to get up in the mornings in 1380?

Q**554**. George Stephenson designed this early locomotive. Was it called *Lightning*, *Iron Horse*, or *Rocket*?

Q**555**. Where was paper money first printed: Syria or China?

Q**556**. Was gunpowder invented before concrete?

Q**557**. Were the first plows made in Canada, China, or Iraq?

German moldboard plow, invented before 700 to work heavy soils in northern Europe

Q**558**. Which was built first, the electric motor or the internal combustion engine?

Q**559**. The velocipede was first invented in 1839. What is it called today?

Q**560**. Which were produced first, Christmas cards or postage stamps?

Q**561**. In 1783 Louis Lenormand jumped from a tower with his new invention. What was it?

European spinning wheel, called the Great Wheel

Q**562**. Was the spinning wheel invented in Europe or in Asia?

Q**563**. Were the first false teeth made by the Etruscans or the Egyptians?

Q**564**. Was paper invented in China, Greece, or India?

An early locomotive and car

TURN TO PAGE 124 FOR ANSWERS

The Earth

Old seismograph instrument

Q 565. Which is the world's largest ocean?

Q 566. Which is the largest continent?

Q 567. What are glaciers made of?

Q 568. What is the layer of the Earth between the crust and the core called?

Q 569. What does a seismograph measure?

Q 570. Where is the world's largest rock?

Q 571. Which is the hardest mineral in the world?

Q 572. What does the Richter scale record?

Q 573. What are tsunamis?

Q 574. How old is the Earth: 2.6, 3.6, or 4.6 billion years old?

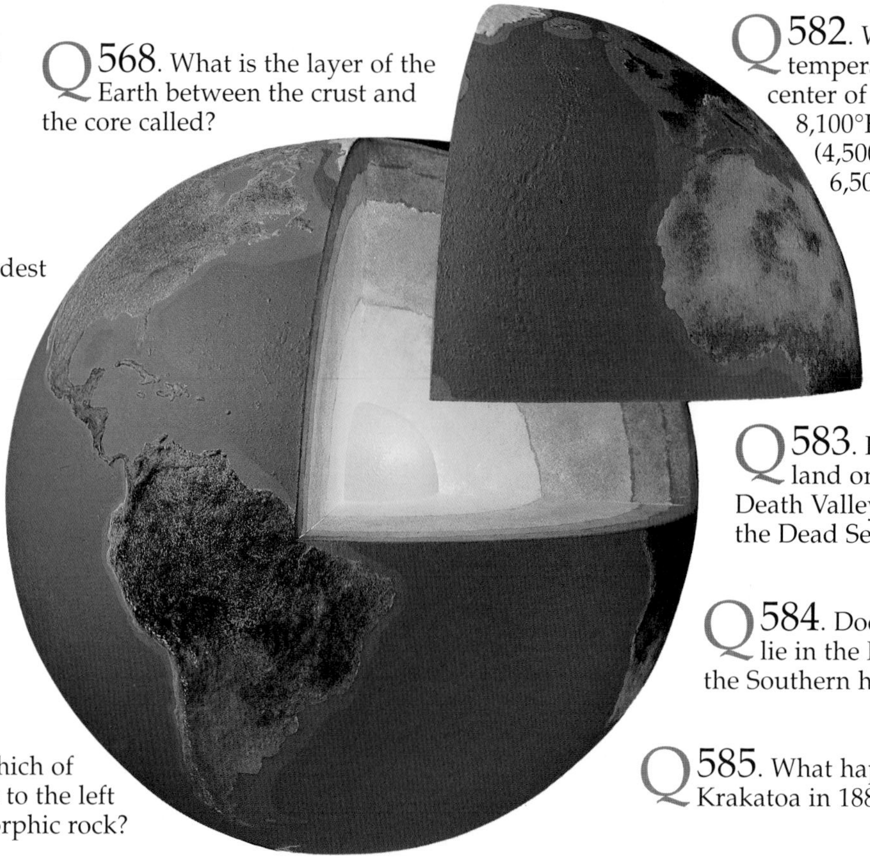

Q 575. Which of the rocks to the left is a metamorphic rock?

Granite rock

Eclogite rock

Q 576. Where rock folds to form ridges, are the steeper or the shallower slopes called "scarps"?

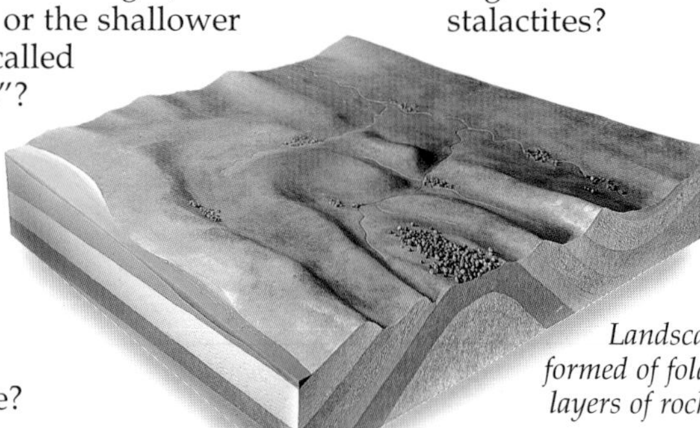

Q 577. Do geysers spout hot or cold water?

Q 578. What is the name of the world's highest mountain range?

Q 579. Gold, silver, and platinum are precious metals. Which is the most valuable?

Q 580. Which is the longest of all rivers?

Q 581. Why was mercury sometimes called quicksilver?

Mercury

Q 582. What is the temperature at the center of the Earth: 8,100°F or 11,700°F (4,500°C or 6,500°C)?

Model of the Earth

Q 583. Is the lowest land on Earth in Death Valley or beside the Dead Sea?

Q 584. Does most land lie in the Northern or the Southern hemisphere?

Q 585. What happened on Krakatoa in 1883?

Q 586. What are stalagmites and stalactites?

Q 587. What does a petrologist study: oil, volcanoes, or rocks?

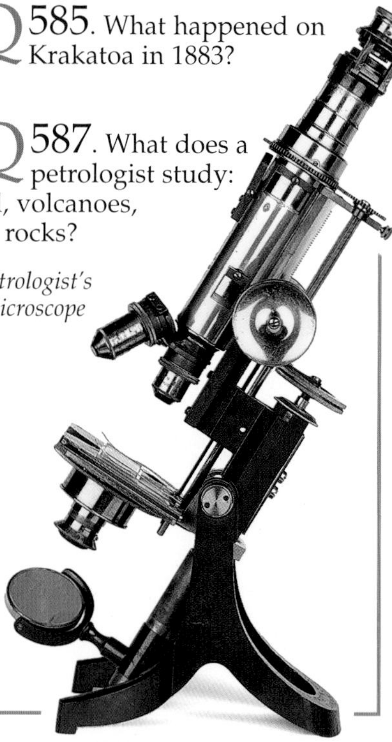

Petrologist's microscope

Landscape formed of folded layers of rock

Q 588. What do hydrologists study?

TURN TO PAGE 124 FOR ANSWERS

Astronomy

Q589. Which planet was named after the Roman goddess of love?

Q599. Which Italian scientist first studied the planets with a telescope?

Replica of 17th-century telescope

Q590. Which two planets lie between the Earth and the Sun?

Q591. What is our galaxy called?

Q600. How long is a year on Mars: 365, 550, or 687 days?

Soviet Vostok rocket

Q592. By what name is the star Sol better known?

Q601. What did Yuri Gagarin do in this rocket in 1961 that only dogs had ever done before?

Q593. In a nursery rhyme, what did the cow jump over?

Q602. What is named after Edmund Halley?

The largest planet

Q594. Which is the largest planet in the Solar System?

The Moon

Q595. In modern science, what is "the fourth dimension"?

Q596. Are the dark patches on the Moon flat areas or mountains?

Q603. Where is the *Hubble Space Telescope* located?

Q597. Who worked out the Theory of Relativity?

Q604. Which film introduced C3PO, R2D2, and Chewbacca?

18th-century moving model of the Solar System

Q605. Was the first woman in space Chinese, Russian, or American?

Q606. Which planet was the last to be discovered?

Q607. Which is the red planet?

Q608. Was the first space station Russian or American?

Q609. What do scientists call the event that began the Universe?

Newton's telescope

Q598. Olympus Mons, Etna, or Vesuvius: which is the biggest volcano on Mars?

Q610. What did Isaac Newton discover after seeing an apple fall from a tree?

TURN TO PAGE 124 FOR ANSWERS

The Human Body

Q**611**. How many times does a heart beat every day: 100,000, 500,000, or 1,000,000 times?

Q**612**. Who has more bones: a child or an adult?

Q**613**. What is the hardest substance in the human body?

Components of the chest

Q**614**. How many pints of air can a pair of lungs hold: 5, 18, or 26 (3, 10, or 15 liters)?

Q**615**. Which country has more hospitals than any other?

Q**616**. Can you name the horny substance in nails, hair, and skin?

Q**617**. Can you name the female organ in which a baby develops?

Q**618**. Which is the largest organ of the human body?

Q**619**. Which doctor founded psychoanalysis, a treatment for mental illness?

Q**620**. Can you name the bony cage that protects the chest organs?

Q**621**. In how many directions can the knee joint bend?

Leg and foot bones

Q**622**. Which intestine is longer: the small intestine or the large intestine?

Q**623**. About how many muscles are there in the human body: 200, 400, or more than 600?

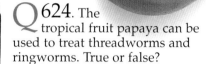

Tropical papayas

Q**624**. The tropical fruit papaya can be used to treat threadworms and ringworms. True or false?

Q**625**. In what year were X rays discovered by Wilhelm Roentgen: 1800, 1850, or 1895?

Thoracic vertebra

Q**626**. In which part of the human body would you find this bone?

Q**627**. How heavy is the human head: 4.4 lb, 8.8 lb, or 17.6 lb (2 kg, 4 kg, or 8 kg)?

Medicine chest

Q**628**. In which century were the medicines above used: the 17th, 18th, or 19th?

Q**629**. Are fish, eggs, and meat made up of carbohydrates or proteins?

Q**630**. Which part of the human body does a doctor examine with a gastroscope: the stomach, heart, or lungs?

Q**631**. Which is the longest bone in the human body: the femur, tibia, or humerus?

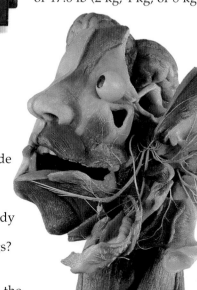

Inside the head and neck

TURN TO PAGE 124 FOR ANSWERS

Q632. Which French scientist developed vaccines and invented pasteurization (heating to destroy bacteria)?

Q633. How many bones are there in the human body: 106, 206, or 306?

Q645. Which year was the first test tube baby born: 1978, 1986, or 1990?

Q646. Where is the smallest bone in the human body: in the ear, the foot, or the wrist?

Q634. Which Polish-born French woman discovered the chemical element radium and was awarded the Nobel Prize for chemistry in 1911?

Q647. When was the first successful heart transplant performed: 1937, 1967, or 1987?

Q635. What is the difference between a local anesthetic and a general anesthetic?

Q648. When did dentistry become a recognized profession: in the 15th, 17th, or 19th century?

Q636. Who discovered penicillin?

Q649. Which fluid secreted by the liver aids digestion?

Q637. What is the function of arteries?

Q650. What does a midwife do?

Q638. Why did doctors apply bloodsucking leeches to their patients?

Leeches

Q651. Which instrument does a doctor use to listen to the heart and lungs?

Q639. When did the first woman graduate from medical school in the United States: 1810, 1849, or 1934?

Q652. Which year was a syringe first used to inject drugs directly into the body: 1753, 1853, or 1953?

Human skeleton

Hypodermic syringe

Q640. Before 1600 in England why did human dissection take place in secret?

Q653. How many bones are there in the hand: 12, 20, or 27?

Q654. In which year was the World Health Organization (WHO) set up by the United Nations: 1908, 1928, or 1948?

Q641. What did a doctor do with the saw above at the Battle of Waterloo?

Q655. Can you name the bone to which the ribs are attached?

Q656. Can you name 2 of the 5 main senses of the human body?

Saw and glove

Q642. Can you name 2 of the major blood groups?

Q657. Why do people get goose bumps?

Ether inhaler

Q643. How many muscles does the average adult use when going for a walk: 50, 100, or more than 200?

Q658. When were anesthetics introduced: in the 1840s, 1880s, or 1920s?

Q644. Which ancient form of Chinese medicine involves the insertion of needles into various points of the body to treat illnesses?

TURN TO PAGE 124 FOR ANSWERS

Biology and Chemistry

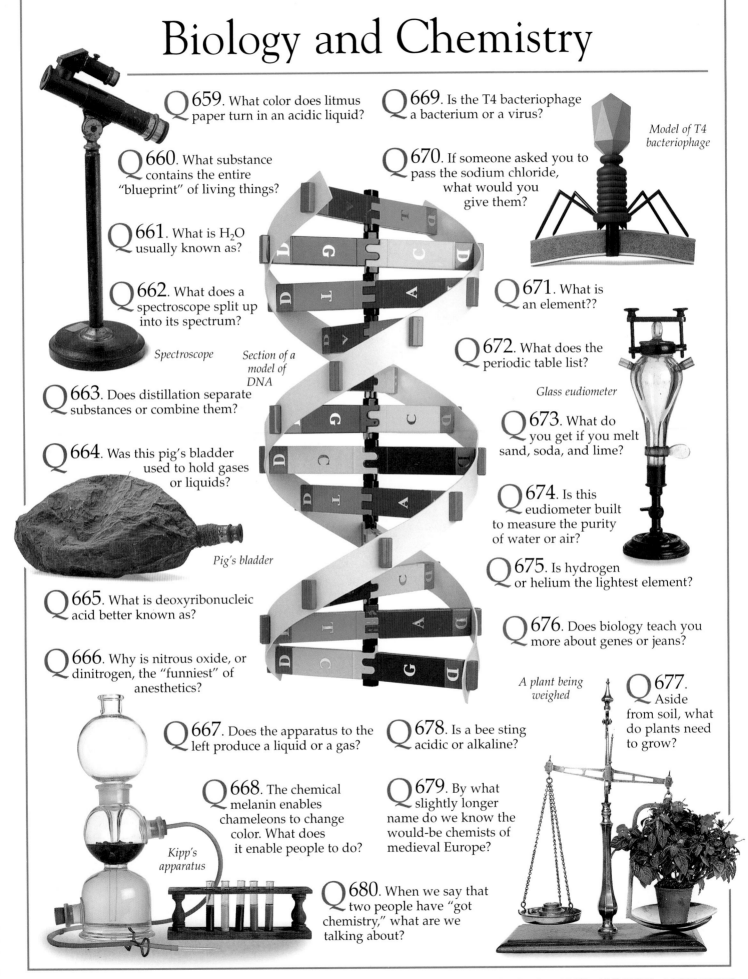

Q659. What color does litmus paper turn in an acidic liquid?

Q660. What substance contains the entire "blueprint" of living things?

Q661. What is H_2O usually known as?

Q662. What does a spectroscope split up into its spectrum?

Spectroscope

Section of a model of DNA

Q663. Does distillation separate substances or combine them?

Q664. Was this pig's bladder used to hold gases or liquids?

Pig's bladder

Q665. What is deoxyribonucleic acid better known as?

Q666. Why is nitrous oxide, or dinitrogen, the "funniest" of anesthetics?

Q667. Does the apparatus to the left produce a liquid or a gas?

Q668. The chemical melanin enables chameleons to change color. What does it enable people to do?

Kipp's apparatus

Q669. Is the T4 bacteriophage a bacterium or a virus?

Q670. If someone asked you to pass the sodium chloride, what would you give them?

Model of T4 bacteriophage

Q671. What is an element??

Q672. What does the periodic table list?

Glass eudiometer

Q673. What do you get if you melt sand, soda, and lime?

Q674. Is this eudiometer built to measure the purity of water or air?

Q675. Is hydrogen or helium the lightest element?

Q676. Does biology teach you more about genes or jeans?

A plant being weighed

Q677. Aside from soil, what do plants need to grow?

Q678. Is a bee sting acidic or alkaline?

Q679. By what slightly longer name do we know the would-be chemists of medieval Europe?

Q680. When we say that two people have "got chemistry," what are we talking about?

TURN TO PAGES 124 AND 125 FOR ANSWERS

Weather and Climate

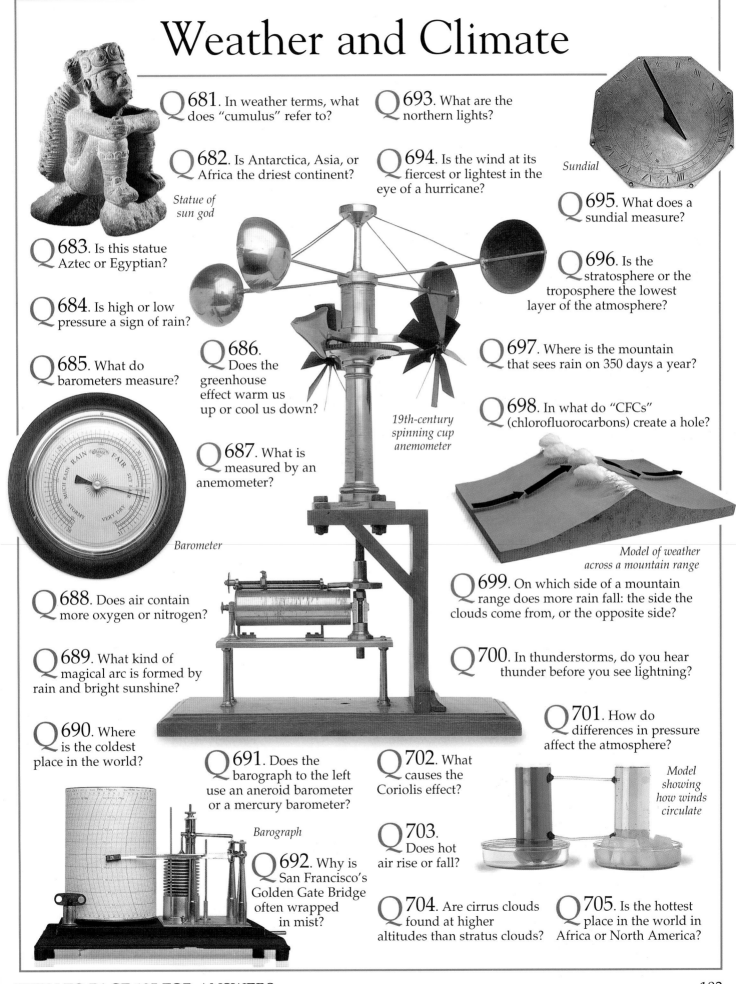

Q681. In weather terms, what does "cumulus" refer to?

Q682. Is Antarctica, Asia, or Africa the driest continent?

Statue of sun god

Q683. Is this statue Aztec or Egyptian?

Q684. Is high or low pressure a sign of rain?

Q685. What do barometers measure?

Q686. Does the greenhouse effect warm us up or cool us down?

Q687. What is measured by an anemometer?

Barometer

Q688. Does air contain more oxygen or nitrogen?

Q689. What kind of magical arc is formed by rain and bright sunshine?

Q690. Where is the coldest place in the world?

Q691. Does the barograph to the left use an aneroid barometer or a mercury barometer?

Barograph

Q692. Why is San Francisco's Golden Gate Bridge often wrapped in mist?

19th-century spinning cup anemometer

Q693. What are the northern lights?

Q694. Is the wind at its fiercest or lightest in the eye of a hurricane?

Sundial

Q695. What does a sundial measure?

Q696. Is the stratosphere or the troposphere the lowest layer of the atmosphere?

Q697. Where is the mountain that sees rain on 350 days a year?

Q698. In what do "CFCs" (chlorofluorocarbons) create a hole?

Model of weather across a mountain range

Q699. On which side of a mountain range does more rain fall: the side the clouds come from, or the opposite side?

Q700. In thunderstorms, do you hear thunder before you see lightning?

Q701. How do differences in pressure affect the atmosphere?

Model showing how winds circulate

Q702. What causes the Coriolis effect?

Q703. Does hot air rise or fall?

Q704. Are cirrus clouds found at higher altitudes than stratus clouds?

Q705. Is the hottest place in the world in Africa or North America?

TURN TO PAGE 125 FOR ANSWERS

Inventions: 1850-1950

Long-playing record, 1948

Q706. What did the Wright brothers do in 1903 that no one had ever done before: fly an airplane, split the atom, or watch TV?

Q707. Which was invented first, the telephone or the fax machine?

"Box telephone"

Q714. Where did the world's first motorway, the Avus Autobahn, open in 1921: Germany, France, or the United States?

Q715. Electric toasters existed at the end of the 19th century, but when was the pop-up toaster invented: in about 1920, 1930, or 1940?

Q708. How long did the first LP (long-playing record) play on each side: 23 minutes, 33 minutes, or 53 minutes?

Hair dryer

Q716. Emilé Berliner created the forerunner of modern records (disks). What did he invent so he could listen to them?

Q709. In which year was the first handheld hair dryer introduced in the United States: 1850, 1870, or 1920?

Q710. What does the car owe to the French Michelin brothers André and Edouard?

Q717. The first motorbike had a wooden frame and wooden wheels. Was it made in 1865, in 1885, or in 1905?

Q711. Which invention, fitted to motor taxicabs in 1896, stopped passengers from arguing with their drivers when they reached their destination?

Q712. Which was the first car to be built on a moving assembly line: the Model T Ford or the Benz Velo?

Q718. Which was invented first, the jet airplane or the helicopter?

First automatic photocopier

Q713. Was the first car built in Germany, the United States, or France?

Q719. In which year did Chester Carlson invent the photocopier: 1859, 1903, or 1938?

An early car

TURN TO PAGE 125 FOR ANSWERS

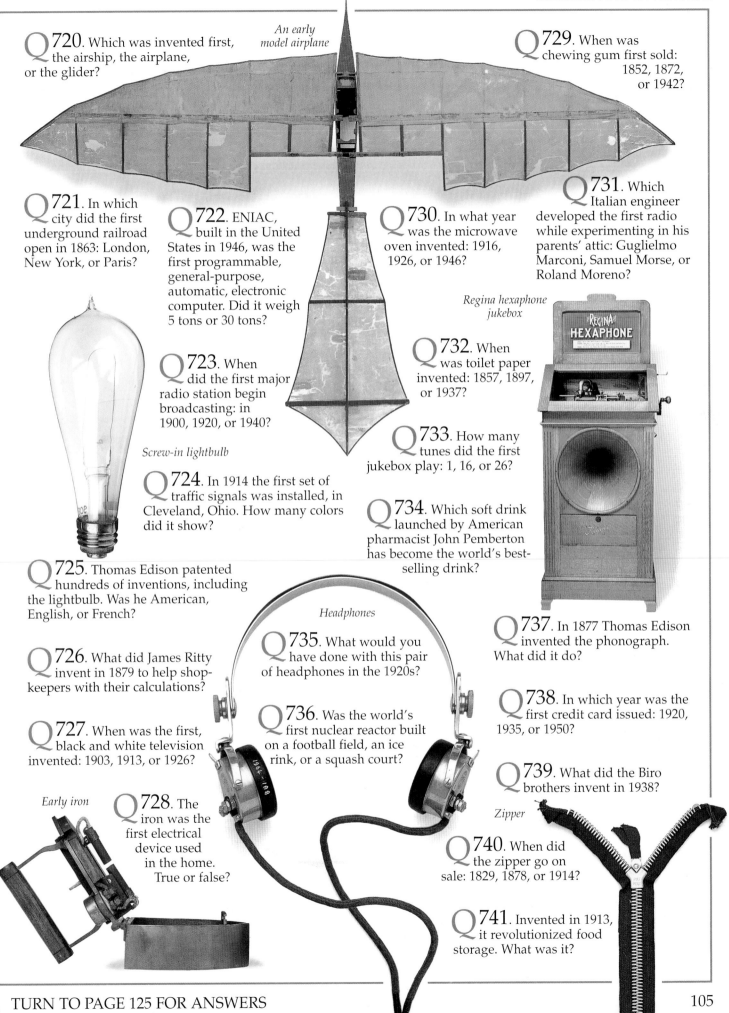

Q720. Which was invented first, the airship, the airplane, or the glider?

An early model airplane

Q729. When was chewing gum first sold: 1852, 1872, or 1942?

Q721. In which city did the first underground railroad open in 1863: London, New York, or Paris?

Q722. ENIAC, built in the United States in 1946, was the first programmable, general-purpose, automatic, electronic computer. Did it weigh 5 tons or 30 tons?

Q730. In what year was the microwave oven invented: 1916, 1926, or 1946?

Q731. Which Italian engineer developed the first radio while experimenting in his parents' attic: Guglielmo Marconi, Samuel Morse, or Roland Moreno?

Regina hexaphone jukebox

Q723. When did the first major radio station begin broadcasting: in 1900, 1920, or 1940?

Q732. When was toilet paper invented: 1857, 1897, or 1937?

Screw-in lightbulb

Q724. In 1914 the first set of traffic signals was installed, in Cleveland, Ohio. How many colors did it show?

Q733. How many tunes did the first jukebox play: 1, 16, or 26?

Q734. Which soft drink launched by American pharmacist John Pemberton has become the world's best-selling drink?

Q725. Thomas Edison patented hundreds of inventions, including the lightbulb. Was he American, English, or French?

Headphones

Q737. In 1877 Thomas Edison invented the phonograph. What did it do?

Q726. What did James Ritty invent in 1879 to help shop-keepers with their calculations?

Q735. What would you have done with this pair of headphones in the 1920s?

Q738. In which year was the first credit card issued: 1920, 1935, or 1950?

Q727. When was the first, black and white television invented: 1903, 1913, or 1926?

Q736. Was the world's first nuclear reactor built on a football field, an ice rink, or a squash court?

Q739. What did the Biro brothers invent in 1938?

Early iron

Q728. The iron was the first electrical device used in the home. True or false?

Zipper

Q740. When did the zipper go on sale: 1829, 1878, or 1914?

Q741. Invented in 1913, it revolutionized food storage. What was it?

TURN TO PAGE 125 FOR ANSWERS

The Modern World

Satellite television dish

Q742. What comes out of a black hole?

Q743. What can high-tech tinned food now do?

Q744. What is a PC?

Q745. Apart from satellites what other new means of transmitting TV programs is very popular?

Q746. How many telephone subscribers were there in the world at the end of 1991: 537 million or 1,537 million?

Q747. Which came first, microchips or videotape?

Q748. What busily buzzing aid to tooth care was first seen in 1961?

Q749. Does superconductivity work at high or low temperatures?

Q750. What travels down optical fibers?

Q751. What does a smart bomb follow?

Q752. What is a Walkman?

Personal computer

Q753. Which part of the body does a pacemaker assist?

Q754. Was the first artificial heart implanted in 1962 or 1982?

Q755. What kind of disk would you insert here?

Q756. Which were made first, 3-dimensional holograms or personal computers?

Q757. What is one of these called?

Q758. Can the world's most powerful microscope magnify objects 1 million times, 100 million times, or 10 billion times?

Q759. What makes Harriers different from ordinary aircraft?

Pacemaker

Q760. What is the circuit board to the left a part of?

Q761. Were the first home video games made in the 1960s or 1970s?

Q762. What is a fax?

Q763. What is a smart card?

Q764. Which country produces the most domestic waste per person: Japan or the United States?

Q765. In 1971, which French invention did more than just mix food?

Q766. What do you do to an icon with a mouse?

Microchips on a circuit board

Credit cards

TURN TO PAGE 125 FOR ANSWERS

Scientific instruments

Q What are the names of the objects below, all of which are used in scientific experiments?

786.

787.

788.

789.

790.

791.

Nuclear fuel rods of uranium from a nuclear reactor

Digital thermometer

Q777. What is this kind of display called?

Q778. Was *Sputnik* a satellite or a boat?

Q779. What does a wind farm produce?

Q780. Which device works through Light Amplification by Stimulated Emission of Radiation?

2 CDs

Q767. What is the difference between nuclear fission and nuclear fusion?

Q768. Which device provided a new way to listen to music in 1963?

Q769. In 1992, could the world's most powerful computer chip process 4 million, 40 million, or 400 million instructions per second?

Q770. Which missiles can turn corners and follow computerized maps to their targets?

Q771. Which came first, the industrial robot or the digital watch?

Q772. Are the most accurate clocks atomic or mechanical?

Q773. How does genetic fingerprinting identify people?

Q774. What first flew on a cushion of air in 1959?

Q775. Was the first space shuttle launched in 1971, in 1976, or in 1981?

Space shuttle

Q776. Which passenger plane was the first to move faster than sound?

Q781. What does CD stand for?

Q782. What game did Erno Rubik invent?

Q783. What do catalytic converters do?

Q784. What is a modem?

Q785. What kind of machines are CD-ROMs designed for?

TURN TO PAGE 125 FOR ANSWERS

Soccer

More people play soccer than any other team sport, and professional soccer is the most popular spectator sport in the world. Soccer encourages friendship, discipline, and the ability to work with others. Sponsorship and television are major influences on soccer and leisure activities. Many soccer and sports personalities become millionaires, and sports and leisure events attract huge international audiences.

Lightweight pads

Q795. On which part of the body must you wear these pads?

Controlling the ball with the thigh

Q792. How long does a soccer match last: 60, 90, or 120 minutes?

Q793. In which country was the 1986 World Cup held: Mexico, Spain, or Italy?

Q794. What is the longest time that anyone has juggled a soccer ball in the air without using their hands: 7, 12, or 17 hours?

Q796. Were the first soccer matches played on grass fields or on the streets?

Soccer cleats

Q797. Which South American country has won the World Cup more times than any other country: Bolivia, Brazil, or Argentina?

Q798. How much does the average soccer cleat weigh: 6, 8, or 10 oz (150, 250, or 350 g)?

Underarm throw

Q799. How many players are there on a team?

Q800. Who is the only player who can touch the ball with his or her hands?

Q801. Who patrols the edge of the field to assist the referee?

TURN TO PAGE 126 FOR ANSWERS

Q802. In soccer, what is a bicycle kick?

Q803. The referee uses a whistle to indicate the start and end of a match. For what else does the referee use the whistle?

Push passing

Q804. Other than the feet, what parts of the body are frequently used to direct the ball?

Q805. What are the 2 occasions when back passes are not allowed?

Q806. Which member of the team wears an armband and why?

Q807. How many different countries play soccer at the international level: 80, 100, or 140?

Q809. Which team won the 1982 World Cup: Spain, Poland, or Italy?

Pre-1945 soccer ball

Q810. Is this early soccer ball made of rubber, plastic, or leather?

Q811. Which Brazilian soccer player is known as the "Black Pearl"?

Red card

Yellow card

Q808. How many shots does each team initially get in a penalty shoot-out: 5, 10, or 15?

Goalkeepers' gloves

Q820. Why do goalkeepers dampen their gloves before a game?

Q821. Which African team in the 1990 World Cup was famous for its wiggling hip dance?

Q812. What is a goalkeeper's punt?

Q813. Which country plays Gaelic soccer: Turkey, Ireland, or Norway?

Goalkeepers' clothing

Q814. Which card is a player given when he or she is sent off the field for a serious offense?

Q815. What does FIFA stand for?

Q816. What is the highest score ever recorded in an international soccer match: 9-2, 16-4, or 17-0?

Q817. Who scored 3 goals in the 1966 World Cup Final: Paolo Rossi, Geoff Hurst, or Diego Maradona?

Q818. Which tenor sang *Nessun Dorma* at the 1990 World Cup: Luciano Pavarotti or Placido Domingo?

Q819. In which area can the goalkeeper pick up the ball?

TURN TO PAGE 126 FOR ANSWERS

Indoor Sports

Q822. Which sport follows Queensberry rules: boxing or horse racing?

Q823. In which of these card games is a royal flush a winning hand: bridge or poker?

Q824. Was the world's youngest ever chess champion Bobby Fischer or Garry Kasparov?

Chess pieces

Q825. Which kind of wrestling began in Japan?

Q826. Which sporting birds are the best at finding their way home?

Q827. Which sport features a puck, a goaltender, and a "sin bin"?

A weightlifting bar with weights attached

Q833. Is it easier to lift weights using the "snatch" technique or the "clean and jerk"?

Q834. Are the Toucan Terribles, the Pernod Rams, and the Black Dog Boozers marbles, volleyball, or football teams?

Boxing glove

Q835. Kung Fu, karate, karaoke: which of these is not a martial art?

Q836. Was Muhammad Ali or Rocky Marciano the only world heavyweight boxing champion never to lose a professional fight?

Q837. In snooker, when are you snookered?

Q838. How many basketballs can one person dribble at a time: 4, 6, or 8?

Snooker balls

Two young basketball players

Q828. Which game was "invented" when skittles, or ninepins, was banned in the United States in 1845?

Q829. Which sport involves vaulting, a beam, rings, and several different kinds of bars?

Q830. Were the blades of the first known ice skates made from metal, plastic, or organic materials?

Q831. In which game do knights, bishops, castles, and the queen work together to protect the king?

Q832. Was the tallest basketball player on record 7 ft 5 in or 8 ft tall (2.25 m or 2.45 m)?

Q839. Which game ends when someone pockets the 8-ball: polo, snooker, or pool?

Ice skate

TURN TO PAGE 126 FOR ANSWERS

Outdoor Sports

Q840. Which are bigger: soccer, polo, or football fields?

Q841. In which sport can you bowl a maiden over: cricket, bowling, or tennis?

Q842. In 1985, a 17-year-old German became the Wimbledon men's tennis champion. Who was he?

A tennis player serving

Q843. What is a hat-trick?

Q844. In tennis, what is the difference between a ground stroke and a volley?

Q845. Which sport features birdies, eagles, and bogies?

Q846. In the Scottish Highland Games, the throwing competition is called "tossing the caber." Do the contestants throw a log, a steel cable, or a haggis?

Referee's whistle

Q847. In which of these sports does the referee or umpire use a whistle: tennis, boxing, or soccer?

Q848. Which is the odd ball out: a soccer ball, a football, or a basketball?

Protective shoulder pads

Q849. In which sport would these shoulder pads be worn?

Baseball mitt

Q850. What does a baseball field have that any jeweler in the world would envy?

Q851. If we battled from love to deuce, and then to gain the advantage, which game would we be playing?

Q852. Was the oldest person to finish a marathon 78, 88, or 98 years old?

Q853. Of which nation was it said, "they are good at inventing games and losing them"?

Q854. In which sport is it possible to be stumped by the keeper off a leg-spinner?

A cricket ball hits the stumps

Q855. In car racing, which is the fastest: Formula 1, Formula 2, or Formula 3?

Renault race car

TURN TO PAGE 126 FOR ANSWERS

The Olympic Games

Q856. The Olympic symbol is a set of interlocking rings. How many are there?

Q857. What do the Olympic interlocking rings represent: continents, different kinds of sports, or the founding nations of the Olympics?

Q858. What kind of medal is awarded for finishing third?

Q859. When the end of a race is so close that the clock cannot tell which contestant finished first, what means is used to decide who has won?

A stopwatch, used for timing sporting events

Q860. Who was the first gymnast to record a perfect score of 10 at the Olympics: Olga Korbut or Nadia Comaneci?

Q861. When high jumpers use the technique called the "Fosbury Flop," do they go over the bar forward or backward?

Q862. Which sport in the Winter Olympics takes place on "the large hill" and "the normal hill"?

Q863. In the 1988 Olympics, Canadian Ben Johnson won the 100 meter race in world record time, but he did not take home the gold medal. Why not?

Sports shoe, with spikes for better grip on running tracks

Q864. Do the Olympics take place every 2 years, every 4 years, or every 6 years?

A gymnast doing a floor exercise

Q870. How many events are there in the decathlon?

Q871. Which event includes pistol shooting, show jumping, fencing, a swim, and a cross-country run?

Q872. Which all-female Olympic sport involves floor exercises with ribbons, balls, hoops, ropes, and Indian clubs?

Q873. Which infamous world leader objected to handing out medals to the most famous athlete at the 1936 Berlin Olympics?

Q865. Which is the longest distance run at the Olympic Games?

Q866. How is a horse used in gymnastics?

Q867. In which country was the site of the ancient Olympic Games: Italy, Greece, or Israel?

Q868. Only 1 person has ever won 7 gold medals at a single Olympic Games. Was the person who won them a skater, a swimmer, or a runner?

Q869. Which are the only team Olympic track and field events?

Target pistol, used in pistol-shooting competitions

Q874. In pistol-shooting competitions, do the competitors stand up or lie down?

Q875. Which can be thrown farther, the shot put or the discus?

A women's shot put, a men's shot put, and a discus

TURN TO PAGE 126 FOR ANSWERS

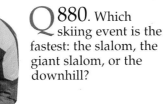

Q880. Which skiing event is the fastest: the slalom, the giant slalom, or the downhill?

A skier tackling the slope

Q881. Did the film *Chariots of Fire* feature Olympic sprinters, cyclists, or tobogganists?

Q882. Was the person who received 35,000 love letters after winning the gold medal a swimmer, a skier, or a skater?

Q876. How many people are there in the crews of the biggest rowing boats at the Olympics: 5, 8, or 9?

Q877. What is the greatest number of gold medals won by 1 person in their Olympic career: 8, 10, or 12?

Q883. How long was the longest Olympic career to date: 30 years, 40 years, or 50 years?

Q878. Do boxers in the Olympics wear headguards or not?

Q879. Two of the elements of the triple jump are a step (or skip) and a jump. What is the third element?

Q884. In show jumping competitions, do the competitors aim for a high or a low score?

Q885. The biathlon is made up of two sports. One is cross-country skiing. What is the other?

Q886. Which is the fastest of the swimming styles for which there are Olympic events?

Q887. How do Olympic swimmers stop the clock at the end of their races?

Q888. Which can be thrown farther, the hammer or the javelin?

Q889. Which track race is run over solid, sturdy barriers and a water jump: the high hurdles, the marathon, or the steeplechase?

Q890. Where do the competitors usually live during the Olympic Games?

Q891. Which Olympic symbol is never allowed to go out?

Q892. In which sport do the competitors pose with nose clips on their noses?

Swimmer poised to dive

Q893. Who are the best dancers at the Winter Olympics?

Q894. Which of these is *not* an Olympic sport: sailing, basketball, tennis, or bodybuilding?

Q895. When were the first modern Olympics held: 1846, 1896, or 1926?

Horse and rider approaching a jump

Q896. How many nations competed in the 1992 Olympic Games: 109, 139, or 169?

Q897. Which city was successful in its bid to host the Olympics in the year 2000: Manchester, Atlanta, or Sydney?

Q898. Is dressage a competition for figure skaters, horse riders, skiers, or bodybuilders?

Q899. Which country won the most gold medals at the 1944 Olympics: Germany, the United States, or Britain?

TURN TO PAGE 126 FOR ANSWERS

Art and Architecture

Q900. What do architects do?

Q901. What is the difference between artists and artisans?

The Villa Savoye, designed by the Swiss-born Le Corbusier, whose real name was Charles Édouard Jeanneret

Q902. Where on a church might you find onions and saucers?

Q903. Was this concrete and glass house built during the 18th century, the 19th century, or the 20th century?

Q904. A viaduct is a bridge that carries a road or railroad across a valley. What does an aqueduct carry?

Model of the spire of Notre Dame cathedral in Paris, France

Q905. What do painters do with oil?

An Australian opera house, finished in 1973

Q906. This famous opera house sits on the water's edge and resembles a ship with billowing sails. Where is it: Sydney or Perth?

Q907. Medieval churches often have grotesque heads such as this one carved on the outside. Are they called thunderheads or gargoyles?

Devil with batlike ears

Q908. Which artists make statues?

Q909. Are Corinthian, Doric, and Ionic styles of arches, columns, or windows?

"The Scream," by Norwegian artist Edvard Munch

Q910. Is the style of this painting known as Impressionism or Expressionism?

Q911. What color do you get when you mix blue and yellow paint?

Q912. What art form is created by sticking together tiny pieces of glass or stone?

Tubes of red, yellow, and green paint

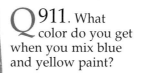

Q913. When artists say that they are going to a life class, what are they doing?

Q914. Many bricks are made by baking a soft, squishy material at a high temperature. What is this material called?

Q915. Is it true that Norman arches are pointed and Gothic arches are rounded?

Q916. What is the name given to the very tall buildings first erected in the United States in the late 19th century?

Q917. Out of which material are the best brushes made: sable or horsehair?

Bristle brushes

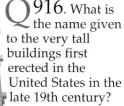

TURN TO PAGE 127 FOR ANSWERS

Dance

Q918. When did ballerinas first dance on pointe (on tiptoe): in the 18th, 19th, or 20th century?

Q919. How many positions of the feet are there in classical ballet: 5, 7, or 10?

Q920. Which elegant and graceful dance originated in Austria in the 18th century?

Jazz dancing

Q921. Which 1980 US film was set in a school for the performing arts?

Q922. Which ballet dancer starred in the 1948 musical *The Red Shoes*: Moira Shearer, Marilyn Monroe, or Doris Day?

Q923. What did the French gymnast Jules Léotard invent in the 19th century?

Q924. Which legendary dancing duo starred in the 1935 film *Top Hat*?

Jazz dancer

Q925. Which 1977 film made John Travolta a disco dancing icon?

Q926. Which strutting, stamping Spanish dance has become famous worldwide?

Q927. Which dance style developed in the streets of New York in the 1980s?

Q928. What fills the tips of pointe shoes?

Q929. Which famous fashion dance was popularized by Madonna?

Ballet shoes

Q930. Which Russian ballet dancer had a meringue-based dessert named after her in Australia?

Q931. Which French king started the first ballet school in 1661: Louis XII, Louis XIV, or Louis XVI?

Q932. What do you call the short, stiff skirt worn by a ballerina?

Q933. Which American actor sang and danced in the rain in 1956?

Q934. Which modern musical is famous for the dancers' daredevil acrobatics on roller skates?

Square dancing

Q935. Who is the person who composes the steps for a ballet or dance?

Q936. Where did square dancing originate: North America, Africa, or Europe?

Music

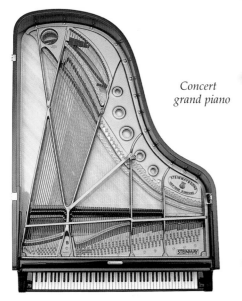

Q937. What do an alto, baritone, wind synth, and tenor have in common?

Q938. Which Italian composer wrote the opera *Aida* in 1871: Antonio Vivaldi, Giuseppe Verdi, Georges Bizet or Richard Wagner?

Q939. Which singer received a platinum record in 1960 to commemorate the sale of his 200 millionth record: Bing Crosby, Frank Sinatra, or Tom Jones?

Baritone

Q940. Which is the biggest of these stringed instruments: a cello, a guitar, a violin, or a double bass?

Q941. What do Maria Callas, Kiri Te Kanawa, and Luciano Pavarotti have in common?

Q942. What do *The Marriage of Figaro*, *Don Giovanni*, and *The Magic Flute* have in common?

Guitar

Concert grand piano

Q943. Who uses a baton as a tool?

French horn
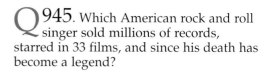

Q944. Of which family of instruments are the horn, trombone, and trumpet members: brass, wind, or string?

Q945. Which American rock and roll singer sold millions of records, starred in 33 films, and since his death has become a legend?

Q946. Which piece of classical music composed by George Frederick Handel in 1741 sets parts of the Bible to music?

Q947. What was the popular music of the 17th and early 18th century that was named after the elaborate architectural style of the day: Romanesque, Baroque, or Gothic?

Q948. Who wrote many well-known ballets including *Romeo and Juliet*, *Swan Lake*, and *Sleeping Beauty*?

Q949. When was the first opera composed: 1297, 1597, or 1897?

Q950. Which 2 members of the Beatles wrote most of the songs?

Q951. How many keys are there on a grand piano: 44, 66, or 88?

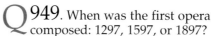

20th-century Indian instrument

TURN TO PAGE 127 FOR ANSWERS

String quartet

Q952. Which of the following is an American folk singer most famous for his protest songs of the 1960s: Bob Dylan, Miles Davis, or Jimi Hendrix?

Q953. Who revolutionized jazz in the 1920s with his brilliant solo trumpet playing?

Q956. Which large, many-stringed instrument is often associated with angels?

Q957. Which legendary, Jamaican reggae star sang *Buffalo Soldier*, *No Woman No Cry*, and *Exodus*?

Q958. Can you name the Swedish group that won the 1974 Eurovision song contest with the hit *Waterloo*?

Q959. This group of musicians is called a string quartet. Can you identify the four instruments being played?

Flute from Fiji

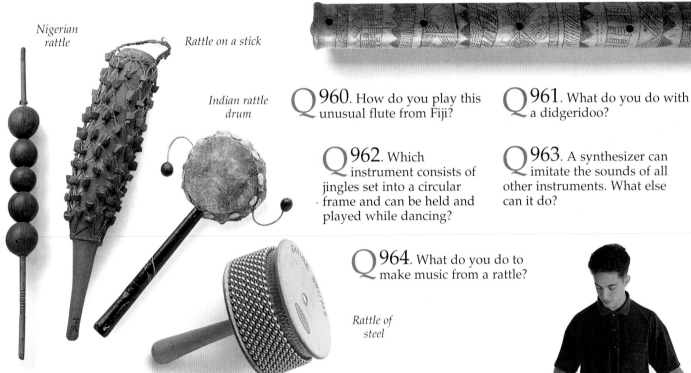

Nigerian rattle

Rattle on a stick

Indian rattle drum

Q960. How do you play this unusual flute from Fiji?

Q961. What do you do with a didgeridoo?

Q962. Which instrument consists of jingles set into a circular frame and can be held and played while dancing?

Q963. A synthesizer can imitate the sounds of all other instruments. What else can it do?

Q964. What do you do to make music from a rattle?

Rattle of steel

Synthesizer

Q954. What do you call a large group of musicians that performs classical music?

Q965. Can you name the famous musical that opened in London in 1968 and celebrated the ideals of the 1960s, such as peace, love, and freedom: *Hair*, *Grease*, or *The Phantom of the Opera*?

Q966. Can you name the 1961 musical set in New York that is based on *Romeo and Juliet*?

Q955. What is the name of this popular Indian instrument?

Q967. When did the Beatles separate: in 1950, 1960, or 1970?

TURN TO PAGE 127 FOR ANSWERS

Movies, TV, and Theater

A spool of film

Q972. Who created Mickey Mouse, Donald Duck, *One Hundred and One Dalmations*, and a "magical land" named after himself in California?

Q973. Which country was the first to have a regular TV broadcasting service: the United States, Britain, or France?

Q979. What is a film story called?

The storyline of a film

Q968. How much film is used in each minute of a movie: 23 ft, 90 ft, or 155 ft (7 m, 27 m, or 47 m)?

Q969. How many Olympic swimming champions have gone on to play the role of Tarzan in the movies: 1, 2, or 4?

Q980. In which country did European theater begin: Greece, Britain, or Italy?

Q981. Which fictional character has appeared in more films than any other: Dracula or Sherlock Holmes?

Technicolor three-strip movie camera of 1932

Q982. What happened in the United States in 1983 to lift up television broadcasting to new heights?

Q970. He wrote *Hamlet*, *King Lear*, and *Twelfth Night*, and many of his plays were first performed at the Globe Theatre. Who was he?

Q983. In an animated film, how many pictures are needed for each second of action: 6, 12, or 24?

Materials for animation

Q974. Why was this camera called a "three-strip" camera?

Q975. In theater, what is the opposite of comedy?

Q976. Which sports event has the greatest television audience: the Olympic Games or the soccer World Cup?

Q977. What made the 1927 film *The Jazz Singer* a landmark in movie history?

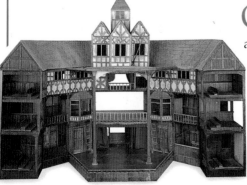

Q971. What is a couch potato?

The Globe Theatre in Southwark, London, England

Q978. Where are you likely to find stalls, boxes, a tier, and an upper tier?

TURN TO PAGE 127 FOR ANSWERS

The inside of a 1930s television set

Movie memories

Q With which films, film stars, or characters are the following objects linked?

A zoopraxiscope; it was rotated as light was projected through it

Q984. What was the zoopraxiscope designed to create?

Q985. Is this device a personal organizer, a traffic monitoring computer, or a TV?

Miniaturized design

Q986. Which town in California is the most famous center of movie production in the world?

Q987. Who directed *Jurassic Park*, *E.T.*, and *Jaws*: Steven Spielberg or George Lucas?

Film director's chair

996.

997.

998.

999.

1000.

1001.

Q988. How many times a second is a TV image renewed: 5, 25, or 50 times?

Q989. In a film crew, what does a boom operator operate: a tape system or a microphone?

Q990. In films, when sound engineers are creating special effects, what gruesome sound do they imitate by sawing a cabbage in half?

Q991. Was this camera made in the United States or France?

Hand-cranked camera used in silent films

Q992. On a film set, what does the director say to stop the cameras?

Theater ticket

Q993. In which country are the most films made: the United States, India, or France?

Q994. In which country do people make the greatest number of trips to the movies in a year: the United States or China?

Q995. Which is the only film to have won 11 Oscars: *Ben Hur*, *Gone with the Wind*, or *Home Alone*?

TURN TO PAGE 127 FOR ANSWERS

Answers

Prehistoric life

1 Yes, a "super-continent" called Pangaea.

2 About 165 million years.

3 Flowers first appeared in the age of the dinosaurs.

4 No, it means "terrible lizard."

5 Three; *Triceratops* means "three-horned face."

6 1842; dinosaurs had been described earlier, in 1824, but the name was not thought up until 1842.

7 *Archaeopteryx*, the only feathered one of the 3.

8 Crocodiles and alligators.

9 65 mya. They disappeared surprisingly suddenly; it is not known why.

10 Turtles are the oldest.

11 It was named after the iguana lizard, in 1825.

12 Amber; sometimes insects are preserved in it.

13 Its tiny brain was the size of a walnut.

14 Spiked lizard; it had spikes on its head.

15 A skin sail; its purpose is not known.

16 Only 5 hen's eggs would make up 1 *Hypselosaurus* egg.

17 The size of a dog.

18 It grew up to 50 ft (15 m) long.

19 Yes, 170 million years before any birds.

20 *Tyrannosaurus*; rex means king.

21 *Jurassic Park*, the highest-earning film of all time.

22 *Pteranodons*; "cousins" of the dinosaurs.

23 On its head; these tiny teeth may have been for hitching rides on other sharks.

24 A plant eater.

25 It was thought to have died out with the dinosaurs. It is a "living fossil."

26 We don't know; colors were not preserved.

27 The spiked thumb was for defense.

28 *Lucy in the Sky with Diamonds* by the Beatles, which was on the radio when she was found.

29 The show is *The Flintstones*.

30 Coal; it has been mined for hundreds of years for use as fuel.

31 Cars cannot move without fuel, which comes from oil, and oil comes from fossils.

32 Woolly mammoths, or the similar mastodons.

33 The Himalayas, which are still growing, slowly.

34 4; "tetra" comes from the Greek word for 4.

35 No; the blue whale is the largest ever.

36 The United States; China ranks second.

37 Yes, and remains of elephants, rhino, and a lion.

Reptiles and Amphibians

38 The saltwater crocodile can be 26 ft (8 m) long.

39 A Marion's tortoise lived more than 152 years.

40 No, but it looks like the poisonous coral snake.

41 Off the coast of Australia. It is a Belcher sea snake.

42 Only 0.7 in (18 mm) long, not counting the tail, it is the British Virgin Island gecko.

43 Some snakes can have up to 400 vertebrae.

44 Temperature; eggs develop faster if warmer.

45 A tortoise; it won a race against a hare.

46 It is an awful-smelling turtle.

47 A lizard; Indonesia's Komodo dragons are the biggest lizards in the world, up to 10.2 ft (3 m) long.

48 It is the size of a basketball.

49 3; the third eye is on the top of its head.

50 They change color to match their surroundings.

51 No, they are cold-blooded.

52 It was a leatherback turtle.

53 Because the ground gets too hot for its feet. It lifts its legs up alternately, as if dancing.

54 Alligators are the missing members.

55 They eat mosquitoes and flies.

56 It is the gaboon viper, found in Africa. Its fangs can be 2 in (50 mm) long.

57 30 minutes, moving at 0.1 mph.

58 A lizard, the six-lined racerunner of the Americas. It has been timed at 18 mph (29 kph).

59 The frog turns into a handsome prince. Unfortunately, in real life this doesn't work.

60 It has special poison glands all over its skin.

61 In water; each egg is surrounded by jelly.

62 Yes; it looks like a worm but has teeth.

63 Frogs; toads usually have dry, warty skin.

64 Because its eyeballs move inward when it blinks and help push the food down.

65 In pouches on each side of its body.

66 It could kill 1,500 people.

67 Kenneth Grahame's *The Wind in the Willows*.

68 In fire, according to legend.

69 A hellbender is a kind of salamander.

70 They are the only amphibians with tails.

71 It can eat as many as 100 in one night.

72 They are 4 weeks old; they become frogs at about 12 weeks.

73 By being brightly colored.

74 Frogmen, who swim underwater.

75 *The Muppet Show*, in which Kermit the frog was loved by Miss Piggy.

76 Goliath; these frogs can be 16 in (40 cm) long.

77 Because most amphibians start their lives in water and later move onto land.

78 Just over 17 ft (5 m) for a single jump.

79 No, those with short legs just walk, crawl, or make short hops.

Life in the Ocean

80 It is an angelfish.

81 The oceans are the largest by far.

82 The narwhal, known as the unicorn of the seas.

83 Bull sharks; they sometimes swim up rivers.

84 Sperm whales; their brains can weigh up to 20.2 lb (9.2 kg).

85 To dig up shellfish from the seabed.

86 The Portuguese man-of-war; it has half a million stingers.

87 No; a shark's skeleton is made of cartilage.

88 Simple animals that filter food from the water.

89 Yes, but they have to wake up every few minutes to surface and breathe.

90 A squid seizes prey with its suckers and then paralyzes it with a deadly nerve poison.

91 The blue-ringed octopus is the deadliest.

92 To confuse their enemies.

93 *Through the Looking-Glass*.

94 Yes, the flying fish has enlarged fins that act as wings, allowing it to glide above the waves.

95 It has a pouch in which babies grow safely.

96 No, it is supported by its shell.

97 Blue whales eat 4 tons of krill a day.

98 They grow a new shell under the old one.

99 A shark is a fish and a dolphin is a mammal.

100 The Philippino dwarf pygmy goby at only 0.3 in (8 mm) long.

101 The razor-toothed piranha of South America; some will attack anything.

102 It uses its arms to force open shellfish, turns its stomach inside out onto the prey, and digests it.

103 The sunfish; one specimen was found carrying 300 million eggs.

104 The orca or killer whale will snatch seals and sea lions on some beaches.

105 It lies on the seabed; its patterned body acts as camouflage.

106 A group of fish swimming together is a school.

107 Because its eggs are eaten as caviar.

108 They are insulated by a thick layer of fat, or blubber, that lies just beneath their skin.

109 They evolved thousands of years ago.

110 It inflates to make itself look as large and ferocious as possible.

111 Pisces; it is the biological group that includes all fish.

112 The archerfish; it can leap out of the water, squirt its prey, and knock it down.

113 The blue clam can live for 100 years.

114 The lungfish, it can breathe air through its lungs.

115 The sperm whale measures up to 66 ft (20 m); a giant squid measures up to 59 ft (18 m).

116 No; sea lions, seals, and walruses are pinnipeds. Dolphins are cetaceans.

117 A great white shark has three rows of teeth.

118 A catfish uses its sensitive whiskers to select food.

119 The swordfish's snout can be 5 ft (1.5 m) long.

120 It stings with its tentacles.

121 The hermit crab will change its borrowed shell for a new one as it grows.

122 It raises spines along its back to sting you.

Dogs and Cats

123 The Tasmanian wolf is a marsupial.

124 False; there are about 400 breeds.

125 Ears back show fear or submission.

126 Pluto is Mickey Mouse's dog.

127 The dingo of Australia is probably the most direct ancestor of domestic dogs.

128 "Dog collar" is slang for a priest's clerical collar.

129 *The Hound of the Baskervilles*.

130 Foxes hunt on their own.

131 The fennec fox, which lives in the Sahara.

132 The prairie dog is a North American rodent.

133 Laika, a Russian dog, in 1957.

134 They walk on their toes.

135 Smell; it uses its nose to hunt and find a mate.

136 Sirius, the Dog Star.

137 Its mane; most dogs have no mane.

138 A female fox is called a vixen.

139 Because they are near-sighted.

140 Romulus and Remus; they founded Rome.

141 The fox cub is 10 weeks old.

142 Up to 386 sq miles (1,000 sq km).

143 16 hours; twice as long as most mammals.

144 He strangled the Nemean lion.

145 The cheetah; it can run 60–63 mph (95–100) kph.

146 The Manx cat has no tail.

147 *The Cat Who Walked by Himself.*

148 The lion has a magnificent mane.

149 To hunt larger animals and protect their young.

150 Lionesses, but the lions always eat first.

151 The cheetah can't retract its claws.

152 T. S. Eliot (*Old Possum's Book of Practical Cats*).

153 Leo is named after the lion.

154 The sand cat, which lives in the Sahara Desert.

155 In London, in 1871.

156 Tigers: male Siberian tigers average 10.3 ft (3.15 m) in length.

157 Black leopards are better known as panthers.

158 The Mochica would have worshiped it.

159 *Puss in Boots* was created by Charles Perrault.

160 The lion in the Narnia stories was named Aslan.

161 The ancient Egyptians believed cats were sacred.

162 Yes, all big cats roar, but they cannot purr.

163 Catnip; when cats smell it, they get excited.

Mammals

164 No, bats have perfectly good eyesight.

165 The result is a mule.

166 To help balance itself when walking along branches high up in treetops.

167 A hedgehog rolls into a ball to protect its belly.

168 The matriarch, responsible for the herd's safety.

169 Yes – it lies on its back and wraps itself in seaweed so it won't be swept away by the current.

170 African elephants are bigger, with longer tusks.

171 A porcupine turns its back on its foe, rattles its quills, grunts, and then reverses into its enemy.

172 A hard substance called ivory.

173 The koala will only eat the leaves of certain eucalyptus trees.

174 It is a warm-blooded animal with fur that gives birth to live babies and feeds its young on milk.

175 Chimpanzees make their own tools.

176 To protect their hoofs from damage.

177 Over 6 months in cold climates.

178 They graze in groups; their stripes make it hard for lions to pick out an individual from the herd.

179 To keep themselves cool in hot weather.

180 Sea cows, which graze on sea plants.

181 22 months, longer than any other animal.

182 An animal with a pouch in which to carry babies.

183 Only the platypus and the echidna lay eggs.

184 In the mountains of South America.

185 The mole.

186 Every 4 weeks.

187 Herbivores only eat plants.

188 Moby Dick was white.

189 Apes are more closely related.

190 Giant pandas eat mainly bamboo; large areas of bamboo forest in China have been cut down.

191 Yes; along with apes and humans. Primates have large brains.

192 A rabbit lives in a warren.

193 Kitti's hog-nosed bat; it weighs 0.5 oz (1.5 g).

194 For social reasons, as well as for fur care.

195 Hamsters "carry" food in cheek pouches.

196 Walking, trotting, cantering, and galloping.

197 True, their wings are really webbed hands.

198 In hands; a hand equals 4 in (10 cm).

199 A baby hare is a leveret.

200 It sprays a horrible smelling liquid at enemies.

201 A sloth; it moves very slowly and only wakes up at night.

202 Zaire (but estimates of elephant numbers vary).

203 Run at each other and clash heads and horns.

204 A male moose may weigh 1,000 lb (450 kg).

205 All bears can swim and are happy in water.

206 Beavers build dams to stop flowing water.

207 A weasel grows a white coat in snowy winters.

Birds and Mini-beasts

208 The ostrich, the world's largest bird.

209 The tundra swan; it has over 25,000 feathers.

210 The peacock; the "eyes" are blue patches.

211 To help determine the sounds of their prey.

212 In his belly feathers, which act like a sponge.

213 Snakes; its long legs have tough scales to protect it against poisonous snakebites.

214 Above; this reduces the air pressure above the wing, which creates an upward lift.

215 90 beats per second have been recorded for the horned sungem, a South American hummingbird.

216 7 miles (11 km); one Ruppell's vulture hit an aircraft at that height.

217 Saliva; they make little cup-shaped nests of it.

218 The peregrine falcon; it has been timed in dives at up to 217 mph (350 kph).

219 The sooty tern stays in the air for 3–10 years after leaving its nesting grounds.

220 The Arctic tern, which migrates between the Arctic summer and the Antarctic summer (the longest migration of any bird).

221 The white dove is a symbol of peace.

222 A robin's heart beats 600 times a minute.

223 The Australian pelican; it has a bill up to 18.5 in (47 cm) long.

224 The bee hummingbird of the Caribbean.

225 Icarus; the wax on his wings melted when he flew too close to the sun.

226 The male emperor penguin.

227 None; the last one died in a zoo in 1914.

228 Hollow; but many flightless and diving birds have solid bones.

229 An albatross; the wingspan of the wandering albatross can reach 12 ft (3.6 m).

230 It is the only bird with a sideways-curving bill.

231 The bee is their model.

232 4 pairs of shoes; it has 8 legs.

233 Bombardier beetles fire a gas from their rear ends, with a pop. It forms a smoke screen.

234 It is called the giraffe weevil.

235 In Brazil; it is called the wandering spider.

236 They are female; the drones are male.

237 Speed; they can run at over 10 mph (16 kmph).

238 511; charmed by a farmer's son.

239 Silk; the silkworm becomes a large white moth.

240 In tests, it supported 850 times its own weight.

241 It is thought that they navigate by the light of the Moon and the stars.

242 0.02 in (0.4 mm); as big as the head of a pin.

243 Elephant beetles are the largest.

244 Ultraviolet light.

245 They become butterflies or moths.

246 Nephila spiders' webs are used for fishing.

247 To attract a mate.

248 20 ft (6 m) for one orb weaver spider's web.

Flowers and Plants

249 They are called blossoms.

250 The sweet chestnut; horse chestnuts are inedible.

251 The leaves fall off.

252 Cedar trees are coniferous; they have needlelike leaves and cones and keep their leaves all year.

253 A young tree is a sapling.

254 It flowers for 1 growing season, then it dies.

255 Yes, aloe vera and jojoba are 2 of many plants used in cosmetics.

256 The sap of the sugar maple.

257 Tulips grow in abundance in Holland.

258 Oak trees are broad-leaved; their leaves drop off in the fall.

259 No; ferns, mosses, liverworts, and lichens don't.

260 The male part of a flower is the stamen.

261 The maidenhair tree of China.

262 The Aztecs were the first.

263 The stems can store water.

264 A monkey puzzle is a coniferous tree.

265 The process is called photosynthesis.

266 They open in dry weather.

267 The US giant sequoia can stand 275 ft (83 m) tall.

268 You can eat the seeds.

269 Because they are allergic to pollen in the air.

270 The female part of a flower is the carpel.

271 True; it is made up of many tiny flowers.

272 To transport water and minerals.

273 The transfer of pollen from the male part of a flower to the female part.

274 By the seashore.

275 The giant rafflesia; its flowers can be 32 in (80 cm) across.

276 A sugary liquid produced by a flower.

277 The petals fall off and the seed ripens.

278 It is called resin.

279 Chlorophyll, it collects energy from sunlight.

280 Pollen is carried by animals, insects, or wind.

281 A simple leaf has only 1 leaf, a compound leaf has several leaves, called leaflets.

282 By night, to attract night-flying insects.

283 It helps the tree by providing it with nutrients.

284 By its prickly leaves or unpleasant taste.

285 A forest in its natural, untouched state.

286 The oak tree produces acorns.

287 Garlic is supposed to repel vampires.

288 Pan was the Greek god of forests and flocks.

289 Yes, Venus's – flytrap.

290 You count the tree rings on a cut stump.

291 To attract animals and insects for pollination.

292 Ray florets.

293 Disk florets.

294 Pollen.

295 Ray florets.

296 Stem.

Ancient Egypt

297 The embalmed body of a person (or animal).

298 The pharaohs were the kings of Egypt.

299 His eye; the eye of Horus was said to protect everything behind it.

300 It was a collection of spells meant to help a dead person on the voyage to the next world. It was often put in tombs.

301 They used papyrus, made from the papyrus reed that grows along the Nile River.

302 The sphinx, a magical creature with the body of a lion and the head of a king.

303 The west, the side of the sunset.

304 It was seen as a way of cleansing the spirit.

305 A hippopotamus; as women gave birth, they prayed to Taweret to protect them.

306 94 years; Pepy II became pharaoh when he was 6, and was still on the throne when he was 100 – the longest known reign of any monarch.

307 As special tombs for the pharaohs.

308 The Sun god; the Egyptians believed that Khepri, who was a form of the Sun god, rolled the sun across the sky in the same way that the scarab beetle rolls a ball of dung over the ground.

309 Nut; she was the mother of the Sun god.

310 Tutankhamun, whose tomb was discovered intact by Howard Carter in 1922.

311 It was the symbol of life.

312 The cobra goddess. Only kings and queens wore images of the cobra goddess who, it was thought, spat death at their enemies.

313 Cleopatra, subject of plays, books, and films.

314 About 7.2 million tons. It contains over 2.3 million stone blocks.

315 Heh, god of "millions of years."

316 Reed sandals were the most common footwear at all levels of society. Leather was also worn.

317 They were sacred; 4 million mummified ibises have been found in one animal cemetery.

318 The black land, the land along the Nile, named for its rich black soil. The red land was the desert.

319 Mourning; if a pet cat died, a whole household might shave their eyebrows. Cats were sacred.

320 It was a popular board game, in which players made a symbolic journey through the underworld to the kingdom of the god Osiris.

321 From linen; they were usually white.

322 In the Valley of the Kings.

323 It was unlucky. Red reminded Egyptians of the desert and often represented bad fortune.

324 Yes; St. Paul's is 360 ft (110 m) high; the Great Pyramid, built about 2500 BC, is 450 ft (138 m) high. It was once 481 ft (147 m); it has crumbled a little.

325 An ancient Egyptian form of writing; pictures and symbols represent objects, ideas, and sounds.

Ancient Greece

326 For Zeus, king of the gods.

327 Piraeus; the modern Greek name is Piraius.

328 Greek foot soldiers were called hoplites, from the Greek word *hoplon*, meaning "shield."

329 Pegasus, tamed by the hero Bellerophon.

330 A doctor who recommended good diet and exercise.

331 Go shopping: it was the marketplace, and a meeting place.

332 They dedicated them to the god Apollo and the goddess Artemis as a sign that they had reached the end of childhood.

333 Helen of Troy; in legend, she ran away from Greece to Troy and a Greek army sailed to Troy, fought a war and destroyed the city to get her back.

334 A banquet or formal drinking party where Greek men discussed politics and philosophy.

335 Electrum, a mixture of gold and silver.

336 You would find it on top of a column.

337 The minotaur, said to live in the palace of Knossos on the island of Crete.

338 A Greek warship with 3 (tri) rows of oars.

339 Wine was the favorite, enjoyed by everybody.

340 The Parthenon, built from white marble in 447–438 BC to honor the goddess Athena.

341 Homer (8th century BC); the *Iliad* tells the story of the fall of Troy. He also wrote the *Odyssey*.

342 Poseidon; for both he was the god of the sea.

343 Democracy, the system in which all citizens have the chance to vote for their rulers.

Ancient Rome

344 In a hospital; these utensils were used to explore wounds and hold incisions open.

345 He used either a trident or a dagger, but his net was his main weapon.

346 Gladiator fights and animal fights, all paid for by the Roman emperor to gain popularity.

347 At the baths; Romans cleaned themselves by putting oil on their skin, then scraping it off with strigils.

348 5,000 foot soldiers, usually.

349 Yes, floors were raised so that underfloor hot air could warm them.

350 4; chariot races were major events, watched by up to 250,000 people.

351 A Roman emperor; the laurel wreath symbolized success and power.

352 Julius Caesar, who conquered Gaul (France).

353 XVI; a hundred would be C.

354 So their foot soldiers could see them and follow them in battle.

Medieval Life

355 Robin Hood, the famous English outlaw.

356 A horse; this enameled pendant was part of an elegant harness.

357 In a kitchen, to lift pieces of meat in and out of cauldrons of boiling water.

358 A kirtle, worn with a skirtlike surcoat.

359 In the 15th century; before then wool was woven into cloth on a loom.

360 A moat; some contain water, others are dry.

361 Round towers; they were built more and more often instead of square ones.

362 A weapon; it was a kind of mace with its head swung on a chain.

363 The hornpipe; a leather band connects its wooden pipe to its hollowed-out cow's horn.

364 No; a villein was a peasant who was tied to his lord, unable to leave him.

365 France; at the age of 19, she led the French army to victory over English invaders.

366 The right to pasture pigs in a forest.

367 The keep (or donjon) is the central tower.

368 A great plague of the 14th century. It caused black swellings on its victims, most of whom died.

369 Retrievers; poachers sometimes trained pigs to fetch the birds that they had shot.

370 A squire; when he became a knight he was given sword and spurs.

371 A horse's head; called a shaffron, the armor usually consisted of a headpiece, spike, and plume.

372 His gauntlet; "throwing down the gauntlet" has come to refer to any kind of challenge.

373 It was called the curtain wall.

374 The rose. They were called the Wars of the Roses because the Lancastrians (symbol red rose) fought the Yorkists (white rose) for the crown.

375 At Christmas in a carol.

376 Soccer, then violent, with few rules.

377 Christian attempts to conquer Palestine (now Israel).

378 They are different kinds of silk.

379 So that the defenders could drop unpleasant substances, such as quicklime and boiling oil, through the holes onto people attacking the castle.

380 William Tell of Switzerland. He was being punished for resisting invaders. He hit the apple.

381 The slapstick; hence slapstick comedy.

382 The dungeon, called the oubliette because prisoners might be left there and forgotten.

Renaissance

383 A doublet, made of black silk velvet heavily overstitched in gold thread.

384 In Florence, in the 15th century.

385 Rebirth, describing a great revival of art and learning in 15th- and 16th-century Europe.

386 Velvet; slashed sleeves were very popular.

387 Nicholaus Copernicus, who suggested that the planets in the Solar System orbit the Sun.

388 Ancient Greece inspired the Renaissance.

389 The Hapsburgs, Holy Roman emperors, whose power reached a peak with Charles V (1519–56).

390 It demanded reform in the Catholic church.

391 Italian Leonardo da Vinci, an all-around genius.

392 Elizabeth I, who gave her name to her age.

393 The Medici family.

394 *Romeo and Juliet*.

395 The Gutenberg press was invented in Germany.

396 Gutenberg's Bible was written in Latin.

Exploration

397 English Captain James Cook, who made 3 voyages to the Pacific in the 1760s and 1770s.

398 Measured distances on charts.

399 American astronaut Neil Armstrong when he became the first person to walk on the Moon.

400 Seafaring explorers from Scandinavia.

401 They used their knowledge of winds, currents, and the stars to estimate distance and direction.

402 To frighten people who saw them coming.

403 An ancient trade route across Asia, linking China and Europe.

404 Timbuktu is south of the Sahara desert. It was for centuries an important trading city.

405 Measured time and longitude.

406 China; he served its emperor from 1275–1292.

407 Longships; Vikings also used larger, fatter ships called knarrs for travel and trade.

408 He thought he was in Asia, which is why the islands are known as the West Indies.

409 To identify landmarks from great distances.

410 *On the Origin of Species*.

411 A sextant. Invented in 1757, it is used to judge latitude.

412 By a Frenchman, Louis Blériot.

413 Ferdinand Magellan, but he never completed the journey. When he reached the Philippines in 1521, he was killed.

414 Mungo Park was a Scotsman who explored the Niger River in 1795–96 and 1805–06.

415 Christopher Columbus was Italian, but his voyage to the New World was sponsored by King Ferdinand and Queen Isabella of Spain.

416 The American Charles Lindbergh. He flew from New York to Paris in 1927.

417 Yes, he did, with 4 other men, on January 17, 1912. But they all died on the trek back to base camp.

418 Sir Walter Raleigh brought back potatoes and tobacco to Europe. Sir Francis Drake was the first Englishman to sail around the world.

419 Sinbad the Sailor.

Aztecs and Incas

420 Drowning, in wells. Other methods were also used.

421 Silver: the eyes are obsidian and shell, and the mosaic pieces are turquoise and coral.

422 The Aztecs: they believed that the world had ended 4 times, and that the Sun would die a fifth time unless they fed it with human blood.

423 Tlaloc was god of rain.

424 The Aztecs' elite warriors were named the Jaguar Knights and the Eagle Knights.

425 The llama (and other animals in its family).

426 The wheel; the Incas (and the Aztecs) may have used it for toys, but not for transportation.

427 To capture prisoners for sacrifice.

428 All Peruvian men carried them.

429 The Mexica, the Aztecs' name for themselves.

430 In Peru; the Nazca made magnificent textiles.

431 The jaguar, often seen as a symbol of power in ancient Central and South America.

432 Grow crops: chinampas were fertile plots of land built up from swampy parts of Lake Texcoco.

433 Horses; the conquistadors brought horses, guns, and steel weapons, all unknown to the Aztecs. They also introduced the cow to the Americas.

434 They all originated in the Americas.

435 It was surrounded by water. Tenochtitlan was built on a swampy island on a lake; Venice is built on islands in a lagoon.

436 Tenochtitlan, with maybe 200,000 people. The population of London was about 40,000.

The Wild West

437 The Stetson, designed by John B. Stetson, whose hat factory opened in 1865.

438 John Wayne, a famous US actor.

439 They are better known as buffalo.

440 The Peacemaker; it was a Colt .45.

441 Rawhide, which shrank to fit the frame as it dried. It was then covered with finished leather.

442 Europeans called the Dakota nation the Sioux.

443 Custer's: General George Custer led 215 men into an ambush by North American Indians. He and his men were all killed.

444 The eagle; dancers wore such masks in spiritual ceremonies in the Northwest.

445 25 years, from the end of the US Civil War in 1865 to the end of the cattle boom in the late 1880s.

446 Rodeos, nowadays a big business.

447 Lacrosse, invented by Native Americans and particularly popular in the Southeast.

448 The Winchester rifle, called "the gun that won the West" because it was so popular.

449 Barbed wire, used to protect crops, good pasture, and water, and to keep cattle in.

450 Buffalo Bill; his show toured the United States

and Europe from 1883 to 1916.

451 A "ten-gallon" hat.

452 A saloon.

453 A knife.

454 For food; it was the cook's wagon.

455 At the OK Corral, in Tombstone, Arizona.

Weaponry and War

456 Sideburns (whiskers grown down the sides of the face). Burnside fought in the Civil War.

457 In France; Allied troops landed in northern France to liberate Europe from the Germans.

458 It is a type of curved sword.

459 Crossbows have a longer range, but are slower to reload. They can be deadly at 200 yds (180 m).

460 A backsword, once used by European cavalry.

461 Lead, hence expressions like "a hail of lead."

462 5; they could fire 6 lb (2.7 kg) cannonballs up to 1,100 yards (1,000 m) 2 or 3 times a minute.

463 5 shots; this model was first made in 1862.

464 A musket was a kind of gun.

465 Covered excavations for soldiers to shelter in.

466 A German submarine; U-boat was short for undersea boat.

467 The great general Hannibal (247–182 BC) from the North African city of Carthage.

468 The Battle of Jutland, fought in 1916.

469 Napoleon Bonaparte, who conquered much of Europe, but was finally defeated at the Battle of Waterloo in 1815.

470 Flint, from which the oldest surviving weapons were made.

471 The tank, first used in battle by the British in France in 1916. It was named the tank while being developed, in order to keep what it was a secret.

472 A colonel is the most senior of the 3, and a corporal the least.

473 A sword, felt to have mystical significance.

474 An AK47 is a gun – a Russian rifle.

475 It is a Zulu thrusting spear from South Africa.

476 Grenadiers, in the 1700s; by the 19th century grenadiers were usually just infantry troops.

477 Caltrops were scattered before a battle to lame enemy horses or soldiers who stepped on them.

478 It weighs about 44–55 lb (20–25 kg).

479 Throwing; the multiple blades mean that it can cause damage whichever way it hits.

480 Abraham Lincoln, assassinated in 1865 at the end of the Civil War.

481 Blitzkrieg: from "blitz" meaning lightning and "krieg" meaning war.

482 6 days: it was the Six Day War of 1967 between Israel and several Arab states.

483 The Ethiopian army smashed an Italian invasion at the Battle of Adowa in 1896.

484 The claw of a tiger.

485 It will fly back to you.

486 Genghis Khan: in the 1200s he founded the Mongol Empire that eventually included lands from China to central Europe.

487 North American Indians used tomahawks.

488 A knuckle-duster, worn on the fingers to cause maximum damage when punching people.

489 A division is the biggest, then a brigade, then a regiment, then a battalion.

490 It is called no-man's-land.

491 30 years: the Thirty Years War raged across much of Europe from 1618–48. Longer wars, such as the 100

Years War, have not been continuous.

492 It is called a gauntlet.

493 Giuseppe Garibaldi (1807–82), who conquered Sicily and Naples for the new Italy in 1860.

494 Rapiers, which were developed in the 1500s.

495 Jousting, a sport in which knights fought mock battles against each other.

496 It was worn on the wrist. The razor-sharp outer edge is covered in this example.

Clothing

497 Hand spindles were used for spinning and weaving textiles.

498 Louis XIV introduced the wig into the French court, some say to hide his own baldness.

499 Jeans, a US invention, first made in the 1850s.

500 It was used to fasten a belt.

501 China, where they had been used for more than 500 years.

502 In the 18th century. They are made of embroidered muslin; cuffs were also made of lace.

503 Men: in the late 18th century men sometimes hung pouch bags on their belts.

504 In the 1960s, in England.

505 To keep a person cool; fans can also be fashion accessories.

506 The toga, a loose, flowing garment.

507 Headdresses worn by aristocratic women.

508 They were cut into various designs and worn on the face.

509 In the early 20th century.

510 Imperial women wore their hair in elaborate designs, using wigs, hairpieces, and tiaras. They needed hairpins to hold everything in place.

511 In Spain. False bellies were created by tailors with horsehair, rags, or wool.

512 A metal or whalebone framework worn under a dress below the waist to make the dress stick out.

513 Overshoes with platform soles, worn in wet weather. Some platforms reached 30 in (76 cm). They were fashionable during the Renaissance.

514 In the 18th century.

515 Silk, which first reached Europe when two monks smuggled silkworm eggs out of China.

516 The Persians were the first people to cut and fit garments in what is now the European style.

517 The crinoline; it was introduced, in Europe, in 1856, replacing layers of petticoats.

518 France influenced fashions until the outbreak of the French Revolution in 1789.

519 A type of plastic, often used in the form of fibers. Its elastic qualities make it suitable for many types of clothes.

520 A very tall hairstyle, popular in the 1700s.

521 Social etiquette demanded that such upper-class women should keep their hands covered.

522 They were popular in the 1970s.

523 Skirts were first worn above the knee.

524 Both men and women wore platform shoes.

525 Around the ankle; it is an African bracelet.

526 Through the nose; it is a Colombian gold ornament.

527 On the wrist; it is a Pictish bracelet.

528 Probably on the chest; it is an Irish brooch, worn to hold a cloak in place.

529 The ears; these are Thai earrings made from animal skin and painted in gold.

530 Around the neck; it is Zulu necklace.

531 Around the head; it is a headband.

532 Around the waist; it is a gold buckle made from precious stones and worn on a belt.

Inventions: to 1850

533 The hot-air balloon, invented by the Montgolfier brothers in 1783.

534 A pendulum; it made clocks far more accurate.

535 Arches, in Egypt, Iraq, and Pakistan, 4000–3000 bc. The oldest record of a tunnel is in 2180 bc in Iraq.

536 The metric system was standardized in France between 1791 and 1795, the imperial system in England in 1824.

537 The cork; bottle corks later (1670) made the champagne process possible.

538 Gas; it did not become popular for a century.

539 In Europe, in England in 1837; but the first really successful telegraph was made by US inventor Samuel Morse, creator of Morse code, in 1844.

540 Baths, which can be traced back to 2500 bc in Pakistan, and perhaps to 3100 bc in Gaza. Egyptian remains of 1350 bc may be the first shower.

541 The first book was printed in China in AD 868. Movable type was invented about 1040, also in China, and was used to publish a book in 1300.

542 In about 1300, in Italy. Bifocal lenses such as those in the picture were invented in 1784.

543 The violin; it dates to the early 16th century; the first piano was made around 1700, in Italy.

544 In England, in 1509.

545 The steam engine; in 1765 he started to improve Newcomen's design of 1712; in 1784 he invented a steam engine that could turn wheels.

546 He improved maps by inventing a better way of copying the Earth's round surface onto flat paper.

547 The wheelbarrow, invented in China in the 3rd century AD. The lawn mower was invented in 1830.

548 He invented the saxophone.

549 In about 1827, by Joseph-Nicéphore Niépce.

550 Metalworking; it was invented about 7000 bc, perhaps in Turkey, the wheel about 3200 bc in Iraq.

551 It was the first battery.

552 Tarmac, originally called Tarmacadam.

553 The alarm clock; one of the first alarm clocks was used in a monastery in Nuremberg, Germany.

554 *Rocket*; it first ran in 1830 at the start of the railroad boom. The first train ran in 1803.

555 In China, under the Tang dynasty (AD 618–906), although it was not widely used until the 1200s.

556 Concrete was invented by Roman engineers about 200 bc, gunpowder in China around AD 950.

557 In Iraq, about 3500 bc.

558 The electric motor: the first one was built about 1831. The first internal combustion engine was not made until 1859.

559 The bicycle; still known in France as the velo.

560 Postage stamps, first produced in 1840; the first printed Christmas cards were made in 1843.

561 It was the parachute.

562 In Asia: the wheel was used to reel silk in China about AD 1000, and to spin yarn in India soon after.

563 The Etruscans of Italy; they were using false teeth made from animals' teeth in about 700 bc.

564 In China, in AD 105.

The Earth

565 The Pacific is the largest ocean. It covers one- third of the Earth's surface.

566 Asia is the largest continent.

567 Ice; glaciers are like rivers of slowly-moving ice.

568 It is called the mantle.

569 Seismographs measure earthquakes.

570 In Australia; it is called Uluru.

571 Diamond is the hardest mineral.

572 The magnitude of an earthquake.

573 Tsunamis are huge waves set off by undersea earthquakes. Some travel at 490 mph (790 kph).

574 The Earth is 4.6 billion years old.

575 Eclogite is a metamorphic rock – it is formed by the alteration of existing rock. Granite is igneous, formed by the crystallization of molten material.

576 The steeper slopes are called "scarps."

577 Geysers spout hot water.

578 The Himalay; they include the world's highest mountain, Everest, which is 29,078 ft (8,863 m) high.

579 Platinum is the most valuable.

580 The Nile is usually considered the longest, at 4,145 miles (6,670 km) long. The Amazon can be figured as longer because it is 4,195 miles (6,750 km) from its source to the *farthest* of its several mouths.

581 Because it is the only metal that is liquid at room temperature and it is silvery in color.

582 It is 8,100°F (4,500°C).

583 On the shores of the Dead Sea, between Jordan and Israel. It is 1,300 ft (400 m) below sea level.

584 Most land lies in the Northern Hemisphere.

585 Krakatoa, a volcanic island, erupted It was the longest eruption in modern history.

586 Columns of calcite that form underground in caves. Stalagmites grow up from the floor and stalactites grow down from the roof.

587 Rocks.

588 Water.

Astronomy

589 The planet Venus.

590 Mercury and Venus.

591 The Milky Way.

592 The Sun.

593 "The cow jumped over the Moon."

594 It is Jupiter.

595 Time is the fourth dimension; modern science sees space and time as a unity, called "spacetime."

596 The dark patches are flat areas. The lighter patches are mountains.

597 Albert Einstein.

598 Olympus Mons, 3 times as high as Everest.

599 Galileo; with his telescope he discovered Jupiter's satellites, and craters on the Moon.

600 There are 687 Earth days in a year on Mars.

601 He orbited the Earth.

602 A comet, Halley's Comet.

603 In space, it orbits around the Earth.

604 The film *Star Wars*.

605 Russian; Valentina Tereshkova, in 1963.

606 Pluto, which was not found until 1930. It is also the farthest away from the Sun.

607 Mars; from Earth it looks like a red disk.

608 Russian; called *Salyut 1*, it was launched in 1971.

609 It is called "the Big Bang."

610 He discovered the force of gravity.

The Human Body

611 100,000 times each day.

612 A child; children have about 300 more bones than adults. In adults, bones fuse together.

613 Tooth enamel is the hardest substance.

614 5 pints (3 liters) of air.

615 China; in 1989 there were reported to be 61,929.

616 Keratin is found in nails, hair, and skin.

617 A baby develops in the uterus, or womb.

618 The skin is the largest organ.

619 Sigmund Freud; he treated patients by listening to them talk about their dreams and thoughts.

620 The ribcage protects the chest organs.

621 It can only bend forward and backward.

622 The small intestine, measuring 21 ft (6.5 m). The large intestine is 6 ft (1.8 m) long. It is thicker.

623 More than 600 muscles.

624 This is true.

625 In 1895.

626 In the spine.

627 The head weighs about 8.8 lb (4 kg).

628 In the 19th century.

629 They are made up of proteins.

630 A gastroscope is used to examine the stomach.

631 The femur; it is found in the thigh.

632 Louis Pasteur; he led the way for the development of antiseptic surgery.

633 206, over half of them are in the hands and feet.

634 Marie Curie.

635 A local anesthetic numbs a part of the body. A general anesthetic makes a patient unconscious.

636 Alexander Fleming, in 1928.

637 To carry blood from the heart around the body.

638 Doctors believed that too much blood in the body was a cause of disease.

639 In 1849. Elizabeth Blackwell was accepted into medical school in 1847.

640 It was forbidden by the church to dissect bodies for scientific study.

641 Amputated shattered limbs.

642 The major blood groups are A, B, AB, and O.

643 More than 200 muscles.

644 This form of medicine is called acupuncture.

645 Louise Brown was born in England in 1978.

646 In the ear; it is called the stirrup.

647 It was performed in 1967.

648 In the 19th century.

649 Bile aids digestion.

650 A midwife delivers babies.

651 A stethoscope listens to the heart and lungs.

652 In 1853; devised by Charles Plavaz in France.

653 There are 27 bones in the hand.

654 It was set up in 1948 to act as an information center concerning health problems facing the world.

655 They are attached to the sternum or breastbone.

656 They are sight, smell, taste, hearing, and touch.

657 When we are cold, tiny muscles lift the body hairs to trap warm air.

658 They were introduced in the 1840s. Patients became unconscious by inhaling nitrous oxide, ether, or chloroform.

Biology and Chemistry

659 It turns pink or red.

660 DNA contains this information.

661 Water, made of hydrogen (H) and oxygen (O).

662 Light; there is a prism inside the scope that splits a light beam into its spectrum, that is, its different colors, or wavelengths.

663 It separates mixtures by boiling and condensing them.

664 Pigs' bladders were used in the 1700s to hold gases before glass equipment was introduced.

665 DNA, the chemical from which chromosomes, "the building blocks of life," are made.

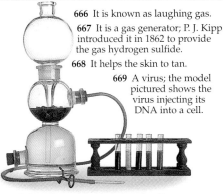

666 It is known as laughing gas.

667 It is a gas generator; P. J. Kipp introduced it in 1862 to provide the gas hydrogen sulfide.

668 It helps the skin to tan.

669 A virus; the model pictured shows the virus injecting its DNA into a cell.

670 Salt; sodium chloride is its scientific name.

671 An element is a substance that cannot be broken down into simpler substances.

672 The chemical elements. There are more than 100.

673 Glass, probably first made in Egypt, 3000 BC.

674 It is designed to measure the purity of air.

675 Hydrogen is the lightest element.

676 Genes; inherited characteristics are passed down the generations in the genes.

677 Water, air, and sunlight to grow properly.

678 It is acidic, so can be relieved by applying cold water containing some bicarbonate of soda, which is alkaline. A wasp sting is alkaline; it is treated with a teaspoon of vinegar, an acid, in half a glass of water.

679 They were called alchemists.

680 Romantic love; this is an unscientific use of the word chemistry.

Weather and Climate

681 Clouds; cumulus clouds are rounded clouds with flattish bases.

682 Antarctica; the central plateau is a cold desert. It is the windiest continent.

683 Aztec, it is the Aztec Sun god, Tonatuich.

684 Low or falling pressure often indicates rain.

685 Air pressure, to help forecast weather.

686 It warms us up; heat trapped by gases in the lower atmosphere keeps the Earth warm. Pollution is increasing the amount of "greenhouse gases" in the atmosphere, and heating the Earth too much.

687 Wind speed; most weather stations use them.

688 Nitrogen; it is 78% nitrogen and 21% oxygen.

689 Rainbows form when the Sun breaks through the clouds after rain and light is reflected in raindrops still falling on the opposite side of the sky.

690 In Antarctica; the coldest temperature ever recorded there was −128.6°F (−89.2°C).

691 An aneroid barometer; in the drum is a vacuum that expands or contracts as air pressure changes.

692 The fog forms as warm, moist, Californian air blows over the cool Pacific ocean currents.

693 Bands of red, green, or yellow light that move across the night sky in northern polar regions.

694 Lightest; the eye of a hurricane is calm.

695 The time of day; the moving shadow cast on the dial by the needle shows what time it is.

696 The troposphere; all that we call weather happens in the troposphere.

697 Hawaii; it is Mount Wai-'ale-'ale in Hawaii.

698 The ozone layer, which shields the Earth from the Sun's ultraviolet rays.

699 The side the clouds come from (the windward side); the farther side (the leeward side) is drier.

700 No; you see the lightning first.

701 They create wind, as air rushes from areas of high pressure to areas of lower pressure.

702 The Earth's rotation; the Coriolis effect describes how this rotation deflects the winds of the world.

703 Hot air rises.

704 Yes.

705 In Africa; the temperature at Dallol in Ethiopia averages 94°F (34°C).

Inventions: 1850–1950

706 They were the first to fly an airplane.

707 The fax machine; an early form of fax machine called the pantelegraph was installed in France in 1856. The telephone was not invented until 1876.

708 It played for 23 minutes.

709 It was introduced in 1920.

710 Pneumatic (inflatable) tires. They had been invented in 1845 and "reinvented" in 1888, but the Michelins were first to make them for cars, in 1895.

711 The meter; it was not quite new to the world, for the ancient Romans fitted a kind of meter to carts.

712 The Model T Ford; the assembly line had earlier been used to make clocks and watches.

713 Germany; Karl Benz made a motorized tricycle in 1885 and had built a 4-wheel car by 1893.

714 Germany; it opened in Berlin.

715 About 1930, in the United States.

716 The gramophone, an early kind of record player.

717 In 1885, by Gottlieb Daimler in Germany.

718 The helicopter; the first practical helicopter was built in 1936, the first jet airplane in 1939.

719 He invented it in 1938.

720 The airship, in 1852. The first glider flew in 1853, but controlled flight in a glider waited until 1891. The airplane first flew in 1903.

721 In London, England.

722 30 tons.

723 In 1920, in Pittsburgh, Pennsylvania.

724 It had a red light and a green light. Yellow came 4 years later.

725 Thomas Edison was American.

726 The cash register.

727 In 1926, invented by John Logie Baird.

728 False; the first practical lightbulb was invented in 1879, the electric iron in 1882.

729 In 1872; chewing gum was an old Native American idea.

730 In 1946, but microwaves in the home did not appear until 1955.

731 Guglielmo Marconi; in 1894 he was sending radio waves across the room, and by 1901 he was sending messages across the Atlantic.

732 It was invented in 1857.

733 It only played 1 tune.

734 Coca-Cola, launched as "the esteemed brain tonic and intellectual beverage."

735 Tuned into a radio broadcast.

736 On a squash court in Chicago, in the United States, in 1942.

737 It recorded and reproduced sound.

738 In 1950, for use in restaurants.

739 The ballpoint pen.

740 In 1914, called the "hookless fastener."

741 The electric refrigerator.

The Modern World

742 Nothing; not even light can escape a black hole.

743 Heat itself; self-heating canned food was invented in 1991.

744 PC stands for personal computer.

745 Cable; it transmits TV down fiber-optic cables.

746 There were about 537 million.

747 Videotape, in 1956; microchips – integrated electronic circuits printed on a single silicon chip – invented in 1959, have made computers far faster.

748 The first electric toothbrush.

749 Very low temperature; some substances lose almost all resistance to electricity at low temperature.

750 Light, laser light carrying vision, sound, etc., in the form of data.

751 A laser beam, directed onto the bomb's target.

752 A cassette player, with headphones, small enough to be worn.

753 Pacemakers help the heart beat regularly.

754 In 1982, in Utah.

755 A floppy disk; a flexible magnetic disk that stores information.

756 3-dimensional holograms, made in 1965. Personal computers arrived in 1975, but the first successful PC was not produced until 1978.

757 A mouse; moving it moves a pointer on screen.

758 The scanning tunneling microscope, invented in 1981, can magnify objects 100 million times.

759 Their ability to take off and land vertically.

760 A computer.

761 In 1972, in the United States.

762 A fax is a document transmitted down a telephone line.

763 A credit card incorporating a computer chip.

764 The United States; Japan produces half as much.

765 The food processor, able to mix, chop, or slice.

766 Click on it; a mouse controls a pointer that can be used to activate functions of a computer by clicking on icons, without using the keyboard.

767 Fission splits atoms, releasing energy; fusion combines them, releasing even more energy.

768 The cassette tape recorder.

769 400 million instructions per second.

770 Cruise missiles, a US innovation.

771 The industrial robot, in 1962; the first digital watch was made in 1971.

772 The most accurate clocks are atomic.

773 By our DNA; we each have a unique pattern.

774 The hovercraft.

775 In 1981; it was the first reusable space launcher.

776 The Concorde, a joint English-French project.

777 It is a liquid crystal display, or LCD for short.

778 *Sputnik* was the first space satellite, launched by the Soviet Union in 1957.

779 Electricity; wind is used to drive wind turbines.

780 The L.A.S.E.R., that is, the Laser.

781 CD stands for Compact Disc.

782 Rubik's Cube, a brain-teasing puzzle.

783 Reduce pollution from car exhausts.

784 A device to link computers via a telephone line.

785 Computers; CD-ROMs store information.

786 A hydrometer to measure the density of liquids.

787 A spring balance for measuring weight.

788 A test tube.

789 A Bunsen burner.

790 A pipette.

791 A micrometer for measuring small objects.

Soccer

792 A soccer match lasts for 90 minutes.

793 It was held in Mexico.

794 Just over 17 hours; this feat was achieved by Huh Nam Jin of South Korea..

795 On the shin, to protect against bruises and cuts.

796 On the streets; there were no time limits and few rules.

797 Brazil; they have won the World Cup 4 times.

798 It weighs 8 oz (250 g).

799 A team consists of 11 players and 3 substitutes.

800 The goalkeeper.

801 A linesman; linesmen use flags to indicate when a player fouls or the ball goes out of play.

802 An overhead kick in which the player back flips to direct the ball behind him.

803 To draw attention to fouls.

804 The chest, head, and thighs.

805 At kickoffs and penalties.

806 The team captain, for identification.

807 140 play at the international level.

808 5 shots for each side.

809 Italy won the World Cup in 1982.

810 It is made of leather.

811 Pelé, who said "make the ball your friend."

812 A kick in which the goalkeeper gathers the ball, drops it, and kicks it before it can hit the ground.

813 Ireland plays Gaelic soccer.

814 A red card; a yellow card is a lesser penalty.

815 Fédération Internationale de Football Association; it is soccer's ruling body.

816 England beat Australia 17–0 in 1951. (This match was a "friendly" and not a full international.)

817 Geoff Hurst; England beat West Germany 4–2.

818 Luciano Pavarotti sang *Nessun Dorma*, which became the theme tune for the 1990 World Cup.

819 In the penalty area.

820 To give them a better grip of the ball.

821 Cameroon.

Indoor Sports

822 Boxing; Queensberry rules were laid down by the English Marquess of Queensberry in 1865.

823 In poker; it is made up of the Ace, King, Queen, Jack, and 10 of a single suit.

824 Garry Kasparov, who won in 1985, aged 22.

825 Sumo, usually the province of large, bulky men.

826 Racing pigeons, which fly vast distances home.

827 Ice hockey. Players hit a puck (a hard rubber disk), the goaltender defends the goal, and players have to spend time off the ice in the "sin bin," or penalty box, when they break the rules.

828 Tenpin bowling: the players added a 10th pin to the 9 with which they had played skittles and arranged them in a triangle instead of a diamond.

829 Gymnastics, which also involves floor exercises.

830 Organic materials, that is, pieces of bone or wood, tied around shoes. Metal blades were first used in the 1600s.

831 Chess; to lose your king is to lose the game, so the king must be protected.

832 Libyan Suleiman Ali Nashaush was 8 ft (2.45 m) tall.

833 The "clean and jerk" is easier: the bar is first lifted onto the chest, then the lifter steadies himself, then lifts it over his head. In the "snatch" the bar is lifted above the head in one movement.

834 They are marbles teams from Britain. Marbles is a game played by flicking marbles at each other.

835 Karaoke; it involves singing along to a prerecorded tune.

836 Rocky Marciano; Muhammad Ali lost several, but came back to be world champion three times.

837 When the direct path from the cue ball to the object ball is blocked by another ball.

838 No one has ever dribbled more than 4 at a time.

839 Pool, or at least the "8-ball" version of the game.

Outdoor Sports

840 Polo fields, which cover 12.4 acres (5 hectares).

841 In cricket: an over is a set of six deliveries (deliveries are roughly like pitches in baseball). If no runs are scored in it, it is called a maiden over.

842 Boris Becker, youngest ever men's champion.

843 In cricket, it is taking 3 wickets in 3 balls. The reason for the name is that in the early days of cricket, bowlers who did this were given a top hat. In other sports, a hat-trick is 3 goals in the same game.

844 A ground stroke is played after the ball has bounced, a volley is played before it bounces.

845 Golf. A birdie is a hole played 1 stroke under par; an eagle is 2 under; and a bogey is 1 above.

846 A log, which is called a caber.

847 In soccer.

848 A football; the other two are round.

849 In football.

850 A very large diamond; the bases are arranged in a diamond shape.

851 Tennis: "love," "deuce," and "advantage" are different tennis scores.

852 He was 98 years old; the oldest woman was 82.

853 England. The English invented soccer, rugby, cricket, tennis, squash, and other games.

854 In cricket. This is one of the ways in which a batsman can get out. The inning ends when 10 of the 11 batsmen on a team are out.

855 Formula 1 is the fastest of these three divisions of motor racing.

The Olympic Games

856 There are 5 rings.

857 They represent the 5 continents.

858 Bronze; people who finish second are awarded silver medals.

859 The photo-finish: pictures of the finish are looked at very closely.

860 It was Nadia Comaneci.

861 They go over backward.

862 Ski jumping; they jump from these two hills.

863 He was disqualified for taking illegal drugs.

864 Every 4 years.

865 The marathon is the longest distance run, although competitors such as the walkers and cross-country (Nordic) skiers race over longer distances.

866 The pommel horse is a key bit of gymnastic equipment; originally created to help soldiers learn riding skills, it is a leather-covered shape with two pommels (handles) along its upper surface.

867 It was in Greece. Only men could compete. Women had their own separate games.

868 US swimmer Mark Spitz won 7 gold medals in 1972. 4 were individual medals and 3 were team golds. US speed skater Eric Heiden, who won 5 golds at the 1980 Winter Olympics, holds the record for individual golds won in a single games.

869 The relays; 4 runners race 100 meters each or 400 meters each, passing a baton between them.

870 There are 10 events: 100 meter, long jump, shot put, high jump, 400 meter, 110 meter hurdles, discus, pole vault, javelin, and 1,500 meter.

871 The men's pentathlon. The women's pentathlon consisted of the 100 meter hurdles, shot put, high jump, long jump, and the 200 meter until 1984, when the javelin and 800 meter were added and the event became the heptathlon.

872 The sport is called rhythmic gymnastics.

873 Adolf Hitler; he refused to present black US athlete Jesse Owens with the 4 golds he had won.

874 The competitors stand. In rifle-shooting competitions they usually lie down.

875 The discus can be thrown 3 times as far.

876 There are 9 people in an "eight": 8 rowers and the cox, who steers and dictates the pace.

877 The record is 10 gold medals, won by Raymond Clarence Ewry of the United States, between 1900 and 1908, in the standing high, long, and triple jumps.

878 Yes; amateur boxers do; professionals don't.

879 The third element is a hop.

880 The downhill; in the other two the competitors have to follow a twisting course marked out with flags. In the downhill, they ski straight down.

881 It featured sprinters in the 1924 Olympics.

882 A skater; the German figure skater Katarina Witt received them after winning the gold in 1984.

883 It was 40 years, achieved by 4 contestants, 3 in yachting and 1 in fencing.

884 A low score, because points are awarded for faults; as in golf, the lowest scorer wins. Only 3 people have won the Olympic show jumping competition without any faults at all.

885 The other sport is rifle shooting.

886 Freestyle is the fastest swimming style, followed by butterfly, then backstroke, then breaststroke.

887 They hit a touch-sensitive board at the end of the swimming pool.

888 The javelin can be thrown slightly farther.

889 The steeplechase, run over 3,000 meters.

890 In the Olympic "village."

891 The Olympic flame, or Olympic torch. It is kept burning always at Olympia in Greece, and a torch is carried by runners to each Olympics, where it is used to light a giant torch at the opening ceremony.

892 In synchronized swimming, now an Olympic sport.

893 The ice dancers; ice dance is one of the skating events.

894 Bodybuilding is the odd one out.

895 In 1896, in Athens.

896 There were 169 nations represented.

897 Sydney won, and will host the Olympics.

898 It is one of the riding competitions.

899 Trick question: the Olympics did not take place in 1944 because World War II was being fought at the time.

Art and Architecture

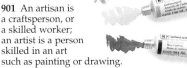

900 They design buildings.

901 An artisan is a craftsperson, or a skilled worker; an artist is a person skilled in an art such as painting or drawing.

902 On the roof; they are different types of domes.

903 In the 20th century, between 1929 and 1931.

904 Water; aqua is Latin for water.

905 Many painters use oil paints; other types of paint include watercolors.

906 In Sydney. It was designed by Danish architect Jørn Utzon.

907 Gargoyles.

908 Sculptors make statues and carve wood, stone, and other materials in 3 dimensions.

909 Columns; all these styles originated in ancient Greece.

910 Expressionism, an early 20th-century artistic movement that aimed to express emotion, rather than to show reality in a natural way.

911 Green; the three primary colors of paint are yellow, blue, and red. All other colors of paint can be made by mixing these 3 colors.

912 Mosaic; mosaics are often found in churches, palaces, or great houses.

913 Going to a class in which they will draw someone or something from life.

914 Clay, a sturdy material for building.

915 No, Gothic arches are pointed and Norman arches are rounded.

916 Skyscrapers; the first was built in Chicago, Illinois, in 1883.

917 Sable. Sable martens are small, carnivorous mammals, and the brushes are made from their fur.

Dance

918 In the 19th century; Marie Taglioni first danced on pointe in *La Sylphide* in 1832.

919 There are 5.

920 The waltz, first danced in Vienna, Austria.

921 *Fame*, set in New York City.

922 Moira Shearer starred in *The Red Shoes*.

923 The leotard, a close-fitting one-piece garment covering the torso.

924 Fred Astaire and Ginger Rogers; they starred in 10 films together.

925 *Saturday Night Fever.*

926 Flamenco; dancers hold their heads up high as they stamp their feet and turn around.

927 Breakdancing; some dancers could spin on their heads.

928 Layers of satin, paper, and a coarse material called burlap glued together.

929 Vogueing, in which dancers imitate the poses of catwalk models.

930 The pavlova, a kind of meringue cake, was named after Russian ballerina Anna Pavlova.

931 Louis XIV; he was an avid dancer.

932 A tutu.

933 Gene Kelly; he starred in the hit musical *Singin' in the Rain.*

934 *Starlight Express*, by Andrew Lloyd Webber.

935 The choreographer.

936 In North America.

Music

937 They all belong to the saxophone family.

938 Giuseppe Verdi; the first performance was part of the celebrations for the opening of the Suez Canal, in 1869 in Egypt.

939 Bing Crosby; his recording of *White Christmas* in 1942 is the biggest-selling record of all time.

940 A double bass is the biggest of them.

941 They are all famous opera singers.

942 They are all operas written by Wolfgang Amadeus Mozart.

943 A conductor; his or her job is to direct the band or orchestra.

944 The brass family.

945 Elvis Presley; he is known as "The King."

946 The *Messiah.*

947 Baroque.

948 Peter Ilyich Tchaikovsky.

949 In 1597, by the Italian Jacopo Peri. It was called *Dafne* and was performed in Florence.

950 John Lennon and Paul McCartney.

951 There are 88 keys.

952 Bob Dylan; his real name is Robert Allen Zimmerman.

953 Louis Armstrong; he devised the first solo style in jazz with his daring improvisations.

954 An orchestra; 200 years ago orchestras were 30-strong, but some music of the late 19th century and 20th century requires more than 100 musicians.

955 A sitar; this one has 7 main strings that pass over arched metal frets.

956 The harp; it is a very difficult instrument to play. While plucking 47 strings with the fingertips the harpist must work 7 foot pedals.

957 Bob Marley; his group was called the Wailers.

958 Abba; they went on to make 13 hit albums.

959 2 violins, a viola, and a cello.

960 The player blows air into it through a nostril. It is called a nose flute.

961 You blow through it, and it makes a deep, resonant sound; it is an Aboriginal instrument.

962 A tambourine; a dancer taps it with the fingers and shakes it or bangs it against the body.

963 It can produce voices, sound effects, and new sounds never heard before.

964 Shake it.

965 *Hair*; it opened the day after the abolition of British stage censorship.

966 *West Side Story* by Leonard Bernstein.

967 1970.

Movies, TV, and Theater

968 90 ft (27 m); a full-length feature film uses 1.5 miles (2.5 km) of film.

969 2; Johnny Weismuller, who won 3 gold medals in 1924 and 2 in 1928, and Buster Crabbe, who won 1 gold in 1932.

970 William Shakespeare, England's greatest playwright, who wrote nearly 40 plays between about 1588 and 1613.

971 Someone who watches too much television; it is a rather rude term, suggesting that they sit in front of the television like a vegetable, not thinking much.

972 Walt Disney, the most famous creator of animated films in history.

973 Britain; the BBC (British Broadcasting Corporation) began regular service in 1936.

974 Because the images it shot were recorded onto three films at once, recording red, blue, and green individually. A special printing process then put the colors back together.

975 Tragedy; both comedy and tragedy were first developed, in theatrical terms, in ancient Athens.

976 The soccer World Cup; the Olympics have perhaps 2.5 billion viewers in all, while the total audience for all the World Cup soccer games may add up to an audience of about 25 billion.

977 It was the first "talkie," the first feature film that featured sound. Most of it was still silent, however. The first all-talking film came in 1929.

978 In a theater; the boxes are at the side, with very good views, and the stalls are the lowest seats. The tier is above them and the upper tier above that.

979 A screenplay, written by a scriptwriter.

980 In ancient Greece; Athens saw the first plays that were like the plays we see today. Many of those 2,500-year-old Athenian plays are still performed.

981 Sherlock Holmes, who has appeared in over 200 films to date. Dracula has featured in over 150.

982 The first satellite broadcasting service was launched.

983 24; an average 90-minute feature film is made up of about 130,000 separate frames.

984 A moving image; when it was rotated very fast, the painted images seemed to become a single moving image on the screen. It was created in England in the 1870s.

985 A miniaturized TV.

986 Hollywood.

987 Steven Spielberg; George Lucas has produced, among other films, the Star Wars series (he also directed the first one) and *Raiders of the Lost Ark.*

988 25 times a second is standard. John Logie Baird's 1926 television sets projected a new image 10 times a second.

989 A microphone; the boom is the long pole on which the microphone is placed so that it can be held above the actor's head. When a camera is placed on a boom, the person operating it is known as a boom man or woman.

990 The sound of someone's arm or leg being chopped off.

991 In France, by the Pathé company, which also built projectors and made newsreel films.

992 "Cut!" When directors want to start filming, they say "Action!"

993 India, where more than 900 feature-length films have been produced in a single year.

994 China, which has recorded over 20 billion movie theater attendances in a single year.

995 *Ben Hur*, produced in 1959, starring Charlton Heston in the title role.

996 A hero turtle, from the 1990 film *Teenage Mutant Ninja Turtles.*

997 Dracula, star of vampire movies since 1921.

998 Charlie Chaplin, the great star of silent comedy, wore them in the film *The Immigrant.*

999 Marilyn Monroe, who wore this dress in the film *Some Like it Hot.*

1000 A gremlin from the film *Gremlins.*

1001 The Pink Panther, symbol of the Pink Panther films, and star of a series of TV cartoons.

What do you know about nature?

THE NATURAL WORLD is full of secrets and surprises, but how many of them do you know? With a series of intriguing questions, this section will test your knowledge of the Earth and its atmosphere, rocks and minerals, and the amazing lives of plants and animals. See if you can answer the questions here, then turn over the pages to see if you were right.

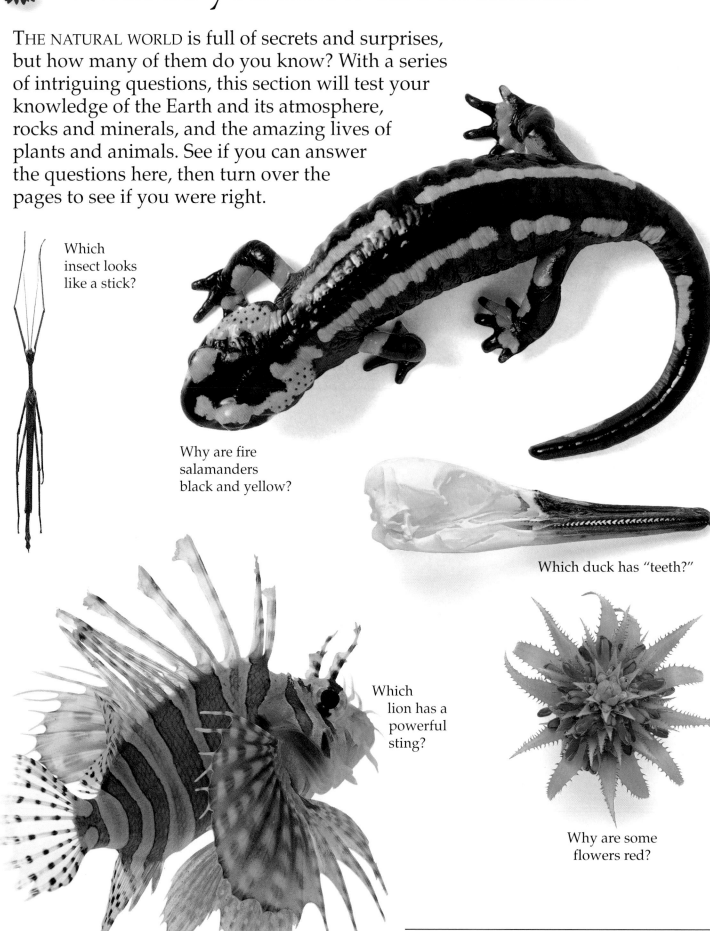

Which insect looks like a stick?

Why are fire salamanders black and yellow?

Which duck has "teeth?"

Which lion has a powerful sting?

Why are some flowers red?

Who or what is an orrery?

How does the poison arrow frog get its name?

How does a snake hatch?

What can a geologist learn from a shellfish called nautilus?

What makes some leaves turn red in autumn?

Why is an elephant like a bridge?

129

Why is the Earth unique?

THE EARTH is the only one of the nine planets in the solar system able to sustain life. Five of the other planets are simply balls of gas, and of the four remaining rocky planets – Mercury, Venus, Mars, and Earth – only Earth has the right kind of atmosphere. Earth's atmosphere not only contains the oxygen all living creatures need to breathe, but it also keeps the surface of the planet at just the right temperature, preventing it from getting ferociously hot like Venus or icy cold like Mercury.

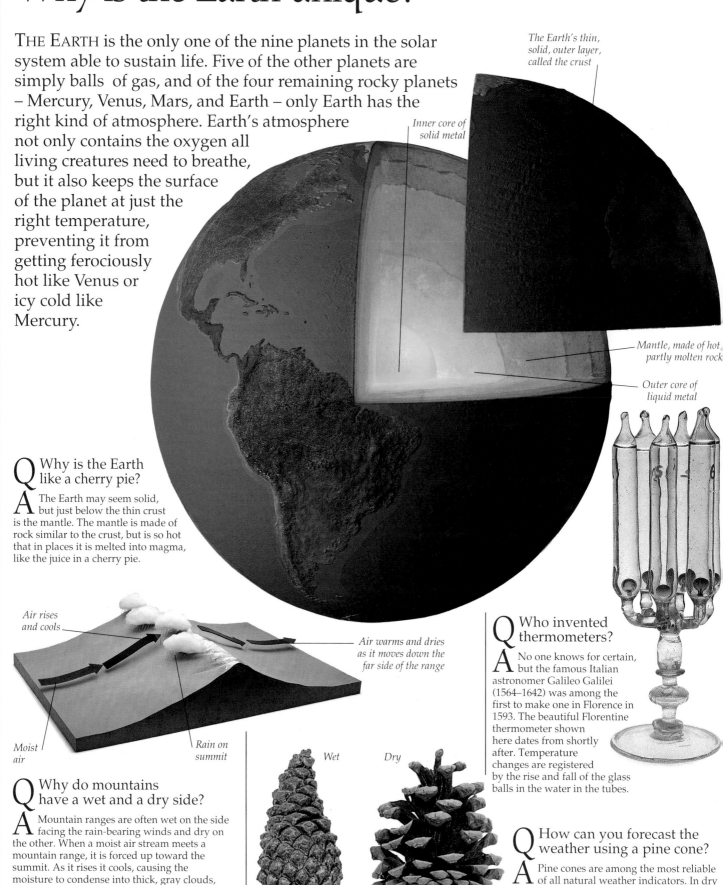

The Earth's thin, solid, outer layer, called the crust

Inner core of solid metal

Mantle, made of hot partly molten rock

Outer core of liquid metal

Q Why is the Earth like a cherry pie?

A The Earth may seem solid, but just below the thin crust is the mantle. The mantle is made of rock similar to the crust, but is so hot that in places it is melted into magma, like the juice in a cherry pie.

Air rises and cools

Air warms and dries as it moves down the far side of the range

Moist air

Rain on summit

Q Why do mountains have a wet and a dry side?

A Mountain ranges are often wet on the side facing the rain-bearing winds and dry on the other. When a moist air stream meets a mountain range, it is forced up toward the summit. As it rises it cools, causing the moisture to condense into thick, gray clouds, which become saturated and fall as rain. As the cold air moves down the far side of the mountain range, it gets warmer and dries out.

Wet   *Dry*

Q Who invented thermometers?

A No one knows for certain, but the famous Italian astronomer Galileo Galilei (1564–1642) was among the first to make one in Florence in 1593. The beautiful Florentine thermometer shown here dates from shortly after. Temperature changes are registered by the rise and fall of the glass balls in the water in the tubes.

Q How can you forecast the weather using a pine cone?

A Pine cones are among the most reliable of all natural weather indicators. In dry weather, the scales dry up and open out. If they start to close up, it is a sure sign that wet weather is on the way.

Q How many sides has a snowflake?

A In the late 19th century, American farmer Wilson W. Bentley photographed thousands of snowflakes under a microscope and never found two the same. But all snowflakes have six sides and are usually formed from flat, platelike crystals, though occasionally the crystals may be needle- or rod-shaped. Outside the tropics, most rain starts as snow. Snow falls when the temperature of the air is just cold enough for the snowflakes to flutter to the ground before they melt. Sometimes, snow can be falling on the mountain tops while it is raining in the valley.

Q What is a mercury barometer?

A A barometer is a device for measuring atmospheric pressure. This is useful to know because a fall in pressure can indicate the onset of stormy weather and a rise in pressure goes with stable, clear weather. Mercury barometers show pressure by the changing level of liquid mercury in a glass tube. As air pressure rises, it pushes the mercury higher up the tube; as it falls, the mercury drops. Mercury is used because it is the heaviest liquid known. A similar barometer filled with water instead would have to be over 32 ft. (10 m) high to work.

Florentine barometer from around 1640

Head points into the wind, indicating the direction the wind is blowing from

The first weather cocks appeared on churches in the ninth century and were probably a reminder of the cock that crowed when St. Peter denied Christ three times

Q How can a cockerel tell you the weather?

A Winds from a particular direction usually bring a certain kind of weather – which is why people often have weathervanes to show wind direction. Many of these are in the shape of a rooster, or cockerel. The cockerel sits on a cross showing north, east, south, and west.

Gnomon

Brass sundial, 18th century

Q How can you tell the time from the position of the Sun?

A Using a sundial, it is possible to tell the time from the position and angle of the Sun. As the Sun appears to move across the sky during the day, the shadow cast by the needle, or "gnomon," moves around the dial. The dial is marked to indicate the time wherever the shadow falls. Since the path of the Sun varies from place to place, sundials must be set up correctly for each place to give an accurate reading.

Moon

Earth

Sun

Q Who or what is an orrery?

A Once it became clear in the 1600s that the Earth circled around the Sun and not the Sun around the Earth, astronomers began to build clockwork models to show how the Earth and Moon moved during the course of a year. These devices are called orreries after Charles Boyle, Earl of Orrery (1676–1731), for whom the first one was made.

Q Why did medieval sailors rely on a quadrant?

A A quadrant was a simple instrument in the shape of a quarter circle used by medieval sailors to measure the height of particular stars in the night sky. From this, they could calculate how far north or south they were. On this quadrant, the central dial can be rotated to show the positions of important constellations, such as the Great Bear, at different times of the year.

Q What was the biggest volcanic eruption in history?

A One of the best ways to tell the size of an eruption is to work out how much ash it blew out. On this basis, the biggest in history was that of Tambora in Indonesia in 1815, which blasted some 50 cubic miles of ash into the air, giving the world cool summers and cold winters for years after. When Mt. Pinatubo erupted in the Philippines in 1991, it blew out 4 cubic miles.

2	50	11	7	.5	.5
Vesuvius Italy AD 79	*Tambora Indonesia 1815*	*Krakatau Indonesia 1883*	*Katmai Alaska 1912*	*St. Helens U.S.A. 1980*	*El Chichón Mexico 1982*

How are rocks formed?

ALL ROCKS ARE FORMED in one of three ways: volcanic rocks form from molten rock within the Earth; sedimentary rocks form when the remains of rocks worn down by the weather are washed into the sea and deposited as layers; and metamorphic rocks are rocks that have been transformed by the effect of heat and pressure inside the Earth.

White quartz

Vein of gold

Q Where does gold come from?

A Gold usually forms in veins along with quartz crystals in volcanic rocks. The veins were once cracks in the rock filled with hot, mineral rich water. When the rock and the water cooled down, solid gold and quartz were left behind. Gold sometimes comes from veins like these, but may also be found as fine dust in rivers, where it is washed down as the rocks containing veins of gold are worn away by the weather.

Q Which rock is used to make blue paint?

A The blue paint pigment called azure was once made by crushing the copper mineral azurite.

Nautilus

Q What can a geologist learn from a shellfish called nautilus?

A A geologist, or rock and mineral expert, can tell the age of sedimentary rocks from the range of fossils in them. Nautilus belongs to a class of sea creatures called cephalopods, which first appeared 500,000,000 years ago. Over time, 10,000 species have come and gone. Identifying species of fossilized cephalopods helps geologists pinpoint the age of the rock.

Q What is tiger's eye?

A Tiger's eye is a crystal made when veins of silk blue asbestos crystals are dissolved by solutions that deposit quartz in their place. The quartz grows exactly in place of the tiny asbestos fibers.

Q What makes granite pink?

A Granite is one of the most common igneous rocks, made from crystals of quartz, feldspar, and mica. It turns pink when it contains a high proportion of potassium feldspar.

Q Which rock makes red paint?

A The pigment in vermilion red paint was once made by crushing the poisonous ore of mercury called cinnabar. The practice began in China in prehistoric times and was introduced into Europe in the Middle Ages.

Cinnabar

Azurite

Q How does amethyst get its color?

A Amethyst is a purple form of quartz. According to a 16th-century verse, Bacchus, the ancient Greek god of wine, declared in a rage that the first person he passed would be eaten by tigers. But when this person turned out to be the lovely maiden Amethyst, the goddess Diana turned her to stone to save her from the tigers. Regretting his anger, Bacchus poured red wine over the stone as an offering to Diana, turning the stone purple.

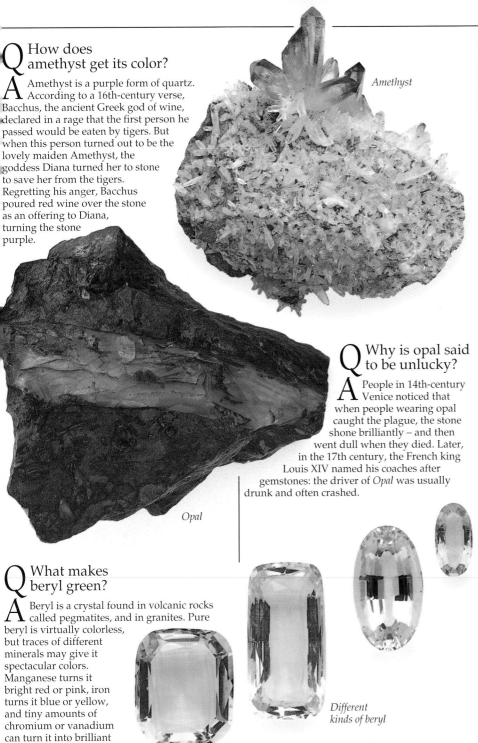

Amethyst

Opal

Q Why is opal said to be unlucky?

A People in 14th-century Venice noticed that when people wearing opal caught the plague, the stone shone brilliantly – and then went dull when they died. Later, in the 17th century, the French king Louis XIV named his coaches after gemstones: the driver of *Opal* was usually drunk and often crashed.

Q What makes beryl green?

A Beryl is a crystal found in volcanic rocks called pegmatites, and in granites. Pure beryl is virtually colorless, but traces of different minerals may give it spectacular colors. Manganese turns it bright red or pink, iron turns it blue or yellow, and tiny amounts of chromium or vanadium can turn it into brilliant green emeralds.

Different kinds of beryl

Q Why is marble not what it used to be?

A Marble is a metamorphic rock, formed when limestone is transformed by the intense heat of a volcanic intrusion – that is, a volcanic upwelling which does not break through the Earth's surface. The smooth, lustrous stone has been popular since ancient Greek times and was used to make the frieze of the Parthenon temple in Athens known as the Elgin marbles.

Q How are crystals thought to bring good health?

A Some people believe that crystals may be able to cure disease. They say that as light reflects off the crystals, the aura, or electromagnetic field, of a person's body absorbs energy. This energy is thought to make the person more aware of the cause of the problem and helps to heal the body.

Q Why is ruby like sandpaper?

A Ruby is a form of the mineral corundum, which is second only to diamond in hardness. Emery is another form of corundum. It is used in a fine form of sandpaper called emery paper, which electricians use to clean electrical contacts.

Different colors of corundum

Q Why do surgeons rely on diamonds?

A Diamond is the hardest substance in the world and so is used in many cutting and abrasive tools. Glaziers use pens with diamond tips to score a line on a sheet of glass to make a clean break. Besides being hard, diamond does not corrode, and so scalpels with diamond blades, such as the one shown here, are often used for delicate surgical operations, such as eye surgery.

Q What does jade mean?

A The Spanish conquerors of Mexico believed the green stones carved by the native people could cure kidney complaints. They called them kidney stones or *piedra de ijada* from which the word jade derives. Jade is a greenish-white rock found as either nephrite or jadeite. It has been treasured in China for over 2,000 years.

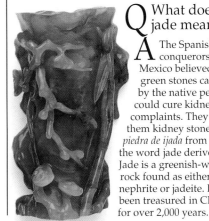

Why are plants green?

ANIMALS MUST FIND AND EAT OTHER LIVING THINGS to survive, but plants can make their own food by absorbing sunlight in a process called photosynthesis. This gives the plant the energy to change carbon dioxide in the air and minerals in water into food. Photosynthesis depends on special organs inside leaf cells called chloroplasts. Chloroplasts contain a green substance called chlorophyll that makes plants green.

Sepal

As the bud starts to burst, the five protective sepals peel back to reveal five petals

Petal

One sepal develops a spur that makes nectar to attract insects

As insects search for nectar, they brush pollen from the male anthers to the female stigma, pollinating the plant

Garden nasturtium

Anther

Stigma

After a few days, the petals shrivel

The flower makes three seeds inside a fruit

Gold head decoration from ancient Greece

Liverwort

Q What makes a plant flower?

A All flowering plants have a mechanism to ensure their blooms develop at just the right time of year. Most respond to the amount of light. Some flower only when days are long and nights are short; others flower only when nights are long and days are short, which is why chrysanthemums will never flower if lit at night by artificial light. The garden nasturtium shown here belongs to a family of plants from South America. It flowers only in midsummer, when the light is plentiful.

Q How did Greek athletes earn their laurels?

A Winners at the Pythian games in ancient Greece were crowned with the entwined twigs of the laurel tree. The laurel was sacred to the god Apollo, who was the patron of all athletes. The Romans adopted the custom and crowned victorious generals with laurel wreaths. Gold laurel wreaths were worn by Roman emperors instead of crowns.

Q Do all plants have flowers?

A No, not all. Most plants – 250,000 different kinds – are indeed flowering plants or angiosperms, including everything from roses to oak trees. But there are 500 or so gymnosperms – that is, conifers and cycads – which make their seeds in cones, not flowers. There are also plants that grow not from seeds but spores, including fungi, lichen, mosses, ferns, and liverworts.

Lid

Q Which plants drown insects?

A At the ends of the leaves of the insect-eating pitcher plant are traps shaped like jugs or pitchers, with a lid to keep out rain. Insects are lured to the pitcher by sweet nectar produced around the slippery rim. When an insect lands on the rim, it slips inside, and drowns in the fluid at the bottom.

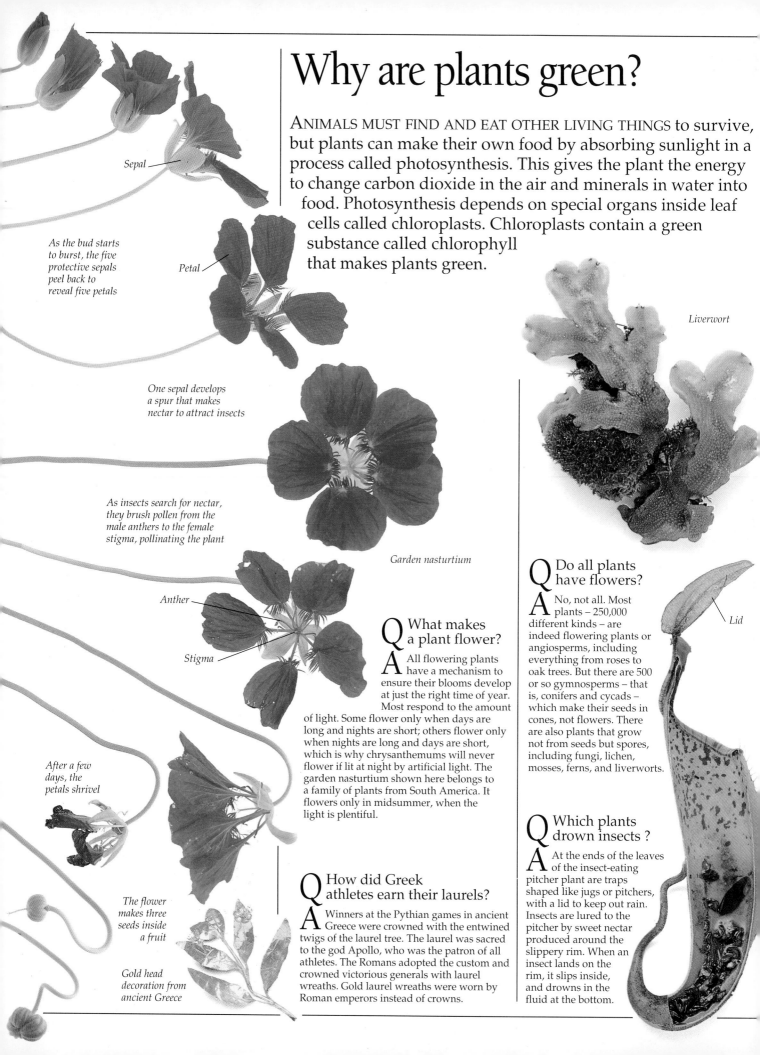

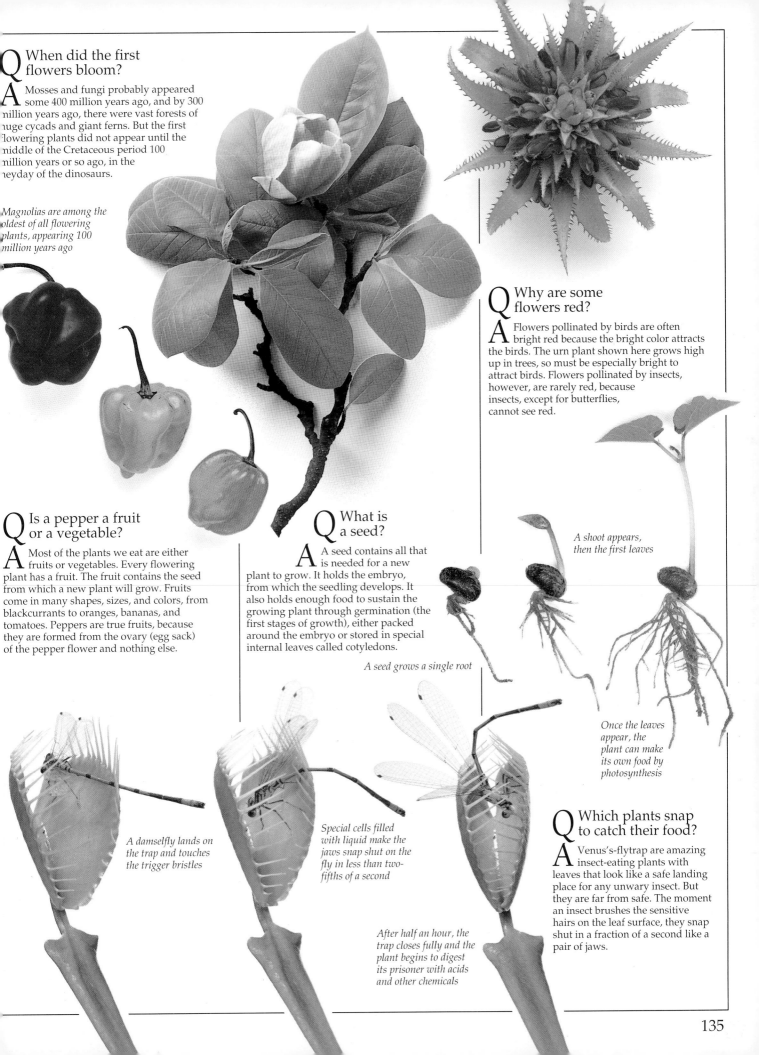

Q When did the first flowers bloom?

A Mosses and fungi probably appeared some 400 million years ago, and by 300 million years ago, there were vast forests of huge cycads and giant ferns. But the first flowering plants did not appear until the middle of the Cretaceous period 100 million years or so ago, in the heyday of the dinosaurs.

Magnolias are among the oldest of all flowering plants, appearing 100 million years ago

Q Why are some flowers red?

A Flowers pollinated by birds are often bright red because the bright color attracts the birds. The urn plant shown here grows high up in trees, so must be especially bright to attract birds. Flowers pollinated by insects, however, are rarely red, because insects, except for butterflies, cannot see red.

Q Is a pepper a fruit or a vegetable?

A Most of the plants we eat are either fruits or vegetables. Every flowering plant has a fruit. The fruit contains the seed from which a new plant will grow. Fruits come in many shapes, sizes, and colors, from blackcurrants to oranges, bananas, and tomatoes. Peppers are true fruits, because they are formed from the ovary (egg sack) of the pepper flower and nothing else.

Q What is a seed?

A A seed contains all that is needed for a new plant to grow. It holds the embryo, from which the seedling develops. It also holds enough food to sustain the growing plant through germination (the first stages of growth), either packed around the embryo or stored in special internal leaves called cotyledons.

A seed grows a single root

A shoot appears, then the first leaves

Once the leaves appear, the plant can make its own food by photosynthesis

A damselfly lands on the trap and touches the trigger bristles

Special cells filled with liquid make the jaws snap shut on the fly in less than two-fifths of a second

After half an hour, the trap closes fully and the plant begins to digest its prisoner with acids and other chemicals

Q Which plants snap to catch their food?

A Venus's-flytrap are amazing insect-eating plants with leaves that look like a safe landing place for any unwary insect. But they are far from safe. The moment an insect brushes the sensitive hairs on the leaf surface, they snap shut in a fraction of a second like a pair of jaws.

135

How high are the world's tallest trees?

THE TALLEST TREES OF ALL are the redwoods or giant sequoias of California, which grow hundreds of feet tall and can weigh more than 6,000 tons. The smallest trees, however, may be only a few inches high. Sequoias are conifers, which have narrow, hard leaves known as scales or needles. The other two main kinds of trees are broad-leaved trees, with broad, flat leaves, and tropical palms.

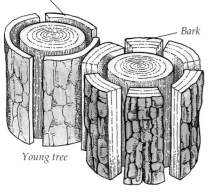

New bark

Bark

Young tree

Mature tree

Q How does a tree grow?

A A tree can get taller and spread wider as cells at the tip of each twig divide to make the twig longer. The trunk and branches grow fatter as cells divide in a layer called the cambium, just below the bark.

Q What grows from a little acorn?

A A tall oak tree. The acorn is the fruit of the oak tree and contains its seed. In a good year, a single oak tree produces over 50,000 acorns. Most are eaten by animals, but a few survive to grow into trees the following spring.

Cinchona bark

Q What bark is better than a bite?

A The bite of a mosquito can give you malaria, but this disease can be treated with a chemical called quinine, extracted from the bark of the Peruvian cinchona tree. Aspirin is another drug based on chemicals from tree bark – this time the willow tree. The chemical name for aspirinlike drugs, *salicylates*, comes from the Latin name for the willow, *salix*.

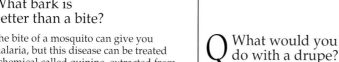

Ripe Victoria plums

Q What would you do with a drupe?

A Eat it! A drupe is a kind of fruit that grows on certain trees, such as Victoria plums, cherries, and walnuts. Drupes are just like any other fruit, except that there are no pips, just a single hard stone containing the seed.

Q How did trees replace reeds?

A When the Egyptians wrote their amazing hieroglyphic script over 5,000 years ago, they used sharpened reed pens on paper made from strips of the papyrus reed that used to grow along the Nile. Nowadays, although the word "paper" comes from papyrus, the paper we write on is nearly always made from pulped wood fiber. And instead of a reed pen, you probably use a wooden pencil.

Ancient Egyptian reed pens

Q How can you tell the age of a tree?

A Trees grow for only a short period each year, and the rings show the amount the cambium has grown in each year. In a mature tree, the cambium typically grows 1 in (2.5 cm) a year, so the rings are 1 in (2.5 cm) wide, but they may be thinner in bad years. By counting the number of rings, you can tell how old a tree is.

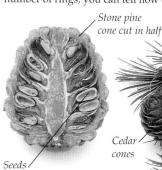

Stone pine cone cut in half

Seeds

Cedar cones

Q Why do conifers have cones?

A Unlike other trees, conifers do not have flowers. The seed develops inside a cone instead. When cones first appear on the tree, they are soft and green and little bigger than a pea. Only after they are pollinated do they grow big and turn brown and hard. Once this happens, a seed gradually develops beneath each of the cone's scales. When it is ripe, the cone breaks up to release the seeds.

Q What is a deciduous tree?

A Deciduous trees are trees that shed their leaves every year. Before the leaves die and fall off, they often turn brilliant reds, oranges, and yellows.

Q What makes some leaves turn red in autumn?

A As the days get shorter and colder, the green pigment in the leaves breaks down, allowing other red, blue, or yellow pigments to shine through. The result is often a brilliant burst of color before the leaves fall off and die.

Leaves of the deciduous European oak

Q Which trees are wooden rowing boats made from?

A Unlike the big sailing ships of the past, which were often made of tough but costly woods, such as oak, rowing boats are generally made from less valuable woods, such as larch. For the boat's hull the wood is cut into flat planks or strakes. It is then softened inside a steam-filled box and bent into the right curved shape. Once bent, the strakes are secured to the boat's inner framework.

Q Why are rowan berries red?

A To help scatter the rowan tree's seeds. Inside every berry is a seed from which a new rowan tree could grow. Birds such as thrushes, fieldfares, and blackbirds are attracted by the bright red and eat the berries. But the hard seeds pass through their system undigested, and so the birds help scatter the seeds far and wide.

Catalpa leaf

Q Which deciduous tree has the biggest leaves?

A Catalpas or Indian bean trees have leaves that reach a giant 1 ft. (30 cm) or more in length in the space of a single growing season. Of course, evergreen leaves can grow much bigger than deciduous leaves because evergreen trees do not lose their leaves every year. Banana leaves, for instance, can grow to several yards long.

Mature catalpa tree

Q Who made bark boats?

A The paperlike bark of birch trees is so light and tough that the natives of North America used it for making canoes. These canoes were even light enough to carry overland to avoid rapids.

137

Why are some animals poisonous?

SOME ANIMALS AND PLANTS just happen to be poisonous to eat – like laburnum seeds, which birds can eat without any ill effects, but which can cause convulsions and death in humans. A few creatures use poison to stun or kill prey. But for many animals and plants, poison is vital for safety – a last line of defense against predators. Most mammals and birds, however, do not have poisons, and must defend themselves in other ways.

Running right down the middle of every spine is a venom gland

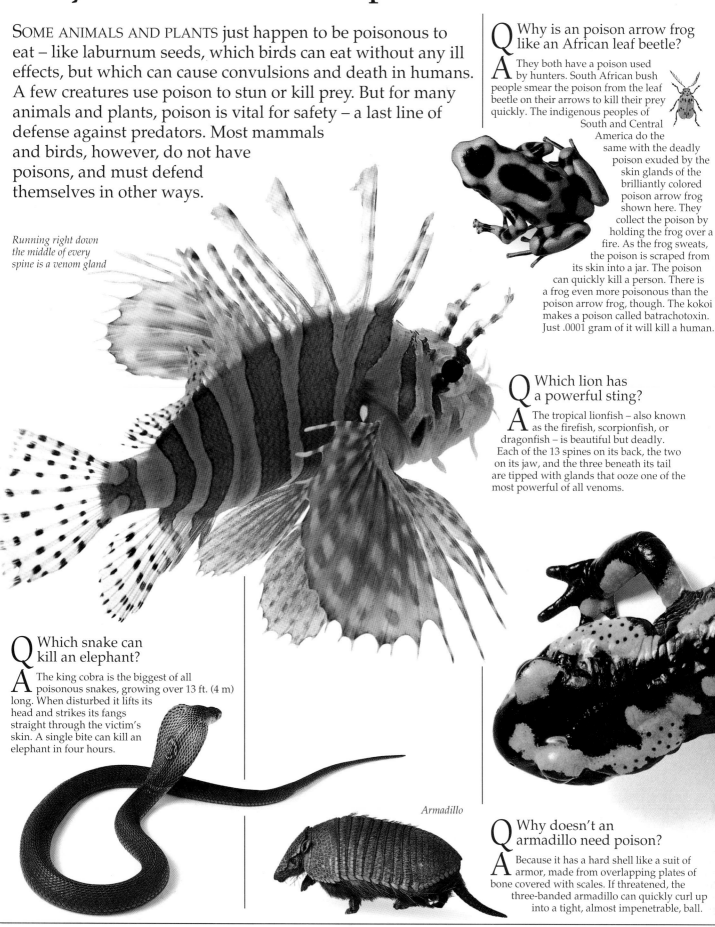

Q Why is an poison arrow frog like an African leaf beetle?

A They both have a poison used by hunters. South African bush people smear the poison from the leaf beetle on their arrows to kill their prey quickly. The indigenous peoples of South and Central America do the same with the deadly poison exuded by the skin glands of the brilliantly colored poison arrow frog shown here. They collect the poison by holding the frog over a fire. As the frog sweats, the poison is scraped from its skin into a jar. The poison can quickly kill a person. There is a frog even more poisonous than the poison arrow frog, though. The kokoi makes a poison called batrachotoxin. Just .0001 gram of it will kill a human.

Q Which lion has a powerful sting?

A The tropical lionfish – also known as the firefish, scorpionfish, or dragonfish – is beautiful but deadly. Each of the 13 spines on its back, the two on its jaw, and the three beneath its tail are tipped with glands that ooze one of the most powerful of all venoms.

Q Which snake can kill an elephant?

A The king cobra is the biggest of all poisonous snakes, growing over 13 ft. (4 m) long. When disturbed it lifts its head and strikes its fangs straight through the victim's skin. A single bite can kill an elephant in four hours.

Armadillo

Q Why doesn't an armadillo need poison?

A Because it has a hard shell like a suit of armor, made from overlapping plates of bone covered with scales. If threatened, the three-banded armadillo can quickly curl up into a tight, almost impenetrable, ball.

*Snake locks
sea anemone*

Q Which fishes blow themselves up like a balloon?

A Porcupine fish and puffer fish look like normal fish most of the time, but when threatened with danger, they can swallow water to inflate themselves into a ball two or three times their usual size. This not only startles predators but makes them difficult to swallow. When danger is past, the fish slowly deflates again.

Puffer fish

Q Why shouldn't you pick flowers or eat jelly in the sea?

A Because most sea flowers are anemones and jellies are jellyfish. These sea creatures, called coelenterates, cannot move fast to catch prey or avoid attack but have tiny, sensitive cells in their tentacles which can give a nasty sting.

Ferocactus

Q Why is a cactus so prickly?

A Cacti are plants of the deserts of the Americas and survive in the parched conditions by storing moisture in their thick, almost waterproof stems. The sharp spines protect them not only from attack by animals, but probably also from heat and cold.

Q Why should you beware of female hornets?

A Because they have the most painful stings of the wasp family. The stinger is an adaptation of the egg-laying ovipositor.

Q What is the world's sleepiest mammal?

A The western European hedgehog spends most of its life asleep. During the summer it sleeps 18 hours day, only waking up a few times at night to forage for food. In winter, it sleeps all the time. It is quite safe when it is asleep, though, for it curls up into an uneatable prickly ball. Only sloths, armadillos, and opossums sleep as long.

Q What do spiders do with their victims?

A Most spiders stun or kill their victims before eating with a bite from their poisonous jaws. Although a spider bite can be painful, few spiders are dangerous to humans – even the giant bird-eating tarantulas. One real exception is the quite small, female black widow spider, whose bite can kill a child.

Q Why are fire salamanders black and yellow?

A To warn potential attackers that they are poisonous to eat. In the natural world, the colors black and yellow are often a sign that an animal is poisonous or has an unpleasant taste. Many wasps and hornets have black and yellow stripes as a warning to enemies that they have a painful sting.

*Tarantula
from Sri Lanka*

139

Why are polar bears white?

POLAR BEARS ARE WHITE so that they blend in with the snow and ice of the arctic landscape in which they live. Many animals use camouflage like this to remain hidden against their background – a huge advantage to both hunter and hunted alike. But not all animals rely on blending in with their background to avoid being eaten. Some scare off any would-be predators with bright colors, while others simply pretend they are something else such as a plant, or a more deadly, poisonous animal.

The Sinaloan milk snake is harmless to humans

Indian leaf butterfly

Citrus swallowtail butterfly chrysalis

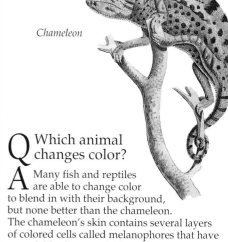

Chameleon

Q What is the difference between a coral snake and a milk snake?

A The coral snake has red stripes bordered by yellow and is highly venomous while the milk snake has red stripes bordered by black and is harmless. Predators are unlikely to attack the milk snake in case it turns out to be a coral snake. An old rhyme goes: "Red to yellow, kill the fellow; red to black, venom lack." Milk snakes were once thought to steal milk from cowsheds.

Q Which insect looks like a stick?

A Stick insects are so long and slender they look just like sticks. They avoid attack by hanging almost motionless in shrubs looking like dead twigs.

Stick insect

Hover fly

Q When does a butterfly look like a dead leaf?

A When it is an Indian leaf butterfly. It has one of the most deceptive natural disguises. At rest, with its wings folded, it looks remarkably like an old leaf on a stem. When it lies on the ground among leaf litter, it is almost totally invisible. Many insects mimic leaves during their vulnerable chrysalis stage.

Q Which animal changes color?

A Many fish and reptiles are able to change color to blend in with their background, but none better than the chameleon. The chameleon's skin contains several layers of colored cells called melanophores that have tentaclelike fingers which wind up through the layers. When the chameleon changes background the melanophores move brown pigments in and out of the upper layers of skin, making it change accordingly.

False-eyed frog

Q Which fly spends its life looking like a wasp?

A This hover fly, with its striped black-and-yellow jacket, looks just like a wasp, but it has no sting and is quite harmless. Most animals are scared off by the disguise and leave the fly alone.

Q Why do some creatures have "eyes" on their backs?

A The *Taenaris macrops* butterfly of New Guinea has two huge eyespots on its rear wings. If it is threatened by a predator while feeding on its favorite banana leaves, it flashes the two eyespots to startle the attacker off. Certain frogs and fish, such as the twinspot wrasse, have similar eyespots.

Twinspot wrasse

A The ground-living
tenebrionid beetle
of Western Australia
cannot easily be spotted
by predators because it
looks just like a seed.

Decorator crab

Q Why does a plaice have both
eyes on one side of its body?

A So it can still see when it is lying flat on
the seabed. The plaice is a flatfish which
spends most of its life at the bottom of the
ocean. Although it starts life like any other fish,
with one eye on either side of its body, as it
grows older the left eye gradually moves
around the head to join the right. After only
three weeks, both eyes are on the camouflaged
right-hand side of the body and the left-hand
side remains white and blind. Like other
flatfish, a plaice is able to change the pattern
and color of the skin on the upper side of its
body to suit the pattern and color of the seabed.

Q Why are some crabs
like Christmas trees?

A Because they are festooned
with decorations. The
decorator crab adorns itself with
all kinds of sea debris, such as
shells and weeds, so it avoids
being spotted by predators.

Q Why are
tigers striped?

A Tigers usually hunt alone at
night among the trees, silently
stalking prey, such as antelope, deer,
and pigs, then pouncing from a few
yards away. The dark stripes of their
yellow fur break up their outline and so
their victims cannot see them lurking in
the shadows of the forest.

Q When do humans
wear camouflage?

A Nearly all the time.
Most clothes and
hairstyles are designed to
make the human body look
more attractive, or hide its
true form. Some people wear
jackets with shoulder pads to
make them look more
impressive, or high-heeled
shoes to make them look
taller. In the 1880s,
women wore a bustle
under their skirts to
make their hips
wider, and a tight
corset for a
narrow waist
and fuller
bosom.

141

What do bones do?

BONES ARE THE RODS AND PLATES that make up a creature's skeleton. Skeletons range greatly in shape and size, from tiny hummingbirds to massive blue whales. But they all provide a rigid, protective framework for the body; the spine is the body's main support; the skull houses and protects the brain and the vulnerable eyes and ears; and the ribs form a protective cage around the heart and lungs.

Q Which duck has "teeth"?

A Unlike mammals and reptiles, birds do not have true teeth, which are made of bone. But mergansers, which are a kind of duck, have toothlike serrations on the sides of their beak. They use their beak "teeth" to catch fish in fresh water and at sea.

"Teeth" are made of the same horny material as the beak

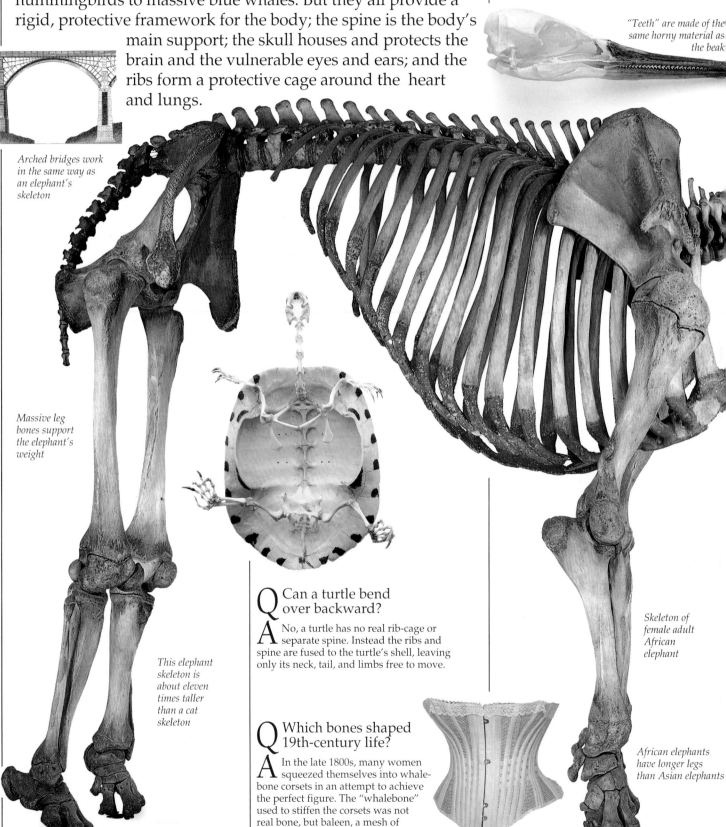

Arched bridges work in the same way as an elephant's skeleton

Massive leg bones support the elephant's weight

This elephant skeleton is about eleven times taller than a cat skeleton

Q Can a turtle bend over backward?

A No, a turtle has no real rib-cage or separate spine. Instead the ribs and spine are fused to the turtle's shell, leaving only its neck, tail, and limbs free to move.

Q Which bones shaped 19th-century life?

A In the late 1800s, many women squeezed themselves into whalebone corsets in an attempt to achieve the perfect figure. The "whalebone" used to stiffen the corsets was not real bone, but baleen, a mesh of gristle in some whales' mouths.

Skeleton of female adult African elephant

African elephants have longer legs than Asian elephants

Australopithecus, 4–1 million years ago

Homo erectus, 1,500,000– 300,000 years ago

Neanderthal 100,000–35,000 years ago

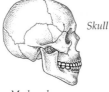

Modern humans from 40,000 years ago

Q How have human skulls changed?

A Over the past 2 million years, human skulls have gradually developed a flatter face, smaller teeth, a less prominent jaw, and the top of the skull has become bigger and rounder to house the larger brain.

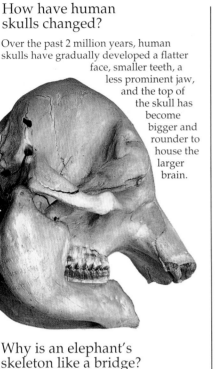

Q Why is an elephant's skeleton like a bridge?

A Elephants, stone bridges, and arches all work on the same mechanical principle, and so have a similar design. They all share the weight of their load between their supports. The load-bearing part curves upward in the middle to give extra strength.

Q Does a car have a skeleton?

A They used to. Old cars had a rigid internal skeleton called a chassis. Today, most cars have a body shell, not a chassis. But trucks and other large vehicles are still built on chassis. A whole range of different bodies can be bolted onto a truck chassis.

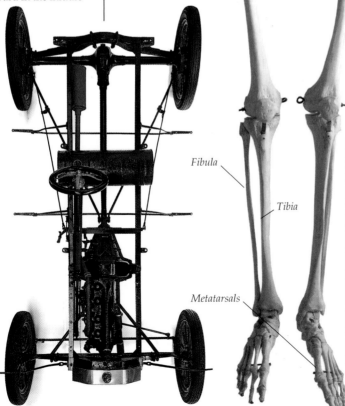

Skull

Clavicle

Ribs

Sternum (breastbone)

Radius

Ulna

Ilium

Sacrum

Cocccyx

Pubis

Ischium

Femur

Fibula

Tibia

Metatarsals

Q How many bones are there in the human body?

A Just over 200. They include 33 vertebrae (backbones), 24 ribs, and a three-part breastbone, besides three large bones in each limb. Each hand has 27 bones, with eight wrist bones to allow them to swivel in almost any direction. Each hip consists of three bones fused together. They are rounded and so allow us to walk upright.

Bullfrog skeleton

Q Why are frogs such good jumpers?

A The frog has one of the shortest spines of all, with only eight or nine vertebrae, so it is well adapted to stand the stresses of jumping. It also has long legs, with the thigh, calf, and foot all about the same length. As a frog jumps, each part of the leg straightens in turn, enabling the frog to leap huge distances.

Stag beetle

Wood-boring beetle

Q Which creatures have skeletons on the outside?

A Insects, spiders, and shellfish all have a hard outer casing, or exoskeleton, instead of bones. Like an internal skeleton, this exoskeleton provides support and protection, but it cannot expand. So the creature grows by molting its exoskeleton every now and then and growing a new one. Above a certain size the exoskeleton becomes too thick and heavy to be molted, which is why animals with exoskeletons tend to be small.

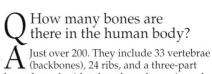

What makes a home?

A HOME IS A PLACE OF SHELTER – from the weather, to hide from enemies, or to bring young safely into the world. For some animals it is just a crack in a tree or a hole in the ground. But many small creatures build burrows and nests. Rabbits and prairie dogs dig elaborate burrows in the ground. Birds and rodents build nests using anything from straw to old bottles. Termites build homes as elaborate in their way as a modern skyscraper.

Termite nest

Cut away of a South American paper wasps' nest

Common wasps' nest

Q How does a bird know how to build its nest?

A Birds rarely live in their nests all the time, but build them to rear their young. Experiments show nest building is instinctive, inherited as reliably as plumage and feeding habits. But each bird improves with practice, building at first rather crudely, but getting better with each season.

Q Which insects live in multistory pagodas?

A In damp African rainforests, the ground is often so sodden that *Cubitermes* termites build their nest on a tall column to keep it dry. Each level has a sloping roof, which sheds rain.

Q Who really invented papier mâché?

A South American paper wasps have made papier mâché nests for millions of years, chewing plant fibers into a papery pulp that hardens as it dries. The result is a material both light and strong, which they use to build huge hanging nests up to 6 ft. (1.8 m) across.

When a hermit crab is moving around, its head, antennae (feelers), front claws, and first two pairs of legs are exposed

Q Where do squirrels live in winter?

A Like many rodents, the gray squirrel is a nest-builder. A squirrel's drey, or nest, is made in autumn, high in a tree from materials such as leaves, straw, feathers, and even old newspapers. The squirrel sleeps there at night or shelters in bad weather.

Squirrel's drey

Beaver

Q Which animals are the best engineers?

A Beavers build elaborate lodges from mud and sticks, with a safe underwater entrance. They also erect sturdy dams in streams to keep the lodge entrance submerged. One beaver dam on the Jefferson River in the U.S. is 2,300 ft. (700 m) long, and can bear the weight of a horse. When building a dam, a beaver may spend a long time selecting the right tree gnawing through it with its sharp incisors in just the right place to make it fall where the beaver wants it.

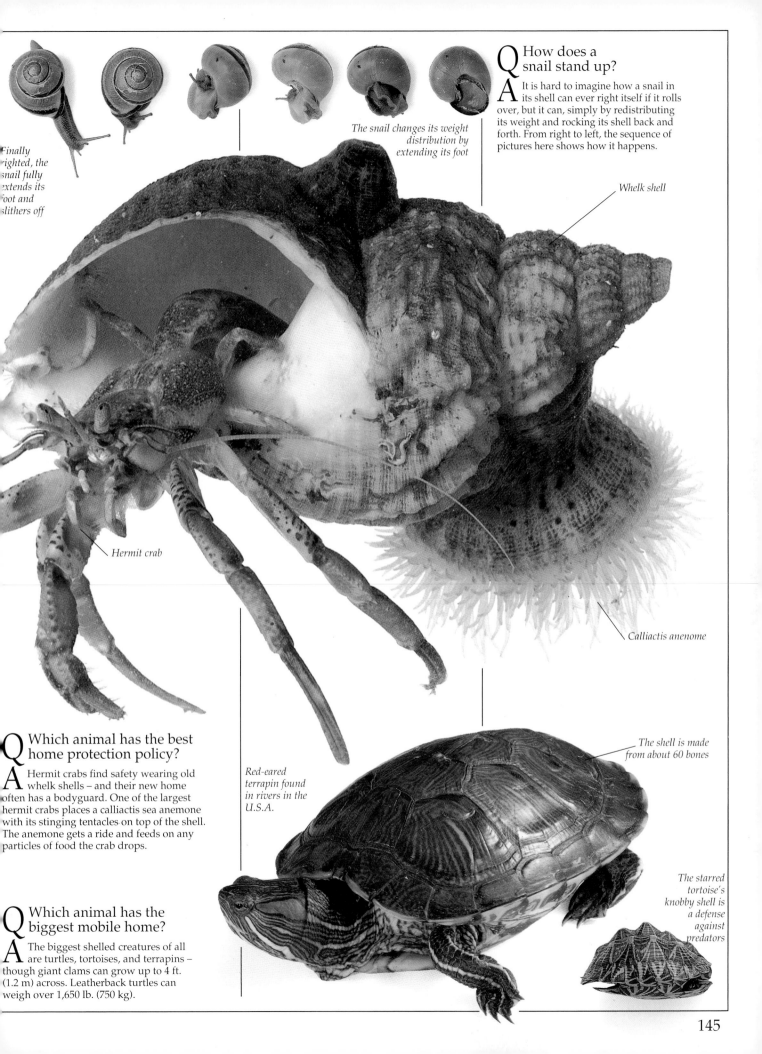

Finally righted, the snail fully extends its foot and slithers off

The snail changes its weight distribution by extending its foot

Q How does a snail stand up?

A It is hard to imagine how a snail in its shell can ever right itself if it rolls over, but it can, simply by redistributing its weight and rocking its shell back and forth. From right to left, the sequence of pictures here shows how it happens.

Whelk shell

Hermit crab

Calliactis anenome

Q Which animal has the best home protection policy?

A Hermit crabs find safety wearing old whelk shells – and their new home often has a bodyguard. One of the largest hermit crabs places a calliactis sea anemone with its stinging tentacles on top of the shell. The anemone gets a ride and feeds on any particles of food the crab drops.

Red-eared terrapin found in rivers in the U.S.A.

The shell is made from about 60 bones

Q Which animal has the biggest mobile home?

A The biggest shelled creatures of all are turtles, tortoises, and terrapins – though giant clams can grow up to 4 ft. (1.2 m) across. Leatherback turtles can weigh over 1,650 lb. (750 kg).

The starred tortoise's knobby shell is a defense against predators

145

Who lays eggs?

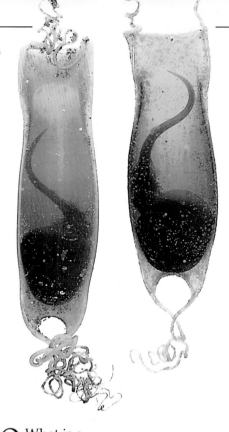

NEARLY EVERY CREATURE starts life as an egg – even humans. Only creatures that reproduce asexually, such as flatworms and hydra, begin life any other way. But though most insects, birds, fish, reptiles, and amphibians actually lay eggs, only a few mammals do, such as the duckbilled platypus of Australia. Most mammals and a few lizards and snakes are viviparous. This means they give birth to fully developed young.

Male midwife toad from western Europe carrying strings of eggs on its back

Q What is a mermaid's purse?

A Mermaid's purses are the hard, horny egg cases of dogfish, skates, and rays. A female dogfish usually lays them in pairs and attaches them to seaweeds by the long, curly tendrils at each corner. The embryos then grow by themselves for six to nine months before wriggling out into the water.

Q What makes a baby spiny anteater special?

A Spiny anteaters are monotremes, which means they are mammals that hatch from eggs. The only other monotremes are duckbilled platypuses.

Q How does a young snake hatch out of its egg?

A A baby snake is ready to hatch from its egg at between seven and 15 weeks. To cut its way through the shell it has a special, sharp egg tooth. Snake eggs vary considerably. Most are round and have a tough papery skin but some hardly look like eggs at all. The mother snake usually buries her eggs in soil or rotting vegetation and then leaves them there to hatch out on their own.

Q Why are guillemot eggs pointed?

A Guillemots are sea birds that lay their eggs on a bare cliff ledge instead of building a nest. The egg's pointed shape probably prevents the mother from accidentally knocking it off the ledge. If it begins to roll, its shape means it will roll right around in a circle.

Some males take on two or even three egg clutches

Eggs

Young larva

Mature larva

Q How does a stag beetle change as it grows up?

A Like many insects, it goes through several changes, or metamorphoses, starting life as an egg, hatching to a larva, then changing through several larval stages to a pupa from which the adult emerges.

Male pupa

Female pupa

Q How long does a bird's egg take to hatch?

A Birds' eggs are surprisingly tough, and it can take a baby bird hours or even days of hard work to break through into the outside world. Typically, though, it takes around half an hour. The pheasant pictured here took 33 minutes from the moment when the first crack appeared.

Q How does the midwife toad get its name?

A Remarkably, it is not the mother midwife toad who looks after the eggs, but the father. After they have been laid, he winds strings of eggs around his back legs and carries them around with him, dipping his legs in pools and streams every now and then to keep the eggs damp. After about three weeks, he returns to water for the eggs to hatch.

Darker color shows egg will soon hatch

Caterpillar cuts its way out with sharp jaws

Caterpillar emerges from shell

Q Who lays the biggest eggs?

A Some dinosaurs laid huge eggs of course, but the biggest birds' eggs are laid by giant flightless birds. The extinct "elephant bird" of Madagascar laid eggs weighing 26 lb. (12 kg). But ostriches and emus lay large eggs, too. An ostrich's egg may weigh up to 3.3 lb. (1.5 kg) and an emu's 1.5 lb. (0.7 kg). The kiwi is no bigger than a chicken, yet lays eggs of 1 lb. (0.45 kg) – more than a quarter of the female's entire weight.

Emu

Kiwi

Q When does a butterfly egg change color?

A Butterfly and moth eggs laid in fall go into a resting stage called diapause in winter. When spring comes and the weather gets warmer, the eggs darken in color as the tiny caterpillars get ready to emerge by biting their way through the shell.

147

When did it happen?

HISTORY is full of fascinating facts about how human life first arose, how primitive hunters and gatherers first settled down to farm, trade, and build towns, and how civilizations and societies slowly grew. But how many of them do you know? Read the questions here, then turn over the pages and check your answers.

Who invented the chronometer?

Who was Darius the Great?

Why did the Spanish go to America?

Who wore "paper" sandals?

Who made the first panpipes?

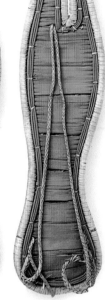

How could you play a goblet?

What did the ancient Greeks keep in an amphora?

Which beetle was sacred to the ancient Egyptians?

Who or what was an ammonite?

How did James Cook know where he was?

Who had tool-shaped coins?

Who were the first shepherd boys?

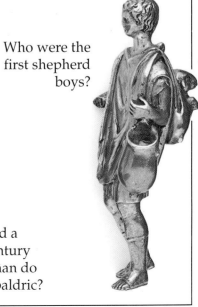

How did a 17th-century gentleman do up his baldric?

When did life begin?

THE EARTH IS ABOUT 4,600 MILLION YEARS OLD, but life probably began in the sea about 3,800 million years ago. Ancient rocks dating from this time contain microscopic specks that may be fossilized, bacterialike organisms, and, in some 3,500-million-year-old rocks, there are ring-shaped fossils called stromatolites, a special kind of algae that grew in warm, shallow seas. But it was not until 400 million years ago that the first primitive creatures walked on land.

Q Who or what is an ammonite?

A An ammonite is a kind of extinct shellfish that had a hard, external shell. Fossils of these creatures are very common in rocks dating from the time of the dinosaurs, 200 to 64 million years ago. In northern England, people believed ammonites were the remains of coiled snakes turned to stone by the seventh-century abbess St. Hilda.

Fern

Cycad frond

Anthracite, the hardest form of coal

Q Why is coal called a fossil fuel?

A Because it is made from the fossilized remains of giant ferns and cycads that grew in the steamy swamps that covered much of the world in the Carboniferous period, 345 to 280 million years ago. Oil and natural gas are also fossil fuels, but they are formed from the remains of sea creatures, not plants.

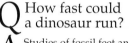

Q How fast could a dinosaur run?

A Studies of fossil feet and footprints prove that not all dinosaurs were cumbersome and slow. Some, especially the two-legged dinosaurs, may have been quite agile. The fossil foot here belonged to an *Iguanodon*, probably one of the slower two-legged dinosaurs, which could shuffle along at around 1 mph (1.5 kmh). Smaller, lighter dinosaurs may have been able to run at over 25 mph (40 kmh).

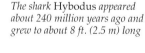

The shark Hybodus *appeared about 240 million years ago and grew to about 8 ft. (2.5 m) long*

Q When did sharks first terrorize the oceans?

A The first sharks appeared in the ancient seas nearly 400 million years ago, which is about 200 million years before dinosaurs roamed the Earth. The remains of some of these early sharks were fossilized when they sank to the bottom of the sea. Hard parts, such as spines or teeth, fossilized more readily than soft parts, such as the sharks' rubbery skeleton of cartilage.

Q Did dinosaurs eat flowers?

A Many plant-eating dinosaurs would have eaten flowers, such as magnolias, which are among the oldest of all flowering plants. Still popular in gardens today, they date from around 100 million years ago.

Magnolia flower

Q How old are sea urchins?

A Sea urchins are among the oldest sea creatures and have lived in the oceans since at least the Cambrian period, about 490 million years ago. Because their skeletons or shells are made from a resistant substance called calcite, they are often preserved as fossils. Fossilized sea urchins are sometimes called thunderstones because some people believed they had fallen from the sky during a thunderstorm.

Q Why did *Triceratops* have three horns on its head?

A The three horns and large bony frill on the head of the fearsome-looking plant-eating *Triceratops* were most probably used as a defense against ferocious meat eaters. *Triceratops* were four-legged and stocky, similar to modern rhinoceroses, and belonged to a group called ceratopians. It is thought that *Triceratops* may have roamed in herds 65 million years ago.

Brow horn

Eye socket

Nose horn

Nostril

Parrotlike beak

Triceratops skull

Flint weapon from Central America

Australopithecine skull

Q Why is Lucy the oldest girl in the world?

A Australopithecines are the most ancient of all our ancestors dating back at least 3.75 million years. In 1974, in Ethiopia, the oldest australopithecine skeleton ever found was excavated and called "Lucy" after the Beatles' song "Lucy in the Sky with Diamonds," which was playing at the time.

Q Is it true that mammoths once lived in New York?

A Until about 10,000 years ago, giant woolly mammoths roamed over much of Europe and North America, including the area now covered by New York. This statue of a mammoth, skillfully carved from an animal's shoulder blade, was made by a hunter at least 15,000 years ago.

Sea urchins

Q When did people learn the secret of fire?

A Fire was one of the most important discoveries ever made. The first fires were probably lit accidentally by lightning. People first learned how to light fires by rubbing sticks together about 250,000 years ago.

Q When was the Stone Age?

A The Stone, or Paleolithic, Age began a million years ago with the appearance of *Homo erectus*, the first humanlike creature to walk upright. It is called the Stone Age because during this period, which lasted for hundreds of thousands of years, people hunted only with shaped and sharpened stones. These stones are virtually all they left behind to tell of their existence. The Stone Age ended some 6,000 years ago with the discovery of bronze and the start of the Bronze Age.

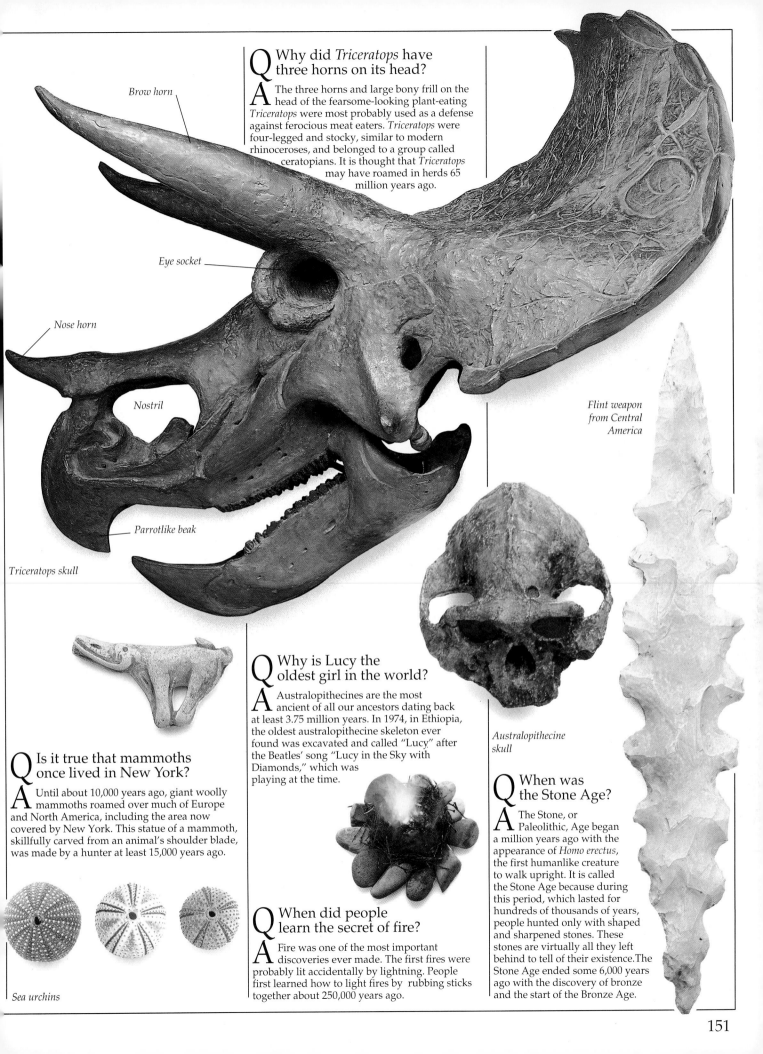

151

Where is the oldest town?

FOR MOST OF PREHISTORY, people were nomads, traveling from place to place to hunt animals and gather wild plants to eat. But around 10 to 12,000 years ago, some people began to settle down and farm the land. Soon after, some small communities grew into towns, and with towns came the first civilizations. The word "civilization" comes from the Latin for town. No one knows for certain where civilization began, but it was probably in the Middle East, where the world's most ancient cities are to be found. The oldest is Jericho, on the West Bank of the Jordan River. It is over 10,000 years old.

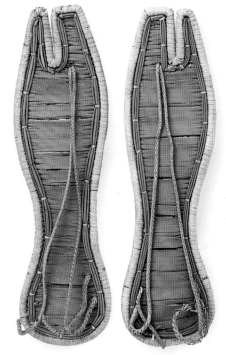

Q Why did Egyptians value Horus' eye?

A The wedjat eye symbolized the eye of the god Horus. It was torn out by Seth in the struggle for the throne of Egypt, but was magically restored. It was said to protect all who stood behind it.

Q Who invented eye shadow?

A People have probably always painted their faces, but the first to wear anything like modern makeup were the ancient Egyptians, over 4,000 years ago. Egyptian men and women both wore eye paint, made from minerals ground on fine slate palettes.

Q Who wore "paper" sandals

A The Egyptians made a kind of paper for writing on, by cutting and flattening strips from the papyrus reed that once flourished along the River Nile. The word "paper" comes from papyrus. They also made sandals from papyrus, which were worn by people at all levels of society. Priests were forbidden to wear any other material on their feet.

Q Did early people play ball?

A Ancient Egyptian children played much the same games as children do today – including leapfrog, tug-of-war, and skipping. They had balls made of clay filled with seeds, which rattled as they were thrown.

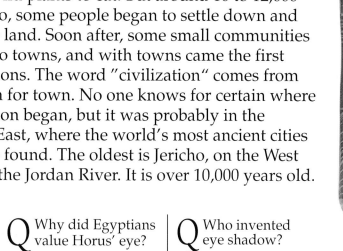

Khnum

Q Did Hapi make people happy?

A Hapi was the god of the River Nile's yearly flood. Ancient Egyptian farmers relied on the Nile flooding to irrigate their land and bring rich, fertile silt deposits, which benefited their crops. Hapi would only rise in flood on the word of the ram-headed god Khnum, who ruled over the wild Nile cataracts. After the flood, happy farmers gave part of their crop to the god's temple in thanks.

Q Which beetle was sacred to the ancient Egyptians?

A To the Egyptians the scarab, or dung beetle, symbolized the sun god Khepri. They imagined Khepri pushed the Sun across the sky in the same way as the beetle pushes a ball of dung around.

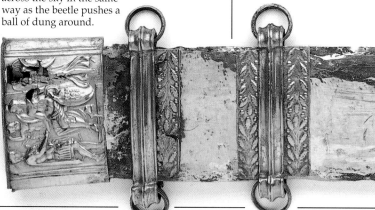

Q Who was Darius the Great?

A Darius the Great was king of Persia from 522 to 485 BC. It was under him that the Persian empire reached its greatest extent, stretching from Egypt to India. Darius divided the empire into regions, or satrapies, and founded the stunning city of Persepolis, which was an important civic and religious center. This silver goat is just one of the treasures found near the remains of the city.

Q Who invented the signs of the zodiac?

A The first evidence of the signs of the zodiac comes from the ancient city of Babylon in what is now Iraq. Babylon was founded over 4,000 years ago and reached its height in the 18th century BC. The Babylonian terracotta plaque here shows the ancestor of the water sign Aquarius carrying streams of water.

Q Which was the most powerful army in the ancient world?

A The Romans had the most powerful and disciplined army in the ancient world, and with it they built an empire that reached from Scotland to the Red Sea. The army played a very important role in Roman society and a talented soldier could expect promotion and rewards. This beautiful scabbard decorated with silver and gold may have been given to a Roman officer by the emperor Tiberius.

Q Where does classical architecture come from?

A Classical architecture is the style first seen in the beautiful temples of the ancient Greeks 2,500 years ago and widely imitated ever since. Greek temples were geometrical in shape with tall, graceful columns and broad horizontal lintels. Shown here is a roof tile from the temple to the god Apollo at Bassae in southern Greece.

Q What did the ancient Greeks keep in an *amphora*?

A The Greeks were famous for their high-quality pots made from clay fired to a rich reddish brown. Pots were made in different shapes according to how they were used. *Amphorae*, like the pot shown here, were used for storing wine. Greek pottery was often beautifully decorated with scenes from Greek myths. In the early sixth century, potters used the black-figure technique, painting black figures on to red. Later they painted the background in black.

Q Did Romans have keys?

A Lock and keys are an ancient invention used by the Egyptians 4,000 years ago. The Romans, too, had locks and keys. Roman keys had a complicated shape which slotted through the keyhole into a pattern of holes in the hidden bolt.

Who believed in gods?

ALL ANCIENT CIVILIZATIONS had their own religions and beliefs. Most were polytheistic, which meant they worshiped more than one god. Much of what we know today comes to us through ancient myths or through archaeological finds that show the lives of the gods. Some of the best-known myths belong to the ancient Greeks.

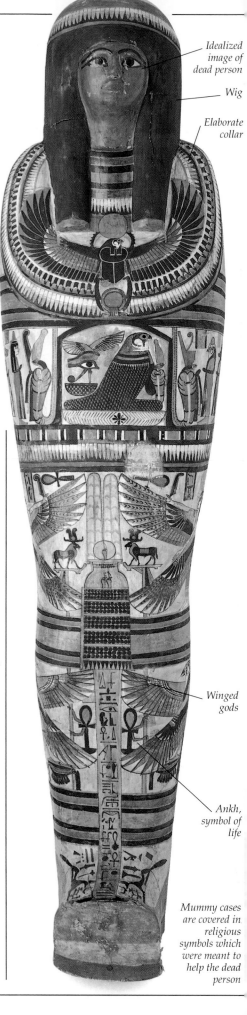

Idealized image of dead person

Wig

Elaborate collar

Winged gods

Ankh, symbol of life

Mummy cases are covered in religious symbols which were meant to help the dead person

Q Why did the Egyptians mummify their dead?

A The Egyptians believed that a person's soul left the body at death. After the burial, the soul was reunited with the body. But, in order for the body and the soul to live on in the afterlife, the body had to be preserved by a mummification process known as embalming. This entailed cutting out the vital organs, then covering the body in crystals of natron, packing it with sawdust and leaves, and wrapping it in linen bandages. The mummified body was then laid in a coffin or mummy case. The technique of embalming developed gradually over ancient Egypt's long history. It reached its peak around 1000 BC, but Romans living in Egypt were still being mummified in the third century AD.

Bronze head from eastern Turkey

Q Who was the ancient Greek goddess of love?

A Aphrodite, known to the Romans as Venus, was the ancient goddess of love. The word "aphrodisiac," meaning a love potion, comes from her name. She was said to have been born from the sea foam and blown by Zephyrs (West Winds) to Cyprus.

Q How many gods did the ancient Greeks have?

A The ancient Greeks had literally hundreds of gods. Besides scores of Olympian gods, each with their own temple, there were many household and local gods attached to places, such as the river god shown in this fired clay face.

Q How did a mirror save Perseus?

A Perseus was a Greek hero sent to behead the terrible she-monster Medusa. But anyone who looked on the Medusa would turn to stone. To avoid this, and succeed in his task, Perseus looked only at her reflection in his shiny shield. In this picture, Medusa sinks to the ground as Perseus escapes with her head in his bag.

Ancient Greek vase painting from 460 BC showing Perseus and the Medusa

Q Who was Horus and why was he important to the Egyptians?

A Horus, represented by a falcon, was the Egyptian sky god from whom all the pharaohs were descended. This royal bracelet depicts him as a child protected by two cobras.

Q What did the letters XP mean in ancient Rome?

A For the ancient Romans, the letters XP were a sign of Christianity. X and P are symbols made from the first two letters of Christ's name in the Greek alphabet, *chi* (X) and *rho* (P). This fragment of gold glass from the last days of the Roman empire shows a Christian family.

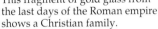

Q Who made this statue – and why?

A This small, white marble statue of a female figure was made in ancient Greece probably about 2,500 years ago during the early Bronze Age. But people today still cannot be certain why it was made, or for whom. As it is of a stylized female figure, it may represent its owner or a goddess, or it may be a fertility symbol.

Q Who was the Babylonian goddess of love and war?

A Ishtar was worshiped as the goddess of love and war by the Babylonians, Sumerians, and Assyrians. She was the Babylonians' chief goddess, and the great blue northern gate of Babylon was named after her. This blue plaque comes from the temple of Ninurta in the Assyrian city of Nimrud and dates from around the ninth century BC. The winged goddess is probably meant to represent Ishtar as goddess of love.

Q Who gave gold pendants to the gods?

A These gold pendants were found in the Fosse Temple, a late Bronze-Age Canaanite sanctuary in the ancient Israeli city of Lachish. They were probably left there by Canaanite people as an offering to the gods.

Q What does the Jewish *menorah* represent?

A *Menorah* is the Hebrew word for candlestick. In the Old Testament it refers to the seven-branched candlestick that stood in the Temple of Jerusalem and was removed by the Romans in AD 70.

Q Who were Zeus and Apollo and how were they related?

A In ancient Greece, many of the gods and goddesses were related. Zeus was the king of all the gods and ruled the Earth and the sky. He is usually shown as a strong, bearded figure throwing a thunderbolt. Zeus had many children, one of whom was the handsome young Apollo. Apollo was the god of sunshine and of poetry, music, and medicine.

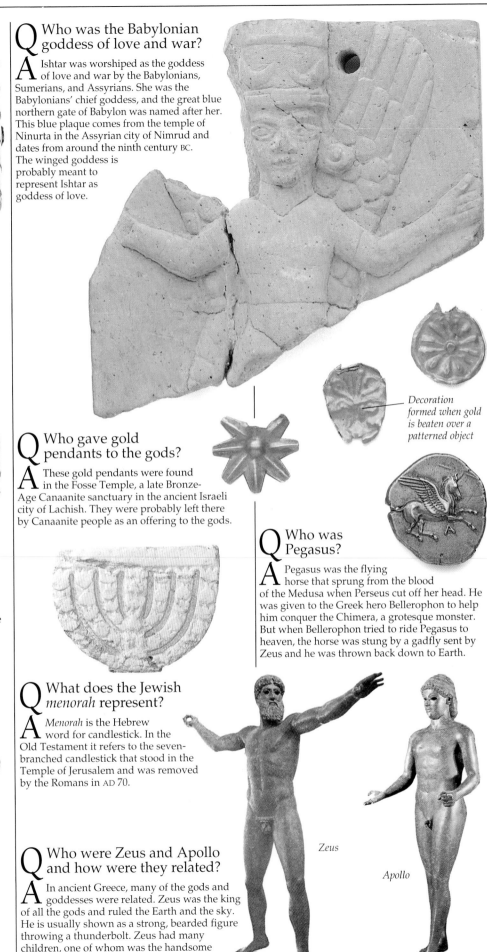

Decoration formed when gold is beaten over a patterned object

Q Who was Pegasus?

A Pegasus was the flying horse that sprung from the blood of the Medusa when Perseus cut off her head. He was given to the Greek hero Bellerophon to help him conquer the Chimera, a grotesque monster. But when Bellerophon tried to ride Pegasus to heaven, the horse was stung by a gadfly sent by Zeus and he was thrown back down to Earth.

Zeus

Apollo

Where is the Fertile Crescent?

FARMING BEGAN about 12,000 years ago in the Middle East. For the first time in human history, people began to form small communities, growing their own food and raising animals. As more and more settlements were gradually established, large areas of land were cultivated, and the whole region became known as the Fertile Crescent. Today, this area, which includes parts of modern-day Israel, Turkey, Iraq, and Iran, is largely desert. But the farming techniques learned there have been adopted worldwide.

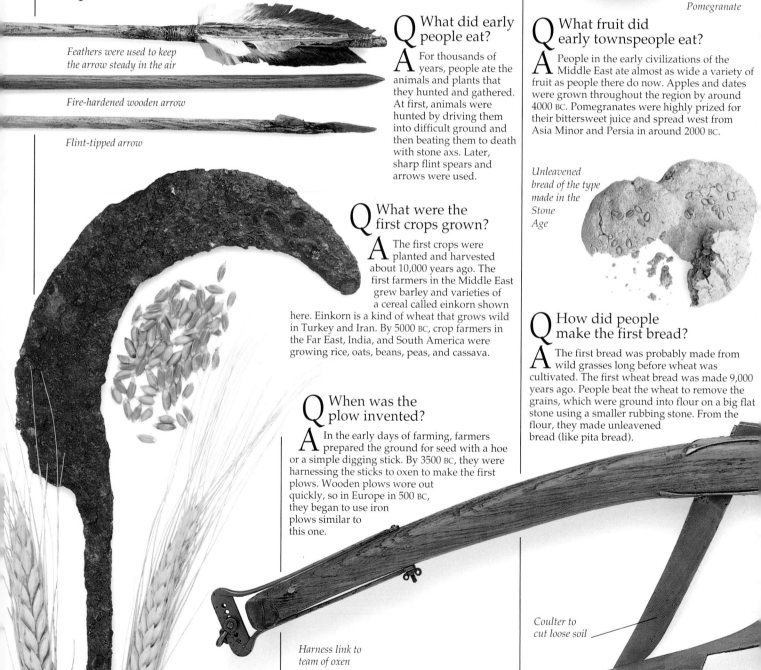

Pomegranate

Feathers were used to keep the arrow steady in the air

Fire-hardened wooden arrow

Flint-tipped arrow

Q What did early people eat?

A For thousands of years, people ate the animals and plants that they hunted and gathered. At first, animals were hunted by driving them into difficult ground and then beating them to death with stone axs. Later, sharp flint spears and arrows were used.

Q What fruit did early townspeople eat?

A People in the early civilizations of the Middle East ate almost as wide a variety of fruit as people there do now. Apples and dates were grown throughout the region by around 4000 BC. Pomegranates were highly prized for their bittersweet juice and spread west from Asia Minor and Persia in around 2000 BC.

Unleavened bread of the type made in the Stone Age

Q What were the first crops grown?

A The first crops were planted and harvested about 10,000 years ago. The first farmers in the Middle East grew barley and varieties of a cereal called einkorn shown here. Einkorn is a kind of wheat that grows wild in Turkey and Iran. By 5000 BC, crop farmers in the Far East, India, and South America were growing rice, oats, beans, peas, and cassava.

Q How did people make the first bread?

A The first bread was probably made from wild grasses long before wheat was cultivated. The first wheat bread was made 9,000 years ago. People beat the wheat to remove the grains, which were ground into flour on a big flat stone using a smaller rubbing stone. From the flour, they made unleavened bread (like pita bread).

Q When was the plow invented?

A In the early days of farming, farmers prepared the ground for seed with a hoe or a simple digging stick. By 3500 BC, they were harnessing the sticks to oxen to make the first plows. Wooden plows wore out quickly, so in Europe in 500 BC, they began to use iron plows similar to this one.

Harness link to team of oxen

Coulter to cut loose soil

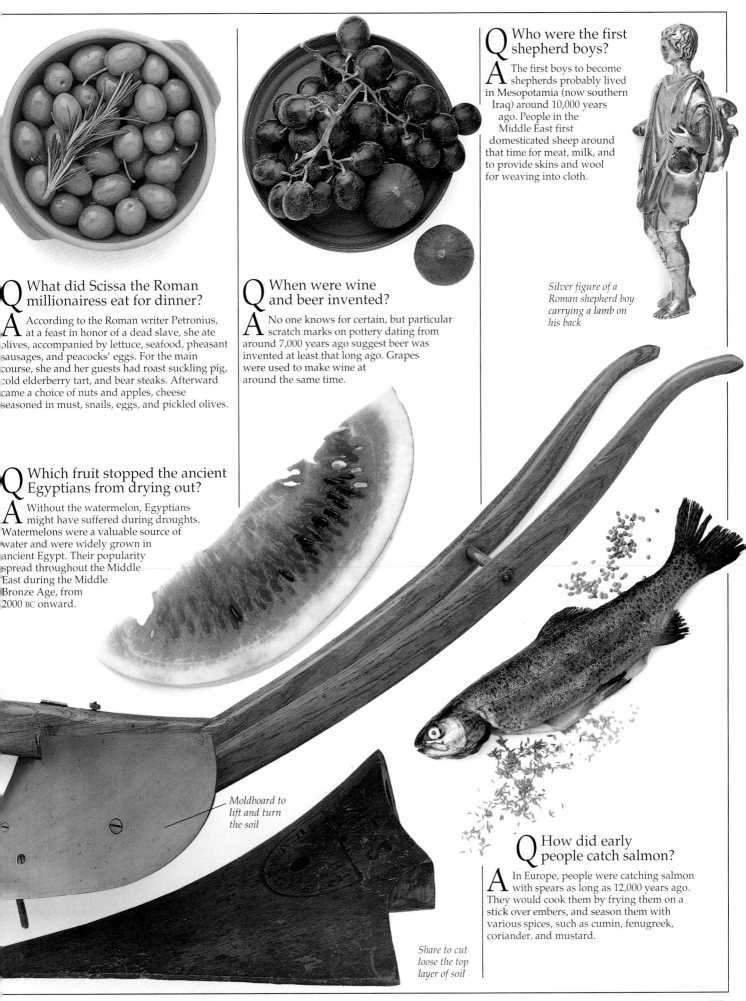

Q Who were the first shepherd boys?

A The first boys to become shepherds probably lived in Mesopotamia (now southern Iraq) around 10,000 years ago. People in the Middle East first domesticated sheep around that time for meat, milk, and to provide skins and wool for weaving into cloth.

Silver figure of a Roman shepherd boy carrying a lamb on his back

Q What did Scissa the Roman millionairess eat for dinner?

A According to the Roman writer Petronius, at a feast in honor of a dead slave, she ate olives, accompanied by lettuce, seafood, pheasant sausages, and peacocks' eggs. For the main course, she and her guests had roast suckling pig, cold elderberry tart, and bear steaks. Afterward came a choice of nuts and apples, cheese seasoned in must, snails, eggs, and pickled olives.

Q When were wine and beer invented?

A No one knows for certain, but particular scratch marks on pottery dating from around 7,000 years ago suggest beer was invented at least that long ago. Grapes were used to make wine at around the same time.

Q Which fruit stopped the ancient Egyptians from drying out?

A Without the watermelon, Egyptians might have suffered during droughts. Watermelons were a valuable source of water and were widely grown in ancient Egypt. Their popularity spread throughout the Middle East during the Middle Bronze Age, from 2000 BC onward.

Moldboard to lift and turn the soil

Q How did early people catch salmon?

A In Europe, people were catching salmon with spears as long as 12,000 years ago. They would cook them by frying them on a stick over embers, and season them with various spices, such as cumin, fenugreek, coriander, and mustard.

Share to cut loose the top layer of soil

Who were the first merchants?

THE FIRST MERCHANTS probably appeared in the Middle East. Archaeologists excavating the remains of the ancient city of Ugarit in modern Iraq have found 10,000-year-old clay tokens that they may have used for buying and selling goods. By 4,000 BC, Sumerian merchants were traveling far and wide, trading food, cloth, pots, and knives for timber, stone, and metals.

Q. When were coins first used?

A. The earliest known coins were made in the 7th century BC in Lydia in what is now Turkey. Lydian coins were simply lumps of electrum, a mixture of gold and silver, but each was weighed and stamped with pictures showing their value.

Ancient Greek silver coin, 6th century BC

Ancient Roman silver coin, 3rd century BC

Ancient Indian gold coin, 1st century AD

Australian aluminum-bronze two-dollar coin, 1988

Ottoman Turkish gold zeri-mahbub, 18th century

Q. Who had tool-shaped coins?

A. Early Chinese coins were always cast from bronze in the shape of tools, such as knives, sickles, and hoes. The bronze coin shown here is in the shape of a hoe and dates from around 300 BC. Eventually, people began to find these shapes awkward, and in 221 BC they were replaced by round coins with square holes.

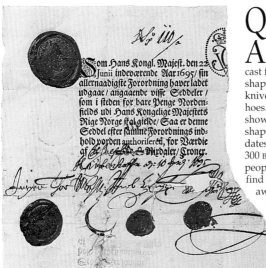

Ancient Roman gold bar, made from melted-down coins, 4th century AD

Q. When did the first banknotes appear?

A. In the 10th century, coins in China were so heavy and worth so little that people preferred to leave them with merchants and use the handwritten receipts the merchants gave them instead. In the 11th century, the government took over and began to issue printed receipts with fixed values – the first banknotes. The idea caught on in Europe in the 17th century, and Europe's first printed notes appeared in Sweden in 1661. The Norwegian note shown here dates from 1695.

Q. Who were the first great iron merchants?

A. People probably discovered how to use iron to make tools and weapons around 8,000 years ago, but for a long time, the knowledge was restricted to a small area of the Middle East. The Hittite people who lived in what is now Turkey made a fortune selling iron in places such as Greece, and were probably the first great iron merchants. Eventually the Greeks learned to make iron themselves as this painting from a Greek urn shows.

Q. What are coins made from?

A. Many early coins were made from precious metals like gold and silver, and the value of the coin depended simply on the value of the metal they contained. Today, however, coins are usually made from cheap alloys such as cupro-nickel (copper and nickel) and the metal in the coin is worth much less than the value stamped on it at the mint.

Q Which blue stone went to Egypt?

A Merchants from what is now called Afghanistan used to trade the beautiful blue stone lapis lazuli with the ancient Egyptians. They brought it to trading centers like Byblos in Lebanon. The Egyptians prized this stone, because they believed the hair of their sun god was made from lapis lazuli.

Lapis lazuli bull set in gold

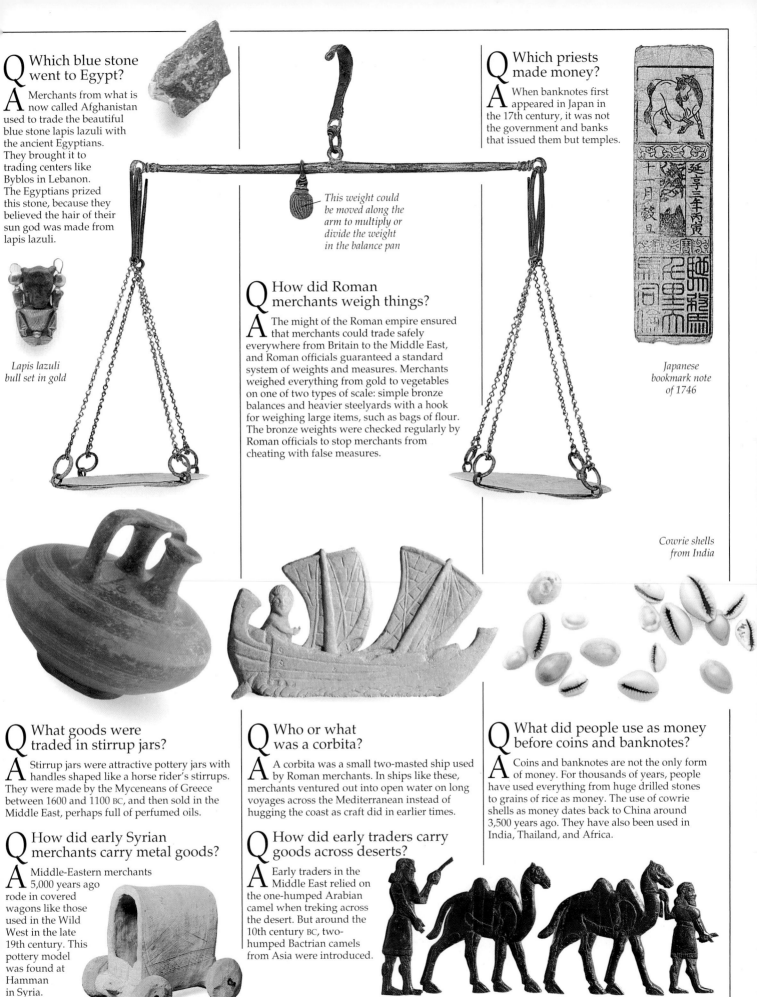

This weight could be moved along the arm to multiply or divide the weight in the balance pan

Q How did Roman merchants weigh things?

A The might of the Roman empire ensured that merchants could trade safely everywhere from Britain to the Middle East, and Roman officials guaranteed a standard system of weights and measures. Merchants weighed everything from gold to vegetables on one of two types of scale: simple bronze balances and heavier steelyards with a hook for weighing large items, such as bags of flour. The bronze weights were checked regularly by Roman officials to stop merchants from cheating with false measures.

Q Which priests made money?

A When banknotes first appeared in Japan in the 17th century, it was not the government and banks that issued them but temples.

Japanese bookmark note of 1746

Cowrie shells from India

Q What goods were traded in stirrup jars?

A Stirrup jars were attractive pottery jars with handles shaped like a horse rider's stirrups. They were made by the Myceneans of Greece between 1600 and 1100 BC, and then sold in the Middle East, perhaps full of perfumed oils.

Q How did early Syrian merchants carry metal goods?

A Middle-Eastern merchants 5,000 years ago rode in covered wagons like those used in the Wild West in the late 19th century. This pottery model was found at Hamman in Syria.

Q Who or what was a corbita?

A A corbita was a small two-masted ship used by Roman merchants. In ships like these, merchants ventured out into open water on long voyages across the Mediterranean instead of hugging the coast as craft did in earlier times.

Q How did early traders carry goods across deserts?

A Early traders in the Middle East relied on the one-humped Arabian camel when treking across the desert. But around the 10th century BC, two-humped Bactrian camels from Asia were introduced.

Q What did people use as money before coins and banknotes?

A Coins and banknotes are not the only form of money. For thousands of years, people have used everything from huge drilled stones to grains of rice as money. The use of cowrie shells as money dates back to China around 3,500 years ago. They have also been used in India, Thailand, and Africa.

How was the world explored?

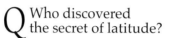

Star
Scale
Crosspiece
Horizon

SOME OF THE GREATEST JOURNEYS into the unknown were on foot, such as Marco Polo's travels in China in the 12th century, Livingstone's in Africa in the 1850s, and Scott's in the Antarctic in the early 1900s. But it was sea voyages, above all, that steadily widened our knowledge of the world – starting 3,000 years ago with the Phoenicians and reaching a peak around 1500 with great seamen like Diaz, Columbus, and Magellan.

Q How did early explorers know where they were?

A On long sea voyages, the heavens provided early explorers with their only clue to where they were. In the 1500s, many used a cross staff to work out the height of stars in the sky and the latitude of the ship.

Q Who discovered the secret of latitude?

A Arab explorers of the sixth and seventh centuries could find their approximate location at sea with a device called a quadrant. This was a quarter circle with a plumbline attached. They could work out latitude – how far north or south they were – by lining up one side with a star and reading off the position of the plumbline.

Q Why did Scott take a chemistry set to the South Pole in 1910?

A Explorers often brought back immensely valuable scientific data. By carrying out simple chemical experiments, Robert Scott hoped to learn more about the minerals in the ancient rocks of Antarctica.

Q What was the seamen's curse – and who broke it?

A Early voyages of exploration were plagued by the disease scurvy – known as the seamen's curse. The first explorer to realize scurvy could be prevented by eating fresh fruit was James Cook (1728–1779), who broke the curse by taking citrus fruits and pickled cabbage on his voyage to the South Pacific in 1768.

Q Were all explorers' tales true?

A No. The temptation for explorers to elaborate tales of strange places and weird creatures must have been great, and in the 1800s all too many explorers were claiming to have discovered new species. By the time Mary Kingsley went to West Africa in the 1890s, naturalists wanted specimens to prove these species really did exist – which is why she carefully preserved this snoutfish found in the Ogowe River to bring it back to Britain.

Q Who first crossed the Atlantic?

A The question of who was the first to make it across the Atlantic arouses fierce passions, but we know the Vikings made the voyage 500 years before Columbus. In 1001, Leif Erikson set out from Greenland with a few longships like the one shown here to investigate rumors of a vast land to the southwest – and reached America. The Vikings called the land Vinland, and settled there for a century or so.

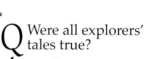

Q How did James Cook know where he was?

A Early seaborne explorers could find their direction with the aid of a magnetic compass – first used by the Chinese over 2,000 years ago. They could also find their latitude from the Sun and stars. But they could only guess longitude – that is, how far east or west they were. On his second voyage Cook could not only find his latitude to within 0.01° with a sextant, but his longitude, too, with a highly accurate clock called a chronometer, designed just a few years before by the ingenious Yorkshire clockmaker John Harrison.

Italian compass from 1719

The sextant used by Cook on his third voyage in 1776

Q What was the secret of Columbus's success?

A None of the great voyages of the 1400s – Diaz's around Africa (1487), Columbus's to the Americas (1492), and Da Gama's to India (1498) – could have been made without the caravel. Though small and light, these boats were fast enough for sailors to risk sailing far out across the ocean.

A chronometer used by Cook on his second voyage to the Pacific in 1772

Crow's-nest – used by the crew to look out for land, or hostile ships

Q Why did the Spanish go to America?

A In the hope, above all, of finding gold. Adventurers such as Francisco Pizarro and Hernando Cortés were lured to the New World by tales of the huge wealth of the Incas and Aztecs.

Q Why did it take so long for Europeans to explore Africa?

A Europeans could get slaves, gold, and other goods from coastal areas. Further inland, travel was treacherous: mountains, deserts, and dense forest barred the way. Tropical diseases could kill in a day, and African peoples strongly resisted any invasion. The arrows below were fired into David Livingstone's boat as he explored the Zambezi River in the 1850s.

Large hold for carrying supplies

Why wear clothes?

HUMANS HAVE NO FUR or feathers to keep them warm and dry, nor do they have thick hides to protect them from thorns or scorching Sun – so they need to make their own body protection. The first clothes were probably animal skins that Ice-Age cave dwellers wrapped around themselves for warmth. Gradually, people learned to fit skins to their bodies with stitching, and about 10,000 years ago, the first woolen cloth was woven. But clothes do not only protect: they hide nakedness and may also show status.

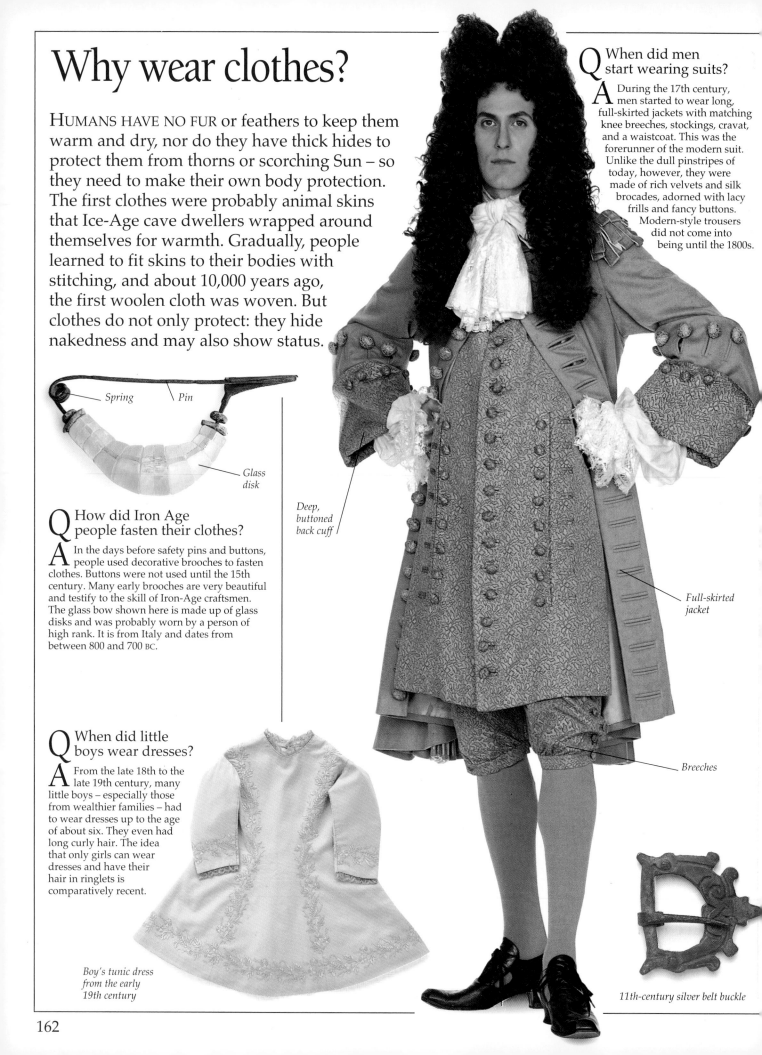

Spring *Pin*

Glass disk

Q How did Iron Age people fasten their clothes?

A In the days before safety pins and buttons, people used decorative brooches to fasten clothes. Buttons were not used until the 15th century. Many early brooches are very beautiful and testify to the skill of Iron-Age craftsmen. The glass bow shown here is made up of glass disks and was probably worn by a person of high rank. It is from Italy and dates from between 800 and 700 BC.

Q When did little boys wear dresses?

A From the late 18th to the late 19th century, many little boys – especially those from wealthier families – had to wear dresses up to the age of about six. They even had long curly hair. The idea that only girls can wear dresses and have their hair in ringlets is comparatively recent.

Boy's tunic dress from the early 19th century

Q When did men start wearing suits?

A During the 17th century, men started to wear long, full-skirted jackets with matching knee breeches, stockings, cravat, and a waistcoat. This was the forerunner of the modern suit. Unlike the dull pinstripes of today, however, they were made of rich velvets and silk brocades, adorned with lacy frills and fancy buttons. Modern-style trousers did not come into being until the 1800s.

Deep, buttoned back cuff

Full-skirted jacket

Breeches

11th-century silver belt buckle

162

Q How did worms color Greek life?

A Ancient Greek women loved to dye their chitons (dresses) in bright colors. One of their favorites was a rich crimson made from the skin of the tiny kermes worm, which lives in the bark of holly and oak trees. During the day, the worms burrow deep inside the bark, but at night they come out on to the surface where girls with long nails picked them off.

Ancient Greek girl wearing a chiton

Q Who dressed in a cage?

A The cage crinoline was devised in 1856 to make skirts fashionably full. Until this time, women in the early 1800s had achieved the desired fullness only by wearing up to six heavy petticoats – one of which was stuffed with horsehair. Women could not wait to dress in cages.

Light steel wire hoops gave shape to the cage crinoline

Q When did children's fashion begin?

A Since the ancient civilizations of Egypt, Rome, and Greece, children have worn the same style of clothes as their parents. It was not until the late 18th century that children's clothes began to have a style of their own and their owners ceased to look like small adults. But during the 19th century children's styles were still very formal as this illustration shows. Only after World War II did children's clothes begin to have the casual style they have today.

Pair of Blackfoot moccasins

Q Who wore gold dolphin earrings?

A The ancient Romans often used dolphin motifs in art and for jewelry, such as these two gold earrings. If a Roman saw a dolphin it was said to be a good omen and a promise of good weather. The Roman author Pliny told the story of a dolphin that carried a poor man's son to school each day. The story was probably inspired by ancient Greek coins that showed a picture of the son of the sea god Poseidon riding a dolphin.

Q When did vandals wear brooches?

A The Vandals were one of the German peoples that began to threaten the Roman empire in the sixth century. The Romans thought all Germans were coarse and barbaric, but their spectacular jewelry proves otherwise. The beautiful brooch above was made by a German group called the Ostrogoths from silver, gold, green glass, and red garnet in about AD 500.

Q When did people begin to wear high-heeled shoes?

A High heels were first worn in the late 16th century – by both women and men. Until this time, shoes had flat heels and took all kinds of bizarre shapes. Early in the 16th century, they were so wide that in England, Henry VIII decreed that no shoe should be wider than 6 in. (15 cm). Back in the 14th century, the fashion was for long, pointed shoes. The toes could be 20 in. (50 cm) long and were stuffed with moss to keep their shape. Such shoes were considered by the Church to be the work of the devil.

14th-century leather shoe

16th-century leather shoe

Q What could a Native American scout tell from a lost moccasin?

A Moccasins were the soft leather or buffalo rawhide shoes worn by Native Americans. Each tribe decorated shoes in a unique way with brightly colored beads. So, if a moccasin was lost, a scout could tell which tribe it came from.

Q How did a 17th century gentleman do up his baldric?

A A baldric was a kind of sash worn over the shoulder to carry a sword or stick – and it was fastened with a buckle. Indeed, in the 17th century, buckles were used to fasten almost everything including baldrics, shoes, belts, and breeches. Until about 1720, shoe buckles were small and plain. But then rich people began to wear huge diamond and silver buckles while poorer people made do with big steel, brass, and quartz buckles.

Baldric buckle from c.1680

Diamond and silver buckle from c.1730

Silk-covered ladies' high-heeled shoe from c.1690

Who started athletics?

SPORTS have always played an important role in every society for players and spectators alike. Even prehistoric peoples may have taken pleasure from kicking a makeshift ball around or enjoyed the glory of winning a race against a rival. But the first regular sporting events were probably the athletic festivals held by the ancient Greeks. Here, young men would compete in the pentathlon, discus, long jump, and track events.

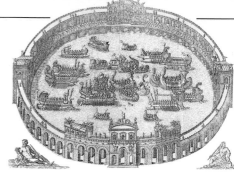

Q What happened if the Roman *retiarius* lost his net?

A The Romans enjoyed much more bloody and sensational sports than the ancient Greeks. Tens of thousands of them would crowd into huge stadia to watch battles to the death between gladiators. One type of gladiator was the *retiarius*, or net man, who was unarmed apart from a net and a Neptune's trident. The aim was for the *retiarius* to catch his opponent in the net and stab him. But if he lost his net, he was usually doomed to die.

Gold glass picture of a retiarius ready to do battle in the arena

Q Why were there ships in the Colosseum?

A As Romans got bored with simple fighting games, they wanted to see more and more spectacular events. When it first opened, the arena of the Colosseum in Rome could be flooded with water so that "sea battles" could be fought between gladiators in small ships.

Competitors in the pentathlon

Q How did the marathon get its name?

A In 490 BC, the Greeks won a heroic victory over the invading Persians on the plain of Marathon, northeast of Athens. At once, a young Greek runner called Pheidippides set off to Athens with the good news. Sadly, he died on arrival. However, over two thousand years later, in 1896, the first modern marathon was named in his honor and run over the distance from Marathon to Athens, 26 miles, 385 yards.

Q Where were the first Olympics held?

A The Olympic Games were the biggest of all the ancient Greek sporting festivals. They were staged every four years in Athens in honor of the god Zeus who lived on Mount Olympus on the Greek mainland. The ancient games died out in the fourth century AD, but the spirit was revived when the first modern Olympics were held in Athens in 1896.

Q When did gloves become compulsory in boxing?

A The bare knuckle fights popular in England in the 18th and 19th centuries were brutal. Boxing was reformed in 1867 with the introduction of the Queensberry Rules. The rules, which included three-minute rounds and wearing gloves, came into force in 1872.

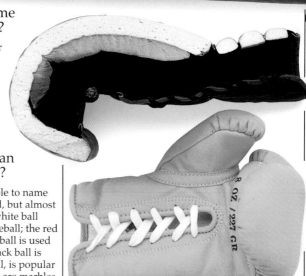

Q How many games can you play with a ball?

A It would be almost impossible to name every ball game in the world, but almost every country has its favorites. The white ball shown here is used for American baseball; the red ball is a British cricket ball; the silver ball is used for the French game of boules; the black ball is a bowl, which like the yellow golf ball, is popular everywhere; and the small glass balls are marbles, which Roman children loved to play with.

Lawn tennis racket from the 1880s

Fashionable fishtail handle racket from the 1900s

Q When were tennis rackets first used?

A Tennis probably originated in the ancient French game of *jeu de paume*, played between two people who hit a ball to each other with the palms of their hands. After a while, players started to use sticks to hit the ball. Then in the 15th century, the first strung rackets were introduced. The basic shape of rackets has changed little since then, though materials are dfferent. Early rackets were made from wood, with gut strings. Modern rackets are molded from light and strong new synthetic materials, such as carbon fiber, fiberglass, boron, and ceramic.

Classic laminated wood racket from the 1950s

Q How did badminton get its name ?

A It is thought to be named after the home of the Duke of Beaufort at Badminton in Gloucestershire, England. There in the 1870s the Duke's dinner guests played a parlor game called battledore and shuttlecock, adapted from a children's pastime. It involved hitting the shuttlecock to and fro over a net with a battledore (bat).

Metal racket from the 1970s enabling players to hit the ball faster

Molded racket from the 1980s

Q How did softball and baseball begin?

A People played games with a ball and long bat as long ago as the Middle Ages, but modern games of baseball and softball are probably based on the old English game of rounders, played with a smaller bat and introduced to North America by settlers during the 18th century.

Q Why do runners wear spiked shoes?

A Track athletes use spiked track shoes. These are tight fitting, lightweight, and the spikes give a good grip on the front of the sole where the foot touches the ground.

Counter of Quarte

Counter of Sixte

Counter of Septime

Counter of Seconde

Q What is a Counter of Septime in fencing?

A A Counter of Septime is one of various circular movements used to deflect the opponent's blade, beginning and ending with the sword angled downward. As with many fencing terms, it originated in the 16th or 17th century, when the light court sword was introduced in France.

Who played a mammoth bone flute?

HUMANS HAVE ENJOYED MUSIC for thousands of years. Around 20,000 years ago, Cro-Magnon people played mammoth bone flutes, and archaeologists have discovered reindeer toe bone whistles that date back 40,000 years. But the first music we know anything about was played by the Sumerians over 5,000 years ago in what is now Iraq. There are Sumerian signs that may be some of the first written music, pictures show lyres and harps, and an 11-string harp was found in the royal tombs at Ur.

Q How could you play a goblet?

A Goblets are single-headed drums which are popular throughout the Arab world. Like the Egyptian darabuka shown here, they are usually made of pottery or wood and have a stretched skin beaten with both hands.

Q Who made the first panpipes?

A Pan was an ancient Greek god. When the nymph that he loved was turned into a reed, he cut the reed into a set of pipes, which he played to console himself. Today panpipes are popular in South America.

Q Which fiddle could fit in a pocket?

A In the 18th century, a dancing master would often use a kit, a pocket-sized violin, when he went to give lessons to young ladies at the great country houses. A kit was only 16 in. (40 cm) long.

Q When is a fish like a recorder?

A This pottery fish doesn't look much like a recorder, but it makes music in just the same way. In both, a short duct (air channel) leads air from the mouth to blow holes in the side. It is the vibration of the air in between that makes the sound.

Tuning peg

Q What kind of music does a Portuguese fish make?

A This fish-shaped *rajao* from Portugal is a kind of lute and would have been used for playing folk music in Madeira in the 19th century. Like all lutes it was plucked, like a guitar. The lute is one of the oldest instruments and the long lute, which has a long neck and short body, dates back at least 4,000 years. The European classical lute evolved from the *'ud*, an Arabian lute that reached Europe in the 13th century.

Lutes are plucked like the guitar and usually have a fretted fingerboard

Flared bell

Valve

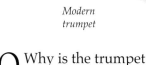

Modern trumpet

Q Why is the trumpet a natural bandleader?

A The lead instrument in many bands and orchestras is often the trumpet because it can play loud, high notes and easily leads over softer and deeper instruments. The trumpet is a brass instrument often favored by jazz musicians who make full use of the different moods that can be created. All the notes on a trumpet are achieved with just three valves.

Q Which dinosaur had a head for music?

A The hadrosaurs, which lived over 70 million years ago, had a long bony tube that extended into a crest behind the head. Dinosaur experts believe that some hadrosaurs, like this *Parasaurolophus*, may have been able to "talk" to each other by making sounds with these tubes – vibrating air inside them just as in a hunting horn.

Q What do Spanish dancers do with their castanets?

A Castanets are cup-shaped pieces of wood that Spanish flamenco dancers hold in the palms of their hands and clap together quickly to create an exciting, rhythmic click as they dance. Castanets are percussion instruments, which produce sounds when they are hit or shaken.

Q Where does the harp originate?

A Harps are among the oldest of all instruments, and were invented independently in many places around the world. The Sumerians had them, and so, too, did the ancient Egyptians. There are wall paintings of Egyptian harps dating back over 4,000 years. The *tsaung* shown here is a modern instrument from Myanmar (Burma), but it is very similar to the harps of ancient Egypt.

Q What was Roman music like?

A The ancient Romans loved wild dances, especially at the riotous feasts of Cybele, when musicians would play frenzied music on a variety of instruments, such as pipes, lyres, horns, and flutes. Although we know much about the people and their instruments, we cannot be sure what Roman music itself was like but it may have been similar to modern Greek folk music.

Q Who invented the record player?

A In 1877, American inventor Thomas Alva Edison invented the first machine for recording sound, called a phonograph. It worked by scoring grooves on paraffin-soaked paper with a steel needle. A year later, he replaced the paper with tinfoil. But when the first recorded music went on sale in 1886, it was on wax cylinders. The gramophone, with flat discs, was invented in 1888 by E. Berliner.

Horn to amplify the sound

The music is recreated as the needle is vibrated by the little bumps in the record's grooves

Early gramophone

Q Which instrument do you strap around your neck and squeeze?

A The accordion can be carried anywhere. It is supported by straps, leaving the musician's hands free to squeeze the bellows and press the keys and buttons. Pressing the keys and buttons allows air from the bellows to pass through sets of free metal reeds. Since they were invented in Berlin in the 1820s, accordions have become popular with folk musicians around the world.

Who invented it?

SCIENCE AND TECHNOLOGY affect all of us in our daily lives. Every day we use machines and tools, travel on planes and trains, watch movies and television, and take books and newspapers for granted. But how much do you know about the people who made and invented these things and why? See if you can answer the questions here – then turn the pages and test your knowledge.

Why are racing cars faster than ordinary cars?

How did a tug-of-war make ships faster?

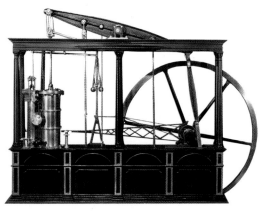

What was special about James Watt's engine?

Who revolutionized the revolver?

What was the first telephone message?

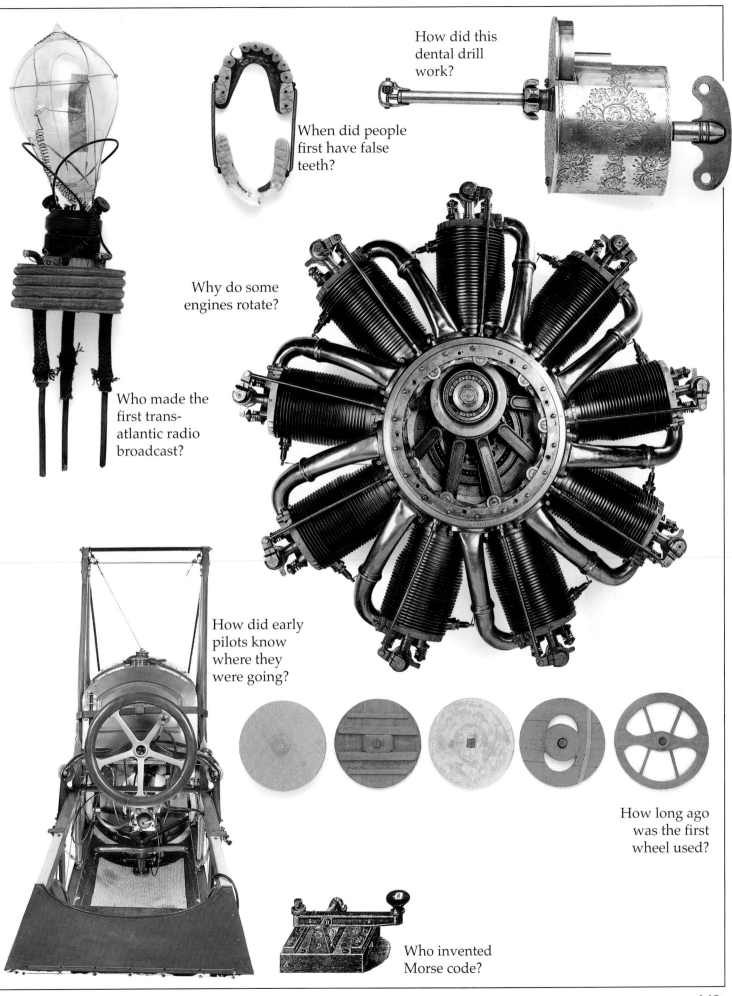

How did this dental drill work?

When did people first have false teeth?

Why do some engines rotate?

Who made the first trans-atlantic radio broadcast?

How did early pilots know where they were going?

How long ago was the first wheel used?

Who invented Morse code?

Who made the first tools?

ALMOST AS SOON as they began to walk upright some 3.5 million years ago, our distant, humanlike ancestors began to use sharp stones for ripping meat and smashing animal bones. But the first real toolmakers were hominids like *Homo habilis* who emerged some 2 million years ago. Not for nothing does *Homo habilis* mean "handy man," for he was extremely handy with stone tools, chipping edges off stones not only to saw meat but to cut hides for clothing. By 400,000 years ago, people had learned to shape flint axes and spearheads.

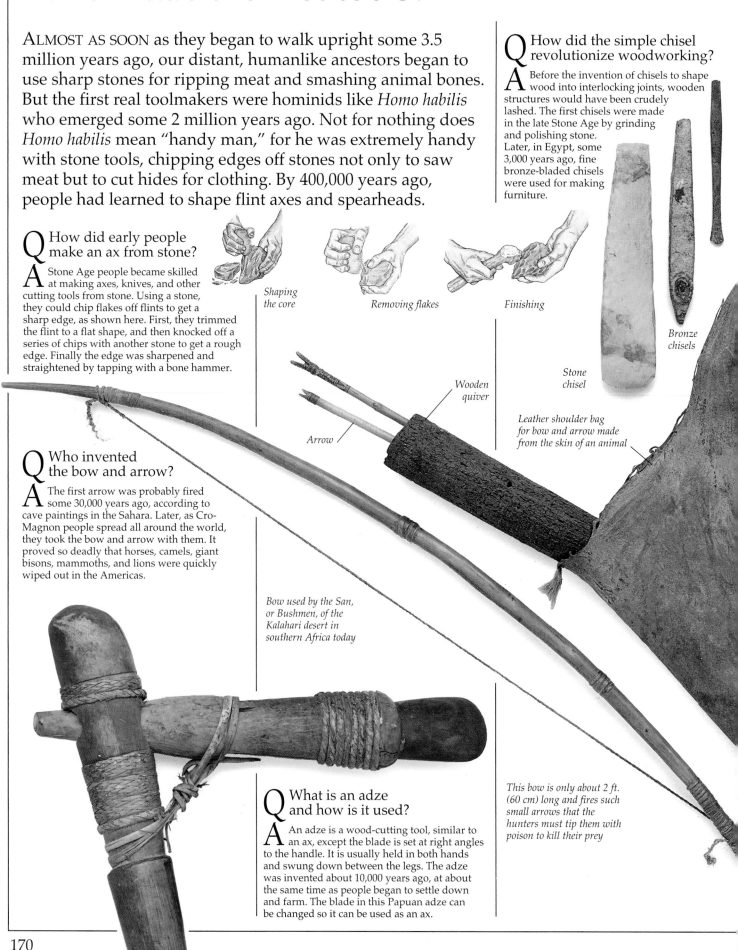

Q How did early people make an ax from stone?

A Stone Age people became skilled at making axes, knives, and other cutting tools from stone. Using a stone, they could chip flakes off flints to get a sharp edge, as shown here. First, they trimmed the flint to a flat shape, and then knocked off a series of chips with another stone to get a rough edge. Finally the edge was sharpened and straightened by tapping with a bone hammer.

Shaping the core

Removing flakes

Finishing

Q How did the simple chisel revolutionize woodworking?

A Before the invention of chisels to shape wood into interlocking joints, wooden structures would have been crudely lashed. The first chisels were made in the late Stone Age by grinding and polishing stone. Later, in Egypt, some 3,000 years ago, fine bronze-bladed chisels were used for making furniture.

Bronze chisels

Stone chisel

Wooden quiver

Arrow

Leather shoulder bag for bow and arrow made from the skin of an animal

Q Who invented the bow and arrow?

A The first arrow was probably fired some 30,000 years ago, according to cave paintings in the Sahara. Later, as Cro-Magnon people spread all around the world, they took the bow and arrow with them. It proved so deadly that horses, camels, giant bisons, mammoths, and lions were quickly wiped out in the Americas.

Bow used by the San, or Bushmen, of the Kalahari desert in southern Africa today

Q What is an adze and how is it used?

A An adze is a wood-cutting tool, similar to an ax, except the blade is set at right angles to the handle. It is usually held in both hands and swung down between the legs. The adze was invented about 10,000 years ago, at about the same time as people began to settle down and farm. The blade in this Papuan adze can be changed so it can be used as an ax.

This bow is only about 2 ft. (60 cm) long and fires such small arrows that the hunters must tip them with poison to kill their prey

Q What is unusual about these knives?

A They were made by Inuit (Eskimos) out of scraps of steel found in ships abandoned in the Arctic by Sir John Franklin on his fatal last trip in 1845. They sharpened the steel and attached the blades to handles made of bone.

Straps made from animal's legs

Inuit knives made from steel and bone

The natural coloring in the safflower, or dyers' thistle, was used 4,000 years ago to dye cloth red and yellow

Early spindle

Q How were the first woolen clothes made?

A The first woolen clothes were probably made about 10,000 years ago by people in the Middle East, which is where sheep were first domesticated. The raw wool was plucked off the back of the sheep when it was shedding, spun into a single thread using a spindle, and then woven into cloth. The first woolen cloth was not colored, but by 2000 BC, people had learned how to dye it bright colors using natural dyes.

Q How did people start fires before matches were invented?

A By turning the point of a kind of wooden drill very fast on a block of wood, early people generated enough friction and heat to start a fire in dry grass. Some people twisted the drill by hand; others used a bow in the way shown below. The leather thong made it easier to twist the drill quickly.

Model of a bow drill

Using a bow drill

Wooden hearth showing holes where the drill has been used

Main handle

Winch

Main wheel

Pinion

Chuck

Q How do gearwheels work?

A This brace drill, used for working in confined spaces, incorporates some of the most basic engineering principles. The wheels are adapted as gears and pinions and the drill bit is in the form of a screw to give it better forward motion. The use of gears means that the turning force of the handle is increased and transmitted down to the bit.

What was the first weapon?

THE FIRST WEAPONS were the stones prehistoric people used for hunting over 300,000 years ago. These were revolutionized by adding a handle or haft to make spears and axes. The invention of the bow some 30,000 years ago was another major step, and the coming of metals in the Bronze Age enabled swords to be made. Swords gave way to firearms in the 1700s.

Q What did a pistol owner carry in his flask?

A Gunpowder. Until self-contained cartridges were introduced in the mid19th century, pistols had to be loaded through the muzzle. First, gunpowder was poured from the flask into the muzzle of the gun. Then the lead bullet was wrapped in a cloth or leather patch and rammed into the muzzle with a metal or wooden ramrod.

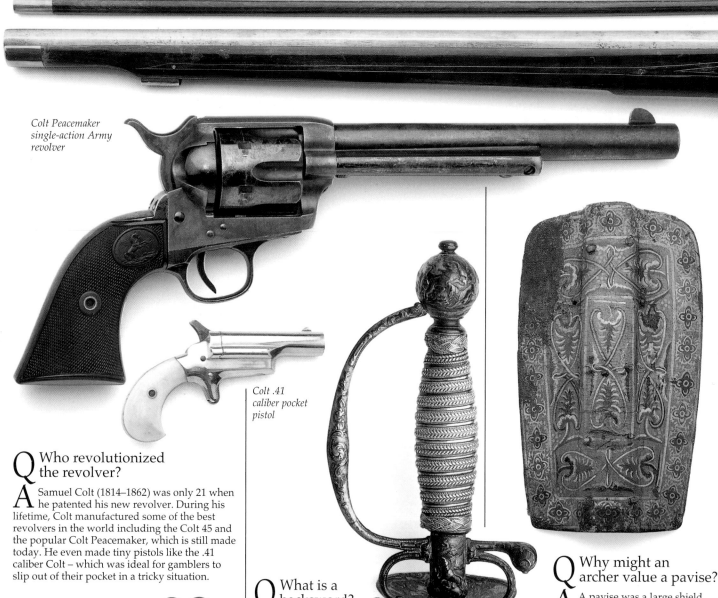

Colt Peacemaker single-action Army revolver

Colt .41 caliber pocket pistol

Q Who revolutionized the revolver?

A Samuel Colt (1814–1862) was only 21 when he patented his new revolver. During his lifetime, Colt manufactured some of the best revolvers in the world including the Colt 45 and the popular Colt Peacemaker, which is still made today. He even made tiny pistols like the .41 caliber Colt – which was ideal for gamblers to slip out of their pocket in a tricky situation.

Q How were lead bullets made?

A Flintlock pistols were popular in the 18th century, replacing swords for duels between gentlemen. The lead ball or bullet was made at home, using a special bullet-shaped mold that came with the pistol. Lead was melted over a fire and poured into the mold. After a few seconds the mold was opened like a pair of scissors and the ball shaken out. Any excess lead was trimmed off with shears.

Q What is a backsword?

A A backsword is a kind of military sword used by European cavalry in the 17th century for both cutting and thrusting at an opponent in battle. Like all swords of the the time, it was much lighter and easier to handle than the massive swords of the Middle Ages. Fighting with swords like these was a highly skilled art.

Q Why might an archer value a pavise?

A A pavise was a large shield that medieval archers and crossbowmen would shelter behind while firing their weapons. Used between the 14th and the 16th centuries, the pavise was as big as a man and made of wood covered with canvas. Since the archer needed both hands for firing his bow, the pavise was usually supported by another soldier. The pavise shown here dates from the mid15th century and was commonly used in siege warfare.

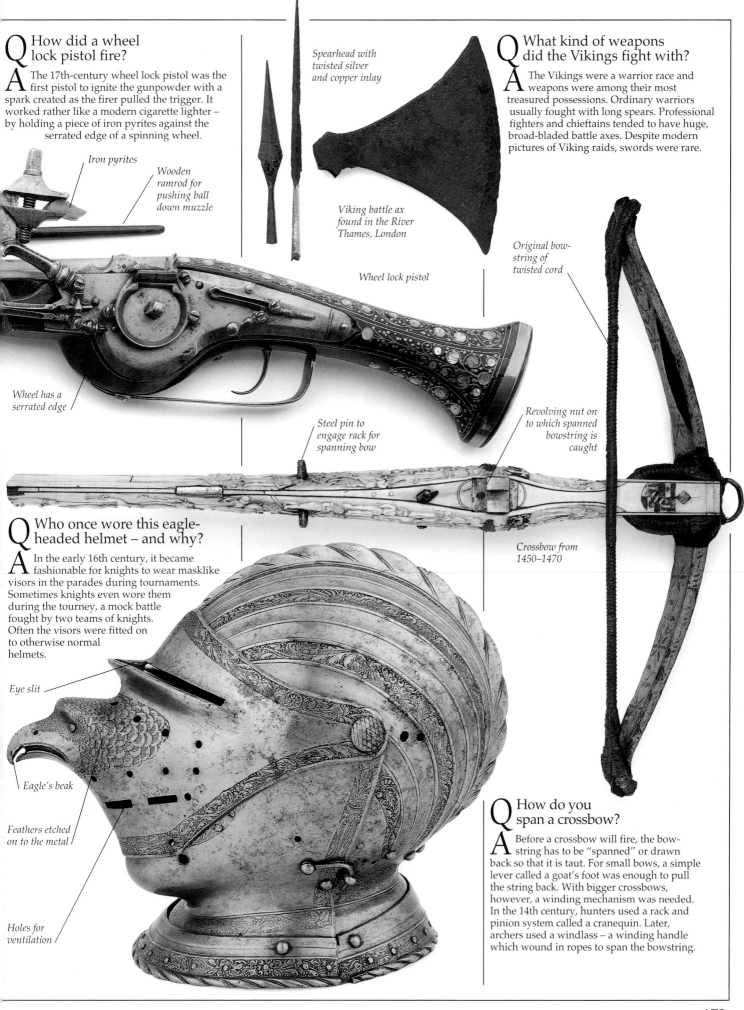

Q How did a wheel lock pistol fire?

A The 17th-century wheel lock pistol was the first pistol to ignite the gunpowder with a spark created as the firer pulled the trigger. It worked rather like a modern cigarette lighter – by holding a piece of iron pyrites against the serrated edge of a spinning wheel.

Iron pyrites

Wooden ramrod for pushing ball down muzzle

Wheel has a serrated edge

Spearhead with twisted silver and copper inlay

Viking battle ax found in the River Thames, London

Wheel lock pistol

Q What kind of weapons did the Vikings fight with?

A The Vikings were a warrior race and weapons were among their most treasured possessions. Ordinary warriors usually fought with long spears. Professional fighters and chieftains tended to have huge, broad-bladed battle axes. Despite modern pictures of Viking raids, swords were rare.

Original bow-string of twisted cord

Steel pin to engage rack for spanning bow

Revolving nut on to which spanned bowstring is caught

Crossbow from 1450–1470

Q Who once wore this eagle-headed helmet – and why?

A In the early 16th century, it became fashionable for knights to wear masklike visors in the parades during tournaments. Sometimes knights even wore them during the tourney, a mock battle fought by two teams of knights. Often the visors were fitted on to otherwise normal helmets.

Eye slit

Eagle's beak

Feathers etched on to the metal

Holes for ventilation

Q How do you span a crossbow?

A Before a crossbow will fire, the bow-string has to be "spanned" or drawn back so that it is taut. For small bows, a simple lever called a goat's foot was enough to pull the string back. With bigger crossbows, however, a winding mechanism was needed. In the 14th century, hunters used a rack and pinion system called a cranequin. Later, archers used a windlass – a winding handle which wound in ropes to span the bowstring.

Who was the first true doctor?

THERE HAVE BEEN HEALERS and medicine men since prehistoric times. But the father of modern medicine was the Greek physician Hippocrates (c. 460–380 BC), who based his treatments on careful study of the body. He believed that a good diet and hygiene were the first essentials of good health. The Hippocratic Oath that many doctors take when they begin to practice is named after him.

The Harrington "Eardo" clockwork dental drill, dating from about 1863

Breathing sack placed over the patient's mouth

Q When did people first have false teeth?

A Crude dentures were made by the Etruscans of Italy about 2,700 years ago. The first full set of false teeth like those today was made in France in the 1780s. The set shown here, though, dates from about 1860 – about the same time as dentists started to drill teeth to try to get rid of decay.

Ancient Egyptian amulets

Q Why might a Roman make a model ear?

A Ancient Romans and Greeks believed injuries and ailments could be cured more quickly if they donated a votive model of the afflicted part to the gods. So when Romans visited the temple to ask for a cure for earache, they would leave behind a model ear. They might also leave a votive offering in gratitude once the ear was better.

Greek model leg offered in thanks for a cure to the god Asclepius

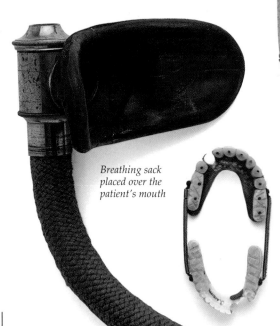

Q Why did the ancient Egyptians wear charm bracelets?

A The ancient Egyptians wore bracelets with special magical amulets dangling from them. Spells were often cast on these amulets and the Egyptians believed they would ward off injury.

Q Which South American plants contain addictive drugs?

A Many do, but the best known are the coca plant and the Mexican mescal cactus. The natives of South America discovered long ago that chewing the leaves of the coca plant dulled pain and prevented tiredness. Today, people derive the stimulating and dangerous drug cocaine from coca leaves. Cocaine is highly addictive and there is a huge illegal trade in it from Colombia. The mescal cactus yields a drug called mescaline, which causes hallucinations. It is often used in religious rituals by native Mexican tribes. Confusingly, the Mexican drink mescal comes not from the mescal cactus but from another plant, *Agave tequilana*.

The drink mescal made from Agave tequilana

Mescal cactus

Coca leaves

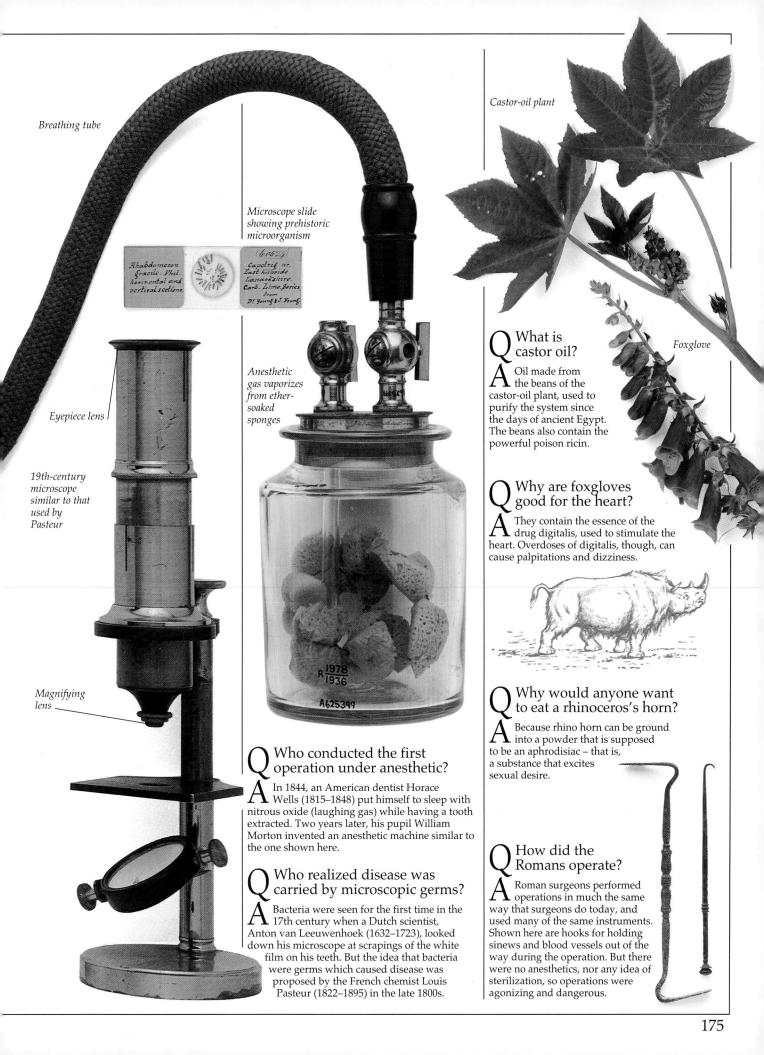

Breathing tube

Microscope slide
showing prehistoric
microorganism

*Rhabdomeson
gracile - Phil.
horizontal and
vertical sections.*

(60524)

*Capelrig nr.
East Kilbride
Lanarkshire.
Carb. Lime Series
from
Dr Young & J. Young.*

Castor-oil plant

Anesthetic
gas vaporizes
from ether-
soaked
sponges

Foxglove

Eyepiece lens

19th-century
microscope
similar to that
used by
Pasteur

Magnifying
lens

R 1978/1936

A625399

Q What is castor oil?

A Oil made from
the beans of the
castor-oil plant, used to
purify the system since
the days of ancient Egypt.
The beans also contain the
powerful poison ricin.

Q Why are foxgloves good for the heart?

A They contain the essence of the
drug digitalis, used to stimulate the
heart. Overdoses of digitalis, though, can
cause palpitations and dizziness.

Q Why would anyone want to eat a rhinoceros's horn?

A Because rhino horn can be ground
into a powder that is supposed
to be an aphrodisiac – that is,
a substance that excites
sexual desire.

Q Who conducted the first operation under anesthetic?

A In 1844, an American dentist Horace
Wells (1815–1848) put himself to sleep with
nitrous oxide (laughing gas) while having a tooth
extracted. Two years later, his pupil William
Morton invented an anesthetic machine similar to
the one shown here.

Q Who realized disease was carried by microscopic germs?

A Bacteria were seen for the first time in the
17th century when a Dutch scientist,
Anton van Leeuwenhoek (1632–1723), looked
down his microscope at scrapings of the white
film on his teeth. But the idea that bacteria
were germs which caused disease was
proposed by the French chemist Louis
Pasteur (1822–1895) in the late 1800s.

Q How did the Romans operate?

A Roman surgeons performed
operations in much the same
way that surgeons do today, and
used many of the same instruments.
Shown here are hooks for holding
sinews and blood vessels out of the
way during the operation. But there
were no anesthetics, nor any idea of
sterilization, so operations were
agonizing and dangerous.

How fast can a message be sent?

FOR THOUSANDS OF YEARS THE ONLY WAY TO get a complicated message over any distance was to carry it physically – which made communication very slow. In 1649, it took over a week for people in northern England to learn that Charles I had been executed. Today, modern electronics enable us to send words, pictures, and sounds almost instantaneously across the world via telephones, radio, television, and other media.

Diode valve

Q Who invented printing?

A The Chinese made printed books like this one as long ago as the sixth century AD. They used characters engraved on a block of wood, clay, or ivory, which was inked and pressed against the paper. By the 11th century, the Chinese were using movable type – single characters on small individual blocks that could be set in any order and used again and again.

Casts of early Turkish type

Q Who was the first person to appear on television?

A When a Scottish inventor, John Logie Baird, was experimenting with television he paid a 15-year-old office boy called Bill Taynton half a crown (18 cents) to appear on the screen in October 1925. Baird gave the world's first public demonstration of television the following January and became famous overnight. Ten years later, the BBC began to broadcast television pictures from its studio at Alexandra Palace in London, shown above.

Q Who printed the Bible first?

A In about 1438, a German goldsmith, Johannes Gutenberg, invented "typecasting"– a way of making type of individual letters from molten metal. These letters could then be set by hand on the page ready for printing. He completed the first printed Bible in 1455.

Q Can a drum talk?

A Yes. Nigerians use this *kalengo* to "talk" by pressing the cords to raise or lower the note produced as they beat the drum. The drum makes the sounds of a tonal, African language and can communicate very complex messages.

Q Who made the first transatlantic radio broadcast?

A In 1901, an Italian inventor, Guglielmo Marconi (1874–1937), sent the first radio signal across the Atlantic from Poldhu in Cornwall, England to St. John's in Newfoundland, Canada. These early radio signals were very faint and were picked up by certain crystals that allowed current to pass only in one direction. In 1904, however, an English electrical engineer John Ambrose Fleming invented the diode or tube, which picked up the signals much better. Two years later, in 1906, an American inventor Lee De Forest added an extra element to make a triode, which enabled the signal to be amplified.

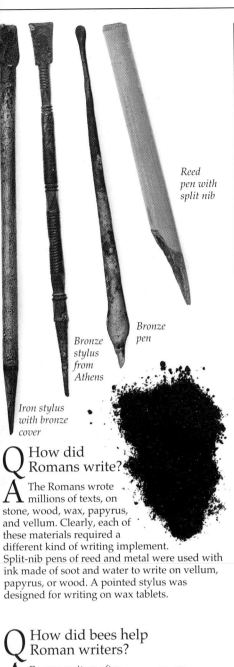

*Reed
pen with
split nib*

*Bronze
pen*

*Bronze
stylus
from
Athens*

*Iron stylus
with bronze
cover*

Q What was the first telephone message?

A In 1875, a Scots inventor, Alexander Graham Bell, constructed the first experimental telephone. Then on March 10, 1876, he transmitted the first telephone message to a colleague in a room upstairs: "Mr Watson, come here. I want to see you." Within a few years, people were calling each other on telephones like the wall-mounted phone shown here, designed by Thomas Edison in 1879.

Earpiece

Mouthpiece

The user had to wind the handle while listening

Q How did Romans write?

A The Romans wrote millions of texts, on stone, wood, wax, papyrus, and vellum. Clearly, each of these materials required a different kind of writing implement. Split-nib pens of reed and metal were used with ink made of soot and water to write on vellum, papyrus, or wood. A pointed stylus was designed for writing on wax tablets.

Q How did bees help Roman writers?

A Roman writers often wrote everyday letters on wax. Beeswax was melted and poured into shallow cavities in wooden tablets. When it hardened, people could scratch their message with a sharp stylus.

Q How do gypsy moths communicate?

A Female gypsy moths produce a very faint scent (a pheromone), which can attract males from as far as 7 miles (11 km) away.

Q Who invented Morse code?

A An American, Samuel Morse, patented Morse code in 1838. Every letter of the alphabet was represented by a series of dots and dashes. Morse's code was adopted by the first electric telegraphs when they came into operation in 1843. The telegraph allowed signals to be sent along a wire by switching on and off an electric current. By tapping on an electric switch, operators could send messages over long distances.

Q What is semaphore?

A Semaphore is a method of signaling with flags in different positions. It was invented in the 18th century to help ships keep in touch at sea, but is very rarely used nowadays.

"Ready" position

The letter E

The letter X

1953-117

Heavy magazines hold three strips of film separately

Viewfinder window shows the camera operator what is being filmed

Matt box (lens hood) keeps stray light out of the lens

Light tight door

Who invented movies

THE FIRST MOVIES were made by a French inventor, Louis Le Prince, as long ago as 1888. He shot pictures of traffic moving on a bridge in Leeds in northern England, using a special camera to take scores of pictures in a few minutes on light-sensitive rolls of paper. The first film lasting much more than a minute, though, was made the following year by the American inventor, Thomas Edison, and his British assistant, William Dickson. In their short film, according to contemporary newspaper reports, a man "bowed and smiled, and took off his hat with the most perfect naturalness and grace."

Q What was the first film in color?

A *Becky Sharp*, a historical drama based on Thackeray's *Vanity Fair*, was the first real color film, made in 1935 with the Technicolor three-strip process. The Technicolor process worked by making three separate black-and-white films for the red, blue, and green parts of the scenes using a special camera with a beam-splitting prism.

Q Who made the first rolls of film?

A Early photographs were all taken on cumbersome glass and metal plates in big, heavy cameras. Paper roll films were first used in 1887 by a French scientist, Étienne Marey. In 1888, American George Eastman launched a small, lightweight camera called the Kodak, which used paper film instead of plates. A year later, Kodak introduced rolls of film on celluloid.

Wet-plate collodion chemicals

Q What did early photographers put on a wet plate?

A Early photographs. In 1851, Frederick Scott Archer invented a way of taking photographs using a glass photographic plate that was more light-sensitive than its predecessors. Called the wet-plate collodion process, it consisted of a glass plate, which was coated with silver salts and a sticky material called collodion. The plate was put in the camera and exposed while it was still wet. It was a messy process but gave excellent results. After exposure the image was developed and fixed using chemicals dispensed from small bottles.

Tripod to keep the camera steady during filming

Wheels made the camera easy to move

Javanese shadow puppets are made of leather, stretched thin and painted to cast colored shadows

Q How do you make a gremlin?

A Monsters in movies like *King Kong* were rubber models which were moved and shot painstakingly frame by frame to create the illusion of movement. Today, movies such as *Gremlins* rely on animatronics which creates working models that move and can be shot just like any live actor. Under remarkably realistic latex skins, electronic motors operate steel joints and muscles to create the most life-like movements. Computerization – especially virtual reality techniques – makes even very complex sequences possible.

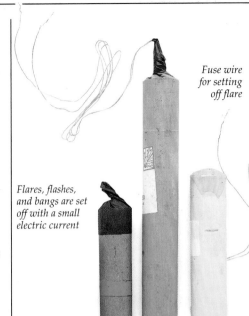

Fuse wire for setting off flare

Flares, flashes, and bangs are set off with a small electric current

Q How did the Javanese make movies over 400 years ago?

A With shadow puppets – puppets designed to cast a shadow that can be moved at will with sticks that swivel jointed limbs. Javanese shadow puppets were used to tell traditional tales with a narrator and orchestra. The idea spread to Europe in the 17th century, and in 1893 the Chicago World Fair featured a shadow show.

Q Who set the *Towering Inferno* ablaze?

A Movies like *Towering Inferno* rely on realistic fire and explosion sequences. Because they are potentially very dangerous, these sequences are always handled by experts called pyrotechnicists, who ensure every fire and explosion is very carefully planned and controlled. For a controllable blaze, sets are built with flaming forks. These are gas jets that burn with real flames that can be extinguished when the director shouts "cut." Explosions are set off from a safe distance with an electric current and some may be big enough to create huge balls of fire.

Cap indicates the color of the smoke in the cylinder

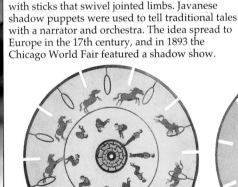

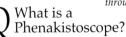
As the disc turns, the horse jumps through the hoop

Q What is a Phenakistoscope?

A A device for creating the illusion of movement by using images on a rapidly spinning disc. It was invented in 1833 by a Belgian physicist, Joseph Plateau (1801–1883). All the pictures on the disc were slightly different, so that as the disc spun, they all blurred together into one apparently moving image.

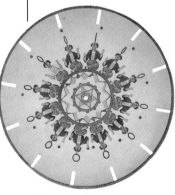

Q What was the first successful photographic process?

A The daguerreotype invented by Louis Jacques Daguerre (1789–1851) in 1839. This process used a plain copper plate coated with a silver compound made sensitive to light by letting iodine vapor pass over it. Once the photograph was taken, the plate was developed by passing mercury vapor over it, and the image fixed permanently with a salt solution. Mercury vapor is highly toxic, so the process could be dangerous.

What is natural energy?

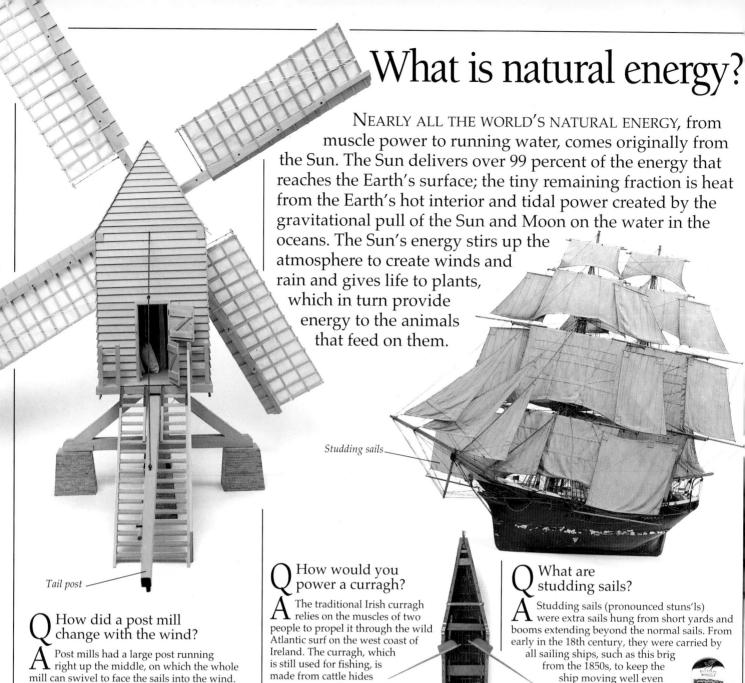

NEARLY ALL THE WORLD'S NATURAL ENERGY, from muscle power to running water, comes originally from the Sun. The Sun delivers over 99 percent of the energy that reaches the Earth's surface; the tiny remaining fraction is heat from the Earth's hot interior and tidal power created by the gravitational pull of the Sun and Moon on the water in the oceans. The Sun's energy stirs up the atmosphere to create winds and rain and gives life to plants, which in turn provide energy to the animals that feed on them.

Studding sails

Tail post

Q How did a post mill change with the wind?

A Post mills had a large post running right up the middle, on which the whole mill can swivel to face the sails into the wind. In early post mills, the miller turned the mill's sails into the wind manually by pushing on a long tail post extending out behind the mill. Later mills had a small wind wheel called a fantail that turned the mill automatically.

Q How would you power a curragh?

A The traditional Irish curragh relies on the muscles of two people to propel it through the wild Atlantic surf on the west coast of Ireland. The curragh, which is still used for fishing, is made from cattle hides or canvas stretched over a light willow frame.

Q What are studding sails?

A Studding sails (pronounced stuns'ls) were extra sails hung from short yards and booms extending beyond the normal sails. From early in the 18th century, they were carried by all sailing ships, such as this brig from the 1850s, to keep the ship moving well even in light breezes.

Q Why do we need sugar to move?

A The sugar we buy is almost pure glucose, the fuel that powers all muscles – which is why athletes often eat sweet glucose tablets to give them extra energy. But the body does not need to rely on purified sugar for muscle power. In a complex chemical process, it can create its own glucose from any food that contains starches.

Q How does sea power make the beach sandy?

A Rocks falling from cliffs are broken down into smaller and smaller pieces as they are hurled together by the power of the waves. Eventually they are smashed into fine sand. Water naturally sorts the grains into different sizes and deposits each in a different place. Generally the biggest pebbles are farthest up the beach where they are flung by storm waves.

Q Where do the world's fastest horses come from?

A The fastest horses are thoroughbred racehorses, which descend from Arabian and Barb breeds. Arabian horses probably orginated not in Arabia as their name suggests but in Egypt, where they were used over 3,500 years ago. The Barb comes from Morocco in northern Africa.

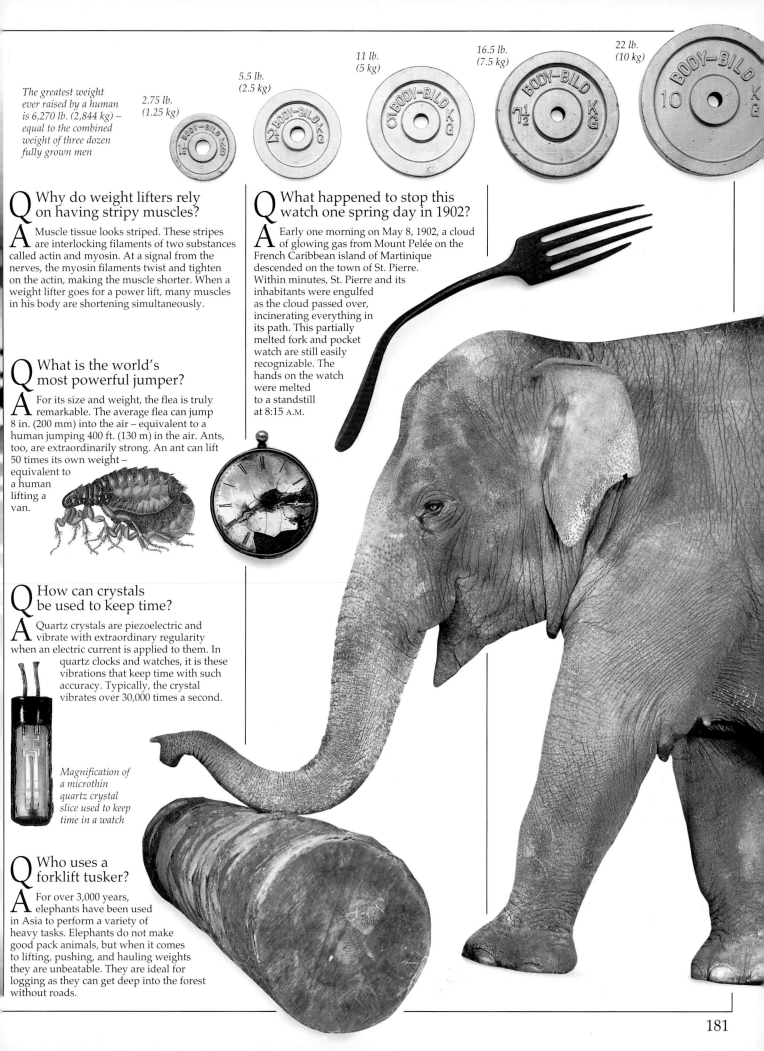

5.5 lb. (2.5 kg)

11 lb. (5 kg)

16.5 lb. (7.5 kg)

22 lb. (10 kg)

2.75 lb. (1.25 kg)

The greatest weight ever raised by a human is 6,270 lb. (2,844 kg) – equal to the combined weight of three dozen fully grown men

Q Why do weight lifters rely on having stripy muscles?

A Muscle tissue looks striped. These stripes are interlocking filaments of two substances called actin and myosin. At a signal from the nerves, the myosin filaments twist and tighten on the actin, making the muscle shorter. When a weight lifter goes for a power lift, many muscles in his body are shortening simultaneously.

Q What is the world's most powerful jumper?

A For its size and weight, the flea is truly remarkable. The average flea can jump 8 in. (200 mm) into the air – equivalent to a human jumping 400 ft. (130 m) in the air. Ants, too, are extraordinarily strong. An ant can lift 50 times its own weight – equivalent to a human lifting a van.

Q What happened to stop this watch one spring day in 1902?

A Early one morning on May 8, 1902, a cloud of glowing gas from Mount Pelée on the French Caribbean island of Martinique descended on the town of St. Pierre. Within minutes, St. Pierre and its inhabitants were engulfed as the cloud passed over, incinerating everything in its path. This partially melted fork and pocket watch are still easily recognizable. The hands on the watch were melted to a standstill at 8:15 A.M.

Q How can crystals be used to keep time?

A Quartz crystals are piezoelectric and vibrate with extraordinary regularity when an electric current is applied to them. In quartz clocks and watches, it is these vibrations that keep time with such accuracy. Typically, the crystal vibrates over 30,000 times a second.

Magnification of a microthin quartz crystal slice used to keep time in a watch

Q Who uses a forklift tusker?

A For over 3,000 years, elephants have been used in Asia to perform a variety of heavy tasks. Elephants do not make good pack animals, but when it comes to lifting, pushing, and hauling weights they are unbeatable. They are ideal for logging as they can get deep into the forest without roads.

How old is steam power?

STEAM POWER dates back to the first century AD when the Greek scientist Hero of Alexandria described the "aeolipile" – a simple device that used steam power to turn a wheel. But it was 1,500 years before people developed a way of using steam to drive machinery. In 1698, Thomas Savery (c. 1650–1715) patented the first steam engine for pumping water from mines and it was only a matter of time before steam power was used to move trains and ships. But people continued to look for more efficient sources of power leading to the development of electric, gas, and diesel engines.

Q How did the first steam pump work?

A Thomas Savery's steam pump was used in mines in 1698. Steam from a boiler passed into a pair of vessels. The steam was condensed back into water, sucking water up from the mine below. Using stop cocks and valves, the steam pressure was then directed to push the water up a vertical outlet pipe.

Q Who made the first battery?

A In 1800, Alessandro Volta (1745–1827) published details of his first chemical battery. It consisted of layers of zinc and silver or copper sandwiched between blotting paper pads soaked in sulphuric acid. Modern batteries, like the ones used in flashlights and radios, are known as "dry" cell batteries. These follow the same basic design of the first batteries, but use modern materials.

Q Why do some engines revolve?

A One of the main problems of early plane engines was that they often overheated. But in 1908, the French Seguin brothers brought out the rotary engine in which the cylinders rotated around the central crankshaft. This created a constant flow of air over them and so kept them cool.

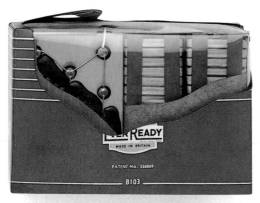

Q Who built a steam plane?

A The first plane engine was a steam engine, built by two Englishmen, William Henson and John Stringfellow, in 1845 to power their "Aerial Steam Carriage." This model steam plane was the first ever practical design for a powered aircraft. But steam engines proved either too weak or too heavy and it was not until the invention of the gas engine that powered flight became possible.

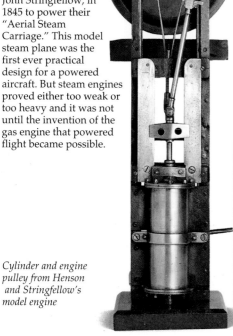

Cylinder and engine pulley from Henson and Stringfellow's model engine

Q How did a frog teach scientists how to store electricity?

A In about 1790, an Italian professor, Luigi Galvani (1737–1798), noted that a dead frog twitched when touched with two different metals at the same time. Galvani put this phenomenon down to "animal electricity." Soon after, Volta proved the twitching was caused as the metals reacted with the moisture in the frog's body and produced electricity. This discovery led him to devise the first battery.

Q Why do some cars have spark plugs?

A All vehicles that run on gas have spark plugs that deliver an electric spark to each of the engine's cylinders at the right moment to ignite the fuel. When the fuel burns it expands and pushes the piston down, giving the engine its power. In diesel engines there is no need for a spark, as the pressure created by the piston when it rises is enough to light the fuel.

Q What was special about James Watt's engine?

A In 1769, James Watt made the first really efficient steam engine. Unlike earlier engines, the steam condensed outside rather than inside the cylinder, which caused it to cool down and reduce the heat.

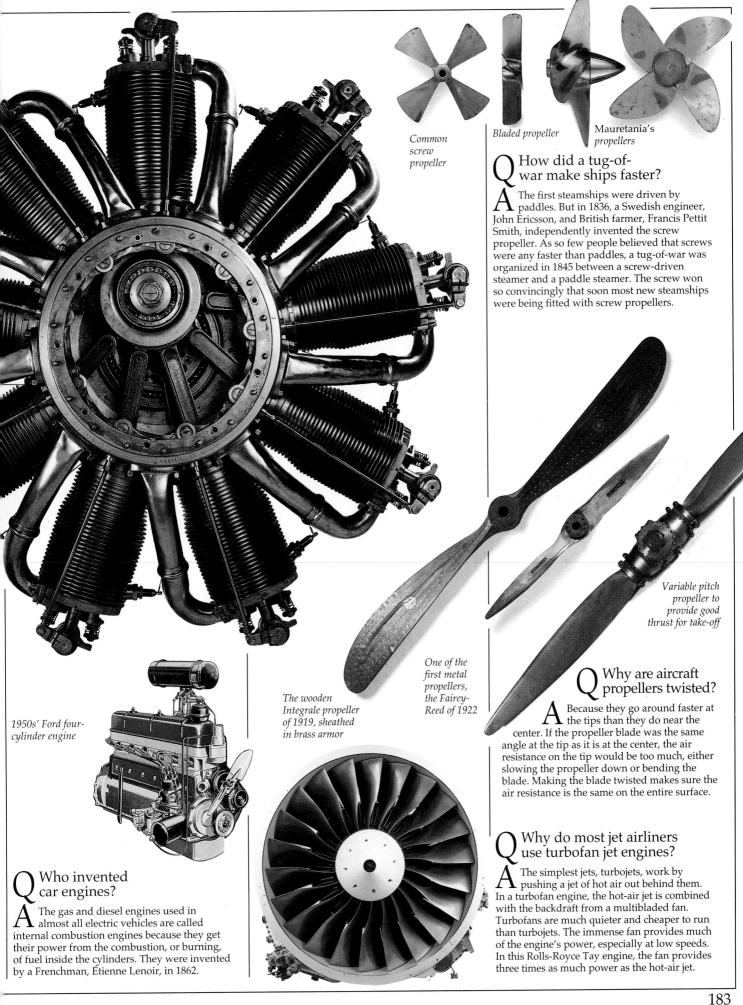

Common screw propeller

Bladed propeller

Mauretania's propellers

Q How did a tug-of-war make ships faster?

A The first steamships were driven by paddles. But in 1836, a Swedish engineer, John Ericsson, and British farmer, Francis Pettit Smith, independently invented the screw propeller. As so few people believed that screws were any faster than paddles, a tug-of-war was organized in 1845 between a screw-driven steamer and a paddle steamer. The screw won so convincingly that soon most new steamships were being fitted with screw propellers.

Variable pitch propeller to provide good thrust for take-off

One of the first metal propellers, the Fairey-Reed of 1922

The wooden Integrale propeller of 1919, sheathed in brass armor

1950s' Ford four-cylinder engine

Q Why are aircraft propellers twisted?

A Because they go around faster at the tips than they do near the center. If the propeller blade was the same angle at the tip as it is at the center, the air resistance on the tip would be too much, either slowing the propeller down or bending the blade. Making the blade twisted makes sure the air resistance is the same on the entire surface.

Q Who invented car engines?

A The gas and diesel engines used in almost all electric vehicles are called internal combustion engines because they get their power from the combustion, or burning, of fuel inside the cylinders. They were invented by a Frenchman, Étienne Lenoir, in 1862.

Q Why do most jet airliners use turbofan jet engines?

A The simplest jets, turbojets, work by pushing a jet of hot air out behind them. In a turbofan engine, the hot-air jet is combined with the backdraft from a multibladed fan. Turbofans are much quieter and cheaper to run than turbojets. The immense fan provides much of the engine's power, especially at low speeds. In this Rolls-Royce Tay engine, the fan provides three times as much power as the hot-air jet.

Did cars or trains come first?

Q Why did early trains need a tall chimney?

A The *Agenoria*, shown here, was built in 1829. Like most early steam locomotives, it looked very similar to the very first working steam locomotive built by Richard Trevithick in 1804, which had four wheels like a cart, a short tube-shaped boiler, and a very tall smokestack, or chimney. A tall chimney improved the draft on the fire and made the locomotive more efficient – but there could be no low bridges on the line.

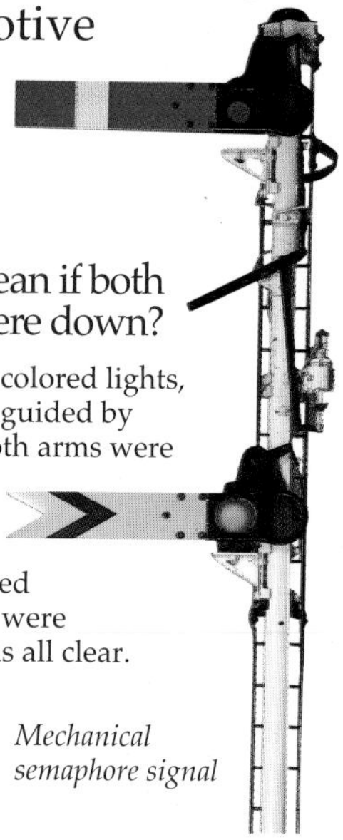

TRAINS AND CARS are much older than you might think. The basic principle of a railway dates back over 5,000 years ago to the ancient Sumerians, who cut grooves in stone roadways to guide wheeled vehicles along a straight course. Surprisingly, though, the first mechanically powered land vehicle was a car, not a train. The first car, a massive steam-driven carriage built by Frenchman Nicolas Cugnot, was made in 1769. The first railway locomotive was not built until 1804.

Q What did it mean if both signal arms were down?

A In the days before colored lights, train drivers were guided by semaphore signals. If both arms were down, they had to stop. If the upper arm only was raised, they could proceed cautiously. If both arms were raised the line ahead was all clear.

Mechanical semaphore signal

Folding hood

Q How did American settlers travel west in the 19th century?

A Without cars or trains, the first settlers in America had to rely on wagons covered with canvas to travel the long distances to the American west. Each wagon was drawn by a pair of horses, and several wagons would travel together with scores of other settlers in a long wagon train. An escort was paid to offer protection and guidance.

Folding windshield for rear seat passenger

Second-class compartment from a 1904 carriage

Q Why did early train passengers loosen their belts in stations?

A For safety, the compartment doors on many trains have no handle on the inside. In early trains, the window was fastened by a simple leather belt and buckle. So passengers had to loosen the buckle and lean out of the window to open the door. This changed after World War II.

Early wheels were solid wooden disks

Tripartite wheels were made of three pieces of wood

Stone wheels were used where wood was scarce

Dystrop wheels had sections cut out to make them lighter

Open wheels could be strengthened with crossbars

Q Why are racing cars faster than ordinary cars?

A Not only do racing cars have much more powerful engines than ordinary cars, but they are made of modern, ultralight materials and are so low slung that they almost scrape the ground. The body is also carefully streamlined to cut air resistance and shaped so that the air flowing over the car helps keep the car stable and on the road. Huge, wide tires give extra grip at high speeds.

Q How long ago was the first wheel used?

A The wheel is one of the most important of all inventions. Wheels were probably first used 5,000 years ago in Mesopotamia, part of modern Iraq, both on carts to move big loads and by potters to help work clay.

Prewar racing cars looked like ordinary road cars

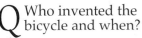

Roll bar protects the driver's head in a crash

Q Who invented the bicycle and when?

A The first bicycle was called a velocipede and was invented by a Scots blacksmith in 1839. Despite its name, the velocipede was very slow: the back wheel turned at exactly the same rate as the pedals, which were linked to the wheel, not by a chain as on modern bikes but by connecting rods. The "safety bicycle" on which most modern bikes are based was introduced in the 1870s by James Starley of Coventry.

Electric sidelight

Rear oil lamp

Wide, treadless tires, called slicks, give extra grip on dry race tracks

Q How did early motorists make sure they were seen at night?

A From 1899 on, many cars carried dim oil lamps for driving at night. But for many years they were considered luxury items. It was not until the 1930s that bright electric lights were standard equipment on most cars.

Q What was the first Rolls Royce called and when was it made?

A Charles Rolls and Henry Royce made one of their first cars in 1906, and the sheer quality of craftsmanship earned it the description of "the best car in the world." Its ghostlike quietness and shiny aluminum body suggested the name "Silver Ghost." The Silver Ghost shown here is a 40/50 from 1909.

Hand brake

"Spirit of Ecstasy" ornament

How do we fly?

IN CHINA thousands of years ago people were carried up into the air by giant kites. But the first long powered flight was made by the American brothers Orville and Wilbur Wright as recently as 1903. Since then nearly all flying machines have been based on the same principle. Specially shaped wings provide lift as they slice through the air, and an engine supplies the power to keep pushing the airplane through the air.

Q What are the smallest powered aircraft?

A Ultralights, which were developed from hang gliders in the 1970s. Many still have flexible delta-shaped fabric wings like hang gliders with a simple tricycle dangling beneath. Others, especially in the U.S.A. and Australia, are more like airplanes and have fixed wings and wing flaps so they can climb or dive.

Q How did early pilots know where they were going?

A The only instrument most early pilots had was a compass, so they found their way simply by aiming for landmarks, such as church steeples. In the Deperdussin cockpit here, the view ahead is obscured by the fuel tank, and the pilot had to lean out to check height and direction.

Q How did the first pilots know how high they were?

A The first airplanes had no instruments, so to find their height, or altitude, pilots would use little pocket altimeters, such as the Elliot shown here. These were very similar to altimeters used by mountaineers for years before and worked simply by responding to changes in air pressure.

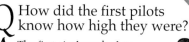

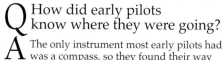

Q What was the first craft to carry people over Paris?

A On November 21, 1783, Jean Pilâtre de Rozier and the Marquis d'Arlandes became Europe's first aeronauts when the Montgolfiers' balloon, filled with hot air, carried them into the skies above Paris. Within two weeks a second flight was made, but this time the balloon was filled with hydrogen. Hot-air balloons disappeared for 170 years until they were revived in the 1960s. Hot-air ballooning is now a popular sport.

Q Why do jet airliners need stressmen?

A Because of the enormous pressure differences they must withstand at high altitudes, airliner bodies have to be tough as well as light – and even a tiny weakness could spell disaster. So the strength and durability of every minute section is carefully assessed – an enormous task once involving scores of stressmen but now made much easier by computers. There are hoop frames and stringers that run along the inside of the aircraft body, but these are small and much of the plane's strength comes from its metal skin.

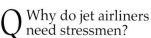

Q What is the black box?

A The black box is a special flight data recorder carried by all modern airliners and military aircraft. It is connected to all the aircraft's main systems and records everything that happens during a flight, monitoring instruments, radio messages, engine data, and so on. If the plane crashes, the box is strong enough to survive, providing experts with a complete history of the flight so the cause of the accident can be found.

Q Why are sycamore seeds like helicopters?

A Helicopter rotor blades are like rotating wings. As they turn they generate enough lift to keep the helicopter in the air. Sycamore seeds are a similar shape and when they fall off the tree they, too, whirl around and around to the ground.

Q How do wings enable birds to fly?

A Birds fly either by gliding with their wings held almost still or by flapping their wings up and down. Since gliding is much less tiring than flapping, birds that stay in the air for a long time, like birds of prey, tend to be good gliders. Even gliding birds flap their wings from time to time, though, if only for landing and take-off. For the downstroke, the bird's main wing feathers are closed together providing maximum push on the air. For the upstroke, the feathers open to allow the air to flow gently through.

Duck flying

Q What were dogfights?

A Dogfights were midair fights between single-seat scout planes in World War I. These planes usually had a single fixed, forward-facing machine gun. This meant the pilot had to aim the whole aircraft at the enemy to shoot, so flying skill was vital. World War I "aces" such as Baron von Richthofen, the Red Baron, became famous for their exploits.

Q How did early balloonists keep a steady height?

A The first balloonists carried a pressure-sensitive instrument called a statoscope which told them immediately they began to rise or fall. If the balloon rose too much the balloonist had to let gas out, which wasted precious gas; if it sank too low, they had to throw out sand ballast. Constant rising and falling in this way soon cut short a flight.

The Blériot planes were the first successful monoplanes (single-winged planes)

Q Who made the first flight across the English Channel?

A Louis Blériot on July 25, 1909. Blériot made the 26-mile (41-km) flight in one of his own machines, a Blériot Type XI, identical to the one shown here. After the flight, Blériot became a celebrity overnight and, when more than 100 of the Type XI were ordered, he became the world's first major aircraft manufacturer.

Index

Acknowledgments

Dorling Kindersley would like to thank the following people for assistance:

Djinn von Noorden and Helena Spiteri for editorial assistance; Ivan Finnegan for design assistance; Ingrid Nilsson for picture research; Jean Cooke and Marion Dent for the index; Gillian Denton, Claire Gillard, and Phil Wilkinson.

Thanks go to the following museums for permission for photography:

The American Museum of Natural History, Arbour Antiques in New York, Ashmolean Museum, Birmingham City Museum, British Museum, Cambridge Museum, Charles Darwin Museum, INAH.-CNCA, Mexico, Museum of London, Museum of the Moving Image, Natural History Museum, Museum of Mankind, National Maritime Museum, National Motor Museum, Beaulieu, Trustees of the National Museums of Scotland (Scottish United Services Museum), Pitt Rivers Museum, Royal Pavilion, Art Gallery and Museum, Brighton, Smithsonian Institution in Washington D.C., National Railway Museum, Royal Geographical Society, Science Museum, Shakespeare Globe Trust, Sir John Soane's Museum, St Bride Printing Library, University Museum, Trustees of the University Museum of Archaeology and Anthropology, Wallace Collection, Warwick Castle, Worthing Museum and Art Gallery.

Dorling Kindersley would also like to thank the following people for special photography:

Peter Anderson, Geoff Brightling, Jane Burton, Peter Chadwick, Andy Crawford, Geoff Dann, Philip Dowell, Mike Dunning, Lynton Gardiner, Phillip Gatward, John Garrett, Christi Graham, Frank Greenaway, Peter Hayman, Chas Howson, Colin Keates, Dave King, Liz McAulay, Andrew McRobb, Ray Moller, Nick Nicholls, Stephen Oliver, Roger Phillips, Karl Shone, James Stevenson, Clive Streeter, Harry Taylor, Kim Taylor, Matthew Ward, Jerry Young, and Michel Zabé.

PICTURE CREDITS

The publishers are grateful to the following individuals and picture libraries for permission to reproduce their photographs.

Abbreviations: t = top, b = below, c = center, l = left, r = right.

Alvis Ltd: 59cra; **American Museum of Natural History:** 151c; **The Ancient Art and Architecture Collection:** 41cr, 49tl, 95cl; **Ashmolean Museum:** 148tl, 155cb; **Aviation Picture Library** 126cl; **Birmingham City Museum** 150br; **Bolton Museum:** 142tl; **The Bridgeman Art Library:** 44cla/British Museum 39c, 39cr, 47tl/Cairo Museum & Giraudon 37br/Christies, London 58cl/Louvre 49cl/National Maritime Museum 36tr/Nasjonalgallertiet, Oslo 174tr/Private Collection 44cra, 49tcr/Queensland Art Gallery 49tr/Staatliche Museen zu Berlin 49cla/The Vatican 47tr; **British Museum:** 142tr, 143tl, 144tl, c, tr, cr, bl, 145tl, bl, br; **Jane Burton** 81cr; Cambridge Museum 155cra; **Bruce Coleman Ltd:** Gene Ahrens 15tr/Brian and Cherry Alexander 10tr/Norman Scwartz 52cl/C.B. & D.W. Frith 8bl/Gerald Cubbitt 21bra/David Howton 14br/Michael Kilmec 59tcl, 67tl/John Markham 42clb/Alfred Pasieka 58bcl/Fritz Penzel 20c/Dr. Eckpart Pott 15br/Warner Stoy 36cl/Norman Tolamin 48tc, 66tc; **Crown:** Public Record Office (E31) 38cb; **Charles Darwin Museum** 149tr; **C.M.Dixon:** 39tc; **Ermine Street Guard** 145tr; **ET Archive:** 46tr, 116tc; **Mary Evans Picture Library:** 8tr, 9cl, 10tl, 11bc, 12cla, 18cl, 22tr, 25cr, 41ca, 41br, 43br, 44crb, 45tr, 45cra, 45cla, 45clb, 45br, 48br, 48bc, 49bcl, 49crb, 51tl, 51br, 54cb, 60tc, 60br, 61cla, 61cr, 61br, 66tl, 66ca, 66c, 66bc; **Florence Nightingale Museum** 160c; **German National Tourist Office:** 12clb; **Giraudon:** 37cra; **Glasgow Museum** 164tl; **Ronald Grant Archive** 179bc (box); **Sonia Halliday:** 45bcr; **Julia Harris:** 59cla; **Jim Henson's Creature Shop** 179bl (box); **Michael Holford:** 40cl/British Museum 38cr; 135cr; 154cl, 155br.; **Hulton Deutsch:** 36bra, 43cl, 44bc, 47br, 48c, 60clb; **Hutchison:** Sarah Errington 13clb, 13tr; By courtesy of **IAL Security Products:** 62crb; **The Image Bank:** 13bl, 15cl, 19cl, 173bl/P.& G. Bower 21crb, 65br/Joseph B. Bribnoto 58bc/Giamalberto Cigolini 62crb/Gary Cralle 20bcr/David W. Hamilton 48cr/Francisco Hidalgo 37tl/Michael Pasczior 19bl/Harold Sand 42cb/Stockphotos Inc. 52cr/Eric Wheater 9bl; **INAH Mexican Museum Authority**

150c, tr, cl; **Ann Ronan at Image Select:** 60cla; **Stephen Kirk:** 35tr; **The Kobal Collection:** 44clb, 59tcr; By courtesy of **Kodak:** 50bl; **Ligabue Studies and Researchers, Venice**/Erizzo Editrice 128/129c; **Museum of London** 146tc, 154tl; **Anne Lyons:** 58br; **The Raymond Mander and Joe Mitcheson Theatre Collection Ltd:** 10bl; **The Mansell Collection:** 47cl; **Museum of the Moving Image** 178tl, 179cr (box); **NASA:** 57tr, 61clb, 159c, 167b; **National Maritime Museum** 149tl, 149tc, 149c, 149cl, 159bl; **National Museum of Scotland** 155cl, 155cla; **National Railway Museum, York** 156/7b; **Natural History Museum** 136tr, 137c, 158br, 158tr; **Network:** Goldwater 13br; **Peter Newark's Western Americana:** 36ca, 39cl, 42ca, 44tc, 45tc, 45crb, 46bl, 49bl, 49cr, 66crb; National Motor Museum, Beaulieu 164b; **The Nobel Foundation:** 46cb; **Novosti:** 45ccr; **Ordnance Survey/© Crown Copyright:** 55crb; **Christine Osborne Pictures:** 9tl; **Osel Group** by courtesy of Quest, Marshall Cavendish: 59tr, 67tr; **Liberto Perugi** 160tl, br; © Renault 171c; **Philips Scientific:** 62cra; **Popperfoto:** 44bl, 45bl, 46br; **Pitt Rivers** 153tl, br, bl, 155ca, car, tcb, tc; **Roger Viollett:** 43tl; **Royal Museum of Scotland** 150bl; **Science Museum:** 178c; **Science Photo Library:** Biophoto Associates 51cl/Ken Briggs 59tl/Earth Satellite Corporation 13crb/Simon Fraser 57br /Eric Grave 62bc/Adam Hart-Davis 53c/IBM 62t/NASA 50tl, 52tl/NIBSC 25cl/David Parker 53bc/Royal Greenwich Observatory 59c/Jim Stevenson 62clb/Dr. T. Thompson 61tl; 71tl, tcl, tc; **Smithsonian Institute** 161r, br, 164cr, 165br, cr, 167cb; **Sir John Soane's Museum** 174bl; **Frank Spooner Pictures:** Eric Bouvet/Gamma 44br; **Sporting Pictures UK:** 21bl, 21clb, 65bl; **Bob Symes** 121bl; **Syndication International:** 44cl, 120t; **Wallace Collection** 147tc, 148bl; **Warwick Castle** 152c; **Werner Forman Archive** 163tl; **Robin Wigington, Arbour Antiques** 152br; **Worthing Art Gallery and Museum** 155br; **Jerry Young:** 34t, 34br, 35tr; **Zefa:** 19br, 20tl/Dr. David Corke 42cla/Damm 11cbl/W.F. Davidson 38tr, 58clb/K. Goebel 44ca/Heilmann 13cla/Messerschmidt 11bl.

Every effort has been made to trace the copyright holders and we apologize in advance for any unintentional omissions. We would be pleased to insert the appropriate acknowledgment in any subsequent editions of this publication.